The Loneliest Revolution

Edinburgh Historical Studies of Iran and the Persian World

Published in association with Elahé Omidyar Mir-Djalali, Founder and Chair, Roshan Cultural Heritage Institute

ROSHAN CULTURAL HERITAGE INSTITUTE

Covering the history of Iran and the Persian world from the medieval period to the present, this series aims to become the pre-eminent place for publication in this field. As well as its core concern with Iran, it extends its concerns to encompass a much wider and more loosely defined cultural and linguistic world, to include Afghanistan, the Caucasus, Central Asia, Xinjiang and northern India. Books in the series present a range of conceptual and methodological approaches, looking not only at states, dynasties and elites, but at subalterns, minorities and everyday life.

Published and forthcoming titles

The Last Muslim Intellectual: The Life and Legacy of Jalal Al-e Ahmad
Hamid Dabashi

The Persian Prison Poem: Sovereignty and the Political Imagination
Rebecca Ruth Gould

The Loneliest Revolution: A Memoir of Solidarity and Struggle in Iran
Ali Mirsepassi

Remapping Persian Literary History, 1700–1900
Kevin L. Schwartz

Religion, Orientalism and Modernity: Mahdi Movements of Iran and South Asia
Geoffrey Nash

Muslim–Christian Polemics in Safavid Iran
Alberto Tiburcio

edinburghuniversitypress.com/series/ehsipw

"The prose of our historiography is changing. Solid scholars with an impeccable academic background are turning to the more publicly accessible genre of memoir, and Ali Mirsepassi's exceptionally insightful new book is a vintage of such fruitful prose. Deeply erudite, and yet intimate, endearing, and irresistibly readable, *The Loneliest Revolution* charts a whole new way of writing history. A bravura performance!"
Hamid Dabashi, Columbia University

"In this searching memoir, Mirsepassi reflects on his country's convulsive history and his own place within it: as a student, as an activist, and finally as an exiled intellectual . . . The result is a daring and powerful work of memoir and intellectual history, and one that is all the more urgent for coinciding with Iran's ongoing struggle for 'Woman, Life, Freedom'."
Adam Shatz, US Editor, *London Review of Books*

"In this wonderful book, Mirsepassi leverages touching personal recollections—of parents, a history-telling grandmother, an upbringing across small-town Iran, and student days in revolutionary Tehran—to reflect on questions of public life . . . A fascinating kaleidoscope of a memoir."
Cyrus Schayegh, Geneva Graduate Institute

"A rich memoir of the intellectual ferment and activism that created the Iranian Revolution. The reader feels what it was like for the author to grow up in a small town amidst surging secular leftist and Islamist ideas, to experience in Tehran the crumbling of the Shah's Iran, and to witness the victory of intolerant Islamism that left the author, and so many others, strangers in their own country. An account this frank and insight-filled is rare."
Sir Richard Dalton KCMG, British Ambassador to Iran 2002–6

The Loneliest Revolution

A Memoir of Solidarity and Struggle in Iran

Ali Mirsepassi

EDINBURGH
University Press

Edinburgh University Press is one of the leading university presses in the UK. We publish academic books and journals in our selected subject areas across the humanities and social sciences, combining cutting-edge scholarship with high editorial and production values to produce academic works of lasting importance. For more information visit our website: edinburghuniversitypress.com

Edinburgh University Press Ltd
The Tun—Holyrood Road
12 (2f) Jackson's Entry
Edinburgh EH8 8PJ

Typeset in Adobe Garamond by
Cheshire Typesetting Ltd, Cuddington

A CIP record for this book is available from the British Library

ISBN 978 1 3995 1141 4 (hardback)
ISBN 978 1 3995 1142 1 (paperback)
ISBN 978 1 3995 1143 8 (webready PDF)
ISBN 978 1 3995 1144 5 (epub)

Contents

List of Figures viii
Acknowledgments x
Note on References xii
Note on Transliteration xiii

Introduction: A Fall Day in 1978 1
1 Dorud and Nahavand, 1956–1966 27
2 Golpayegan, 1966–1970 74
3 Tehran University, 1970–1974 137
4 Zahra's Paradise, 1977–1978 179
5 Our Dreams On Trial, 1979 225
Conclusion: East Coast, U.S., 1980–2021 247

Bibliography 264
Index 273

Figures

1.1	Ali Mirsepassi, three years old, Malayer, 1954	30
1.2	My mother Malekzadeh and sister Susan, Dorud, early 1960s	31
1.3	My mother and her friends, Dorud, early 1960s	34
1.4	My grandmother Batul Khanum, Nahavand, early 1960s	35
1.5	My grandmother, Nahavand, mid-1960s	37
1.6	My father, Mehdi Nahavand, mid-1960s	41
1.7	Ali Mirsepassi, thirteen years old, Nahavand	45
1.8	My father, Nahavand, mid-1960s	46
1.9	Ali Mirsepassi, fourteen years old, Nahavand	47
1.10	Ali Mirsepassi, brother Mansour, and cousin Bijan, Nahavand, mid-1960s	55
1.11	My mother and relatives, Nahavand, mid-1960s	71
1.12	My father, uncle Mohammad Ali, brother Mansour, myself, cousin Bijan, and cousin Farhang, Tagh-e Bostan, Kermanshah, mid-1960s	72
1.13	My mother, brother Masoud, myself, brother Mansour, and sister Susan, Nahavand, mid-1960s	72
2.1	High School teachers, Golpayegan, 1966	79

2.2 High School teachers in front of Ebn-e Sina high school, Golpayegan, 1966 83
2.3 High School teachers, in a classroom, Golpayegan, late 1960s 93
2.4 High School teachers and students, Golpayegan, 1966 94
2.5 High School teachers, Golpayegan, 1966 110
2.6 Ali Mirsepassi, eleventh grade, Golpayegan, late 1960s 115
2.7 Ali Mirsepassi, Golpayegan, late 1960s 135
2.8 Ali Mirsepassi with friends, Golpayegan, late 1960s 136
2.9 Ali Mirsepassi, with high school classmates and vice principal, Golpayegan, late 1960s 136
3.1 Ali Mirsepassi, Tehran, 1971 145
4.1 Ali Mirsepassi, Sar-e Pol-e Zahab, 1975 185
4.2 Ali Mirsepassi and a friend, Bournemouth, U.K., 1977 186
4.3 My grandmother, Nahavand, early 1970s 198

Acknowledgments

Writing a memoir is a rather trying toil. When I set out on this project four years ago, I had no idea how much it would ask of me. Only after months of solitary reflection and some difficult conversations was I able to shake the debris off decades-old memories. Without the support, advice, and inspiration of my family, friends, and colleagues over the past few years, this book would not be. I would like to extend my deepest gratitude to them. They helped me find the courage needed to commit these ideas to paper.

I have been fortunate to benefit from Bita Mousavi's diligent editorial assistance. Bita's contribution to this book goes beyond editorial work, I have benefited from her thoughtful advice on the content and organization of this memoir. My sincere gratitude to Bita for her input and commitment to the project, and for being a genuine team player and devoting so much time to it. Earlier in the process of producing the first draft, Tadd Fernee and Romaissaa Benzizoune helped me with editing the manuscript. I offer my appreciation to both of them for helping get an earlier version of this project off the ground.

Hamid Dabashi, Omid Tofighian, Alejandro Velasco, Todd Porterfield, Kiana Karimi, Ehsan Siahpoush, and Saeed

Zarabian took time to review the manuscript and share extensive comments and advice. Their efforts and feedback helped make the book a much better work, and for their efforts and intellectual companionship, I am very grateful. Christopher Dietrich, Naghmeh Sohrabi, Hossein Kamaly, and Arang Keshavarzian kindly read earlier drafts of various chapters. Their valuable comments pushed me to produce a clearer, more personal work than I otherwise might have. Ismail Fajrie Alatas offered his expertise as I was trying to understand the Karramiyya, a Sufi movement in Khorasan. I am grateful for his kind assistance. Several family members in Iran and the U.S. helped dig through old family documents and locate information. I would like to extend my appreciation to Bijan Esfandiari, Parvaneh Mirsepassi, Susan Mirsepassi, Farzad Esfandiari, and Masoud Mirsepassi.

The unstinting support of the Gallatin School of Individualized Study at New York University has made the pursuit of this and so many other projects of mine possible. I owe a great deal of thanks to the Dean of the Gallatin School, Susanne Wofford, and to the faculty and students at N.Y.U.

Lastly, I would like to convey my gratitude to Stephanie Cronin for looking past convention to offer this book a home in the Edinburgh Historical Studies of Iran and the Persian World Series. Rachel Bridgewater of Edinburgh University Press, and her team, including Louise Hutton, helped steward this project to completion, and for that I thank them.

Note on References

The Loneliest Revolution is a memoir written by a scholar aiming to speak with the widest possible audience. While the book for this reason straddles multiple genres and their conventions, I see my academic training not as a burden on the book but as generative of many of its central insights. Yet the book is not a conventional sociological study either, and rather than force it to conform to the features of an academic monograph, I chose to limit certain features, perhaps most importantly endnotes. The decision to avoid marking the text with them was made out of consideration for the intended audience of both specialists and generalists and the expectation that readers interested in looking for documentation would be able to find it by consulting the bibliography. I have done my best to narrate events that can be generally verified by available sources or that have been touched upon elsewhere, even if those sources are not cited in the form of notes herein. I hope readers consider the trade-off made in favor of readability as one worth making when working with a hybrid text such as this.

Note on Transliteration

The transliteration of Persian words and names follows the system suggested by the journal *Iranian Studies* (available from http://societyforiranianstudies.org/journal/transliteration), with the following exceptions:

- Consonants with the same sound are sometimes not differentiated, depending on the prevailing transliteration of the word. So at times both *ghayn* and *ghaf* are represented by gh and *hamza* and *ayn* are represented by '.
- Current Persian pronunciation has been followed, except for Arabic words in an Arabic context (for instance, in reciting the Qur'an). In such cases *The International Journal of Middle Eastern Studies* transliteration rules were followed.
- For individuals' names, their own preferred transliteration was used if it was accessible. If not, the most common transliteration was used. In cases where the same name is transliterated differently, one form was chosen for the text of the book (but not the bibliography and citation) for consistency. In general, omission of '*ayn* and *hamza* was preferred wherever names are commonly transliterated without them.

Dates

In some cases, two dates are used to cite Persian materials (e.g. 1395/2016). In such cases, the first date is based on the solar *hijri* calendar, which is currently used in Iran, and the second one is its equivalent Common Era date.

Introduction
A Fall Day in 1978

Tehran, 1978

A fall day in 1978 forever altered my life. A day that started like any other tore asunder the life I had worked years to build for myself and my country. For the past forty years, the ghost of that fateful day has trailed my shadow. Today, March 5 2020, as I write these words in the early morning light, sitting in a café on Bleecker Street in Manhattan, the shock of that day still thrums in my mind like a buzzing broken record, while the corresponding images, dark and painful to behold, flash uncontrollably before my eyes.

I have only recently disclosed the details of that day to my family and friends, the people who know me best. It has taken me decades to expose the nefarious underbelly of my political biography to them. Spurring me on has been the realization that burying the ugly face of politics smothers with it hope for change. Neither goodness nor peace can dwell in my mind so long as this darkness remains undisturbed by the light of revelation. It is time to let the "unthought"—those memories I have tried so long to cast into oblivion—speak.

I never intended to hide what happened that day, but the fear that it would overtake and distort memories of my precious, if turbulent, youth led me to push it out of my mind. After all, this event transpired just as I and countless other Iranians were on the cusp of realizing the impossible: toppling a police state indifferent to our wills, hopes, and ambitions. I could see the freedom we had so long been denied materializing as protestors poured daily into Tehran's city streets. Everything I had hoped for, social change on an unimaginable scale directed by and for Iranians, lay within our reach, and all that remained was for us to seize it. Only as we were turning the corner into a future free of the Pahlavi state's modern autocracy did I learn, tragically and violently, that our hopes were fodder for a power struggle that would once again sideline and silence us. When people nurture dreams manipulated by the powerful, any one of them might fall victim to their political caprices.

It was late October 1978 when I almost became such a casualty. I had just pulled off what was perhaps my greatest stunt as a student activist. In front of hundreds of my classmates at the National University in northern Tehran, I delivered a speech arguing for the continuation of an ongoing university strike, a direct challenge to a demand Ayatollah Ruhollah Khomeini had issued just the prior day. University students all over Iran had had been striking for six to eight weeks by this time, refusing to attend classes and occupying university grounds and buildings, bringing whole campuses to a standstill. Khomeini's sudden decree that students and faculty should cease the strikes and immediately allow for the resumption of normal university operations confused most of us, and it was only his supporters gathered among us who left his command unchallenged. The crowd settled on the idea of a debate to keep tensions from growing, and I was elected by the pro-strike faction to make the case for keeping university operations halted. I accepted the assignment with a sense of solemn responsibility and considerable anxiety. My speech stressed the need to maintain unity and a common purpose by making political decisions ourselves. We, as students, should think for ourselves, and do what we think is reasonable. I concluded that if we listened to our hearts and minds, we would vote for the continuation of the strikes. My arguments proved a success, and I left the campus relieved the crowd had voted to continue the strike.

As the last spectators trickled out of the campus, a vast and powerful silence settled over the land. I walked toward the vacant lot where I had parked my old red Paykan. Once the car entered my field of vision, a speck dissolving into the horizon, I hurried toward it, guided by an intuition that arrived seconds too late. Before I could even pull the car keys from my pocket, the world came crashing down on me. When I opened my eyes hours later, there was nothing but the darkness of the ditch I found myself in. Several unfamiliar faces peered down at me. Seeing my eyes flutter open, they yelled: "He's not dead!" It seemed my ability to hear had alone survived the fall. I was completely weak, unable to stand or move, let alone understand what had just happened.

When I next woke, night had fallen, and I was resting in a hospital. The nurse and later a doctor joked that it was divine providence or else extreme luck that had saved me. I had been stabbed twenty-one times and yet survived. A few children playing in a village outside of Tehran, they explained, had noticed a car stop at a local garbage dump. Out from the car climbed a man. He opened the trunk, pulled a body from it, and dumped it into a ditch before quickly driving away. The children informed their parents of this, who immediately called for an ambulance. At the hospital, doctors surveyed the damage done. Some wounds were superficial, others more serious, and a great deal of blood had been lost. But none had been fatal. After being bandaged and recovering from the initial shock, I was released from the hospital that same night. I did not feel mentally prepared to go home and explain the bruises and bandages on my body to my parents. Frail and in poor physical shape, I took a taxi instead to my friend Mozafar's apartment in central Tehran, where I stayed for several days. And with that, the revolution ended for me two or three months earlier that it did for most others.

Educated in Small Towns

The terrible extremity of that day is meaningful only against the cadence of the everyday, against the forgotten and quieter flow of ordinary time. Just as the doctors helped me retrace the moments that put me in that ditch, I have spent the better part of the last forty years retracing the days leading up to it. With photographs, records, and books as my guide, I have revisited the period of rupture that we now call the Iranian Revolution. In a way, the need to retrace, record, and remember is perhaps an extension of my intellectual preoccupation with the history of Iran. I have spent much of my life as an intellectual and a sociologist attempting to understand the national and international forces that shaped the events of the 1970s, a time whose reverberations still echo today.

But before I approached Iran as a scholar, I was its student. I came to the revolution, as did countless other young men and women of my generation who felt they had no way to steer the change enveloping the country, by way of education. Schools and universities were, on the one hand, symbols of state authority, and as sites of censorship and control, they had little to offer young people grappling with what was happening around them. Yet they, on the other hand, were perhaps the only public spaces we occupied every day where curiosity was encouraged. Guided by teachers who suffused, in each their own way, education with ethics, teachers and students of my generation made this state-sponsored space their own.

Education taught me to hunger for a better world, a constant in my life. In the teeming halls and clamorous classrooms of my youth as well as in long, solitary hours of reading, I arrived at an enlightening recognition: Iran was not alone in its struggles against modern incarnations of despotism, and neither was I, despite my outsider status in the cities my family, under the changing duties of my civil-servant father, moved to. The echoes of my schoolteachers' voices, of radio programs broadcast countries away, and of my favorite storybook protagonists colored those realizations. Books, newspapers, and radio were the ingredients in the transnational media space that defined my adolescence, even as they operated alongside a system of routinized disinformation thanks to Pahlavi censorship.

While my friends and I tuned into radio stations broadcasting from East Berlin, Baghdad, Beijing, and London and devoured books about India, China, Vietnam, Latin

America, and Palestine, we could scarcely find commentary on contemporary Iranian politics. The entire modern history of Iran, including the democratic struggles of the Constitutional Revolution of 1905–11, had been rendered a massive void by the masked machinations of the state. If we could find no entry into recent Iranian political history, because those in power wished to hide it, how could information about the wider world educate us? Through a politics of analogy, we looked to the dynamics of oppression and resistance at play in other parts of the world to better diagnose Iran's situation. We fought against this official vacuum in the everyday spaces of schools, universities, and bookshops, sites for reimagining the Iranian nation, which had been reduced to ghost traces by the official Pahlavi political machine.

The memories that animate the following pages, then, are not situated in the recesses of individual memory, but in the commotion of civil society. I experienced the fervor of Iran's revolutionary days as an inexhaustible search for collective truth, a truth arrived at by no way other than open, and sometimes fierce, public debate. Yet important to my formation and understanding of collective action as mass protests were, my political awakening was set in motion years earlier, beginning in seventh grade when my family relocated to the city of Nahavand. Three bookshops there provided me an avenue to American crime novels, which unveiled the social dynamics of New York's streets, to the disturbing socio-psychological novels of Chekhov, Dostoyevsky and Gorky, and to challenging modernist Iranian writers such as Sadegh Hedayat and Bozorg Alavi. On the other end of the spectrum stand instances of spectacular mass mobilization. From a large *minbar* [pulpit] perched upon a balcony in a working-class district of Tehran, the anti-regime preacher Taghi Falsafi recited Qur'anic verses in Arabic before declaring the dawn of a moral transformation so thorough that "nothing will ever be as it once was." Both experiences were public, transformative, and educational in a collective and personal sense. They occurred far from one another, the first in Iran's provincial towns and the other in its capital, Tehran, yet they were the material with which young Iranians braving the upheaval of revolution forged a vision for their future.

Memoirs and Remembrance

Although I have spent much of my adult life pursuing my enduring interest in the sociology of revolutions and in the intellectual history of Iran, tackling these themes within the framework of a memoir is an altogether different task. Memoirs resist the conventions of history writing. A memoir, by its nature, focalizes the life of one person, as recounted at a later date with all the privilege of hindsight in hand. No amount of corroborating or contradicting evidence can alter the composition of my memories. The subjective sensibility of the memoir makes no concessions to empirical reproach and dares even to take on the mantle of evidence for itself. But is it fair to say that individual memories have no claim to the truth? I would say not. While I write as a witness to my own truth, I hope this first-hand account (history in its most rudimentary form) of my introduction to radical politics and subsequent participation in the Iranian Revolution might become a source for further historical and social analysis, subject to all the same rigors of debate and criticism.

Participant accounts make writing histories that accord individuals their full importance in the otherwise spectacular sweep of grand events possible. Even if autobiography treats history as mere scenery to the writer's life, how can one peer into a life remembered without stumbling upon it? Mine, at any rate, is a modest narrative, one that approaches the past through the individual while seeking multiple ways of remembering the same events and stories, and which thus hopes to embrace a principle of humble recollection.

Given these considerations, memoirs not only provide rich material for understanding the historical past but expand what we traditionally take to be its very definition. My story of education and political maturation in the small Iranian towns of Nahavand and Golpayegan approaches the revolution and its aftermath in terms of the people and places that defined my everyday life prior to my being attacked and thrust into exile to appreciate the revolution's reach beyond Tehran.

The Torment of Living in *Ghorbat*

Before introducing these little-known places, I would like to turn briefly to the meaning of the word *ghorbat*, which I believe is key to understanding Iranians' experience of modernization and social change in the 1960s and 1970s. *Ghorbat*, a wandering Arabic word that found a second home for itself in Persian ages ago, invites reflection about the relationship between person and place. The word, which most generally evokes a sense of "strangeness," can mark a place, person, or community. *Ghorbat* can refer to the strangeness of a new place, an outsider's sense of existential unbelonging, or a forlorn nostalgia for home. My early upbringing and family life were defined by the feelings this word conjures. My father's career in the finance ministry moved my family from one city to another. We peregrinated from central to western Iran until my high school graduation, never staying long enough to form a cultural closeness to any one town. My family's middle-class standing was the source of our mobility but also the cause of our *ghorbat*. Each of these movements was a private expression of the "modernization" of Iranian society and culture. For many Iranians, *ghorbat* and modernity were the consequences of a vertiginous life they lived but had little control over.

At a national level, Iranians had been overwhelmingly excluded from participating in the Pahlavi project of economic modernization, which, by its centrally mandated and increasingly autocratic nature, minimized young people's opportunities to participate in and contribute to civil society. My exclusion, however, was dual in character, extending from political exclusion to social exclusion as a stranger to the towns we relocated to. Yet both instances of isolation fed the same hunger I harbored to find new ways of being and living. My yearning to belong, which only grew with my repeated designation as an outsider, transformed me during my final high-school years into an activist, eager to fight for "the cause" as part of a larger movement. While the cause was always framed in national terms, my nationalism was a personal creation motivated by my craving for a home, a place I could proudly feel I was from. If we could imagine and create a new Iran, I thought, then everyone would be welcome to it as equals. Whereas my father loved a distant Iran, an ancient *sarzamin javidan* (eternal homeland) superior to all others and stories of whose past glory filled me with wonder, I wanted an Iran that would accept me and all other Iranians as its children, a homeland rooted in the here and now of our contemporary situation.

In the flotsam-like world of my mobile adolescence, books helped me make sense of my life in *ghorbat*. I was in seventh grade when I discovered my father's small library, a glass-doored cabinet, and devoured the entirety of its contents in a summer. Most of his library consisted of historical novels of little literary or scholarly value, but they nonetheless instilled a fledgling nationalism in me. While I pledged allegiance to no city or clan, I was an Iranian like any other, and these stories nurtured an affinity for Iranian history in me. They narrated the rise and fall of Iran as a civilization tragically overcome by savage nations thanks to corrupt governments and treasonous rulers. Our high school textbooks, which celebrated the *Shahnameh* (Book of Kings) as the pinnacle of learning and lamented the Arab and Mongol invasions as a dark hour in world history, reinforced these tropes.

The world of books and bookshops I built for myself was populated by novelists, poets, journalists, and translators. In the company of writers like Ahmad Shamlu, a leading modernist poet of the 1960s, I realized I was not alone in feeling like a stranger at home. His lyrics articulated an uneasiness with nativism and the beauty of a new kind of humanism, which I found refreshing. An example of Shamlu's poetry is his well-known "Ofogh-e roshan" (The glowing horizon):

> "One day we will find our doves once again
> And kindness and beauty will join hands

One day when the slightest hymn
is a kiss
and each human being
is a brother for all human beings"

In Shamlu's poetic works I sensed an affirmation of the secular and humanist vision of Iranian constitutionalists and the early Tudeh Party, who together redefined radicalism as a worldly project of egalitarian justice and political freedom. While focused on the struggles particular to place, their works referred to human experiences everywhere under capitalism. And it was in this spirit that Shamlu apprehended the cause of our collective alienation or *ghorbat* by simultaneously engaging the local and universal. I admired Shamlu and his broad-mindedness which enabled him to imagine himself as a citizen of the world. His simultaneous wariness with other Iranian thinkers and warm embrace of the world made me realize that *ghorbat* was home to many others.

Another writer who populated my adolescent imagination was Samad Behrangi, who struck me as the opposite of my mother, with her stubborn attachment to her one and only home town. Behrangi, who lived and worked all his life in Iranian Azerbaijan as a schoolteacher and whose children's book *Mahi-ye Siyah-e Kochulu* (The Little Black Fish) made him a national literary figure, pushed the central government to recognize the contributions Azeri people and culture had made to Iran. He seemed equally at home teaching in the grade schools of Azerbaijan's small villages as he did writing about national diversity and the need for individuals and communities to embrace cultural and ethnic differences.

I later learned that other Iranian writers and thinkers, many close to the government, invoked *ghorbat* to describe Iran's supposed alienation from its cultural heritage. This group of influential artists, intellectuals, and political figures, many of whom spent prolonged periods in Europe or the U.S. or lived their whole lives in Tehran (including the likes of Ahmad Fardid, Daryush Shayegan, Ehsan Naraghi, etc.) believed that Iranians ought to preserve their cultural traditions and forsake all that was Western and modern in order to ease the psychological pain of *ghorbat*. A parallel intellectual current diagnosed this alienation as Westoxification or *gharbzadeghi*. Jalal Al-e Ahmad and Ali Shari'ati were two such intellectuals, who dominated the oppositional political culture of 1960s and 1970s Iran.

As someone reared in Iran's small towns, it remains difficult for me to understand the artistic and intellectual romance with rural life, synonymous in so many ways with Iranian "tradition," that flourished in the 1960s and 1970s, not for lack of admiration for the people of these towns and villages but for the pervasive poverty I encountered there. Upon reflection, I see that two distinct *ghorbat* discourses emerged, two cultural outlooks on belonging, place, and authenticity. One believed that the strangeness of the present required a return to an imagined, authentic past, while another believed addressing it required a more hospitable and inclusive bond between "us" and the "other." To overcome the *ghorbat* condition, we must embrace, voluntarily and with open arms, ideas, peoples, and cultures we do not know. This is the principal of humanist hospitality, and it is critical to understanding intellectual traditions and political ideologies that seek to speak on behalf of all Iranians by leveraging an identitarian discourse of "local" legitimacy.

Golpayegan, 1960s, Tehran, 1970s

My adolescence in Golpayegan, where I completed the last three years of high school from 1966 to 1969, would have been familiar to many Iranians who dwelled in the many middling towns like it, which were then neither fully rural nor urban. Golpayegan, a rather conservative city, did not cry out as an ideal breeding ground for political radicalism. Some might ask whether such an unassuming town even participated in the radical upheavals of the 1960s. I am inclined to think it did, and, moreover, that every tucked-away Iranian town, no matter how far-flung or conservative, was touched by the radicalism of the 1960s. Even in Golpayegan, the uproar of student protests in Paris, the anti-war movement in New York, and our own radical groups in Tehran, Tabriz, Mashhad, and Shiraz reverberated, rocking our corner of Iran into a new international consciousness and emboldening my classmates, teachers, and me to link our corner of the world to many others. By turning our attention to Golpayegan, we can unearth local narratives concealed by official ones and better understand acts of resistance against the Iranian elite and the class differences inspiring dissent there.

Despite the local texture distinguishing Golpayegan and towns like it from the revolution's standard-bearer, Tehran, Golpayegan of the late 1960s curiously resembled Tehran of the late 1970s. As in Iran's modernizing capital, in religious towns like Golpayegan, streams of political Islam and Marxism ran together and were nurtured and debated in everyday spaces like high-school classrooms. Golpayegan's two local high schools—Ebn-e Sina and Ferdowsi—were centers of our cultural and political life. Books, newspapers, magazines, and the study of foreign languages, such as Arabic, stretched the imagination of young students there beyond Iran. In our minds, the late 1960s and 1970s were a "place" defined by a synchronous cultural revolution from below despite regime restrictions.

The coming revolution was in some ways the revenge of Golpayegan and Iran's other overlooked peripheries upon Tehrani elities, upon the upper-class fantasy that Iran would soon dispense with its traditions and superstitions to join the arena of modern nations. Official nationalism compelled us to celebrate the Shah as God's gift to the nation, even though we did not accept the state's hallucination that Pahlavi modernization had given birth to a superior modern society. These delusions of Pahlavi grandeur only left us feeling cold. In Golpayegan, the rejection of this chimera did not spring from a reactionary impulse but from a new social consciousness defined by events in Cuba and Russia, France and the United States, and Turkey and India. Our political and emotional affinities were with far away Vietnam, Palestine, Cuba, and India, more so than with the official Pahlavi Iran. Reading Nehru's *Discovery of India* was a sort of rite of passage for young activists living in a country where the United States paraded its influence. The future we envisioned was an amalgamation of Nehru's India, Castro's Cuba, Lenin's Soviet Union, and the spirit of our Constitutional Revolution. And in this sense, the pain of *ghorbat* was overcome by claiming the whole world as our home. It was by knowing the world that we came to know our nation.

Yet part of the appeal of the global had to do with how few channels onto the local the state made available to us. It was easier to access knowledge of the outside world than it was of our own national history under the Shah. Under the Pahlavi dynasty, the entirety of Iran's recent political history—a saga of democratic struggles starting in the late nineteenth century with the 1891 Tobacco Revolt and ending with the labor and nationalist movements of the 1940s and early 1950s—was rendered a massive void. This absence of memory and history reveals the sinister workings of state censorship, which ensconced its citizens in a veritable prison of disinformation. It was only once I left Iran for London before resettling in Tehran two years later that I realized the full extent of the erasure. In England I read works on Iranian political thought written by leftist authors like Ehsan Tabari, Bijan Jazani, the Confederation of Iranian Studies. Suddenly, the hidden histories of Iran's political and intellectual movements opened to me as I read about groups, ideas, individuals, and events I until then only knew by name.

Tajaddod, a Mistaken Modernity

While it was in Golpayegan, the site of frequent debates about Islamism and Marxism and a mix of classes, ethnicities, and ideological affinities, that I came of political age, it was in Tehran that I assumed a new identity for myself. I arrived in Tehran in 1970 to begin my university studies. Then, after graduating, I spent two years in the U.K. (1975–77), before returning to Tehran to participate in the 1978 revolution. It was when I joined Tehran University as a student in the 1970s that my political work began in earnest. While it built on thinking that had germinated in Golpayegan, it was in

Tehran that I, after an encounter with a group committed to the Palestinian cause, became a Marxist. Regardless of my eventual disillusionment, being a Marxist activist in the 1970s was an empowering experience. For the first time in my life, I stood shoulder to shoulder with other men and women committed to realizing a freer, less oppressive Iran. This was at a time when Marxism was ubiquitous. Every political force shaping pre-revolutionary Iranian politics was in dialogue with its chief theoreticians and tacticians. From our European-educated professors at Tehran University to Ali Shari'ati at the Hosseiniyeh Ershad, and from underground leaflets to Radio Moscow, Berlin and Peking, Marxism was the core around which Iran's nascent revolutionary visions circulated.

Three individuals most influenced me in my four years at Tehran University. There was my professor and mentor Dr Hamid Enayat, head of the political science department, with whom I wiled away hours discussing history and politics. Then there was Dr Shafi'i Kadkani, my Persian literature professor, and finally, Abuzar Vardasbi, an older student and experienced political activist. Vardasbi was fully dedicated to the revolution and introduced me to other committed radicals, but he remains in my mind the embodiment of political and intellectual confusion, a confusion that was by no means unique to him but navigated by us all during those days. It was the confusion of *tajaddod* (modernity), a source of unresolved debates and discussion, a political tension dividing Iranians since at least the nineteenth century. Iranian intellectuals were engaged in articulating a vision of modernity that was both cosmopolitan but also grounded in the country's history and culture. As an intellectual and a member of the Mujahedin, Vardasbi was sympathetic to Marxism and happy to mentor a young activist like myself. We discussed the struggles against dispossession raging in Palestine and participated in regular house gatherings in the working-class neighborhood of Tehran-now (New Tehran), which reminded me of my earlier life in Golpayegan. And while he never pressed me to embrace Islam in my politics or faith, ideologically Vardasbi was, to use today's language, an "Islamist" intellectual and activist.

As thinkers, Enayat, Kadkani, and Vardasbi embodied the ambiguity and confusion of *tajaddod* in Iran, which saturated the Iranian political spectrum. For example, Kadkani, a learned literary scholar and poet from Khorasan, was sympathetic to militant left-Islamist groups, like the Fedayeen-e Khalq and Mujahedin, as well as to Marxists. This ambiguity pervaded his academic work as well. He was the first literary scholar I encountered whose theoretical sophistication permitted the application of critical theory to Persian literature. Yet Kadkani's embrace of innovation was tempered by a desire to safeguard Iran's local traditions. He taught us that Greater Khorasan, a historical region comprising northeastern Iran, was a distinctive center of literary and cultural output, with unique literary and philosophical schools.

Another illustration of modernity's confusion is provided by Dr Hamid Enayat, who instructed me in European political theory and Islamic thought at Tehran University. Enayat was once affiliated with the Marxist Tudeh Party, but rumors linked him in the 1970s to Islamists Ayatollah Motahhari and Ahmad Fardid as well. His class on Islamic political thought seemed to confirm a turn away from Marxism, since he spent a great deal of energy detailing the deficiencies of Soviet scholarship on Islam. In Golpayegan I had attributed what "provincial" tendencies I observed to the town's insularity. Enayat, however, had studied at the London School of Economics and been a visiting faculty member at Oxford University. How could I explain the many similarities between him and the religious conservatism of my teachers in Golpayegan, who had never stepped foot outside Iran? These questions perplexed me on the eve of the revolution, but today I find a common thread running through them in the confusion with *tajaddod*.

The *tajaddod* confusion was intimately tied to public space, since it was there—not in the private contemplation of the few—that we forged a path to revolution and that this idea took on its pervasiveness. The truth is sought in open public debate and sometimes violent struggle through—and against—everyday public institutions. Exploring civil society, which was public, contested, noisy, dangerous, and creative, I engaged with the public spirituality of the revolution, the exuberance of which overcame the ordinary barriers that hold different classes and social groups apart.

The "Spirits" of the Crowd

Revolutions nurture their own transcendental moments. In my case, one such moment occurred on the 17 of Shahrivar (September 8, 1978), remembered as Jom'e-ye Siyah (Black Friday) in commemoration of the more than 100 people killed after the Shah's military indiscriminately opened fire onto a crowd of protesters in Jaleh Square. In that moment, I felt the revolutionary crowd had attained a single will or soul.

The crowds commandeered bastions of power—city streets, lecture halls, mosques, and other civil society spaces—in the name of a people united, even as individuals of vastly different backgrounds, parties, desires, and hopes mingled. It was our collective power that transformed these spaces into arenas of revolutionary action. Other such experiences included sit-ins at Tehran University and Aryamehr University, the Ten Nights of Poetry Readings at the Goethe Institute, art exhibitions, theatre performances, teach-ins, and often heated debates that followed in question-and-answer sessions—all of which were living proof for my generation of the possibility of building a freer Iran. These transcendental moments brought us to the brink of revolutionary success and almost overflowed with hope. But they proved to be fleeting and, in many ways, have been overshadowed, both in my mind and in the conventional historical narrative, by the traumatic events that followed.

Some variations of this conventional narrative argue that it was unadulterated contempt for the West that motivated Iranians to follow Khomeini. Yet such a retelling sidelines the more complicated processes of political deliberation and radical organization I lived, witnessed, and remember. My memories of the human rights activist Karim Lahiji provide an antidote to such simplistic histories. My first encounter with Lahiji was at a lecture he gave at Aryamehr University in October 1978, which invoked constitutionalists' struggle against arbitrary state power and political chaos as a parallel to then contemporary challenges to the Shah's corruption and systematic disregard for the rule of law. Several young men in the audience confronted Lahiji after his talk, insisting that the regime's crimes were so evident that making a legal case against it was a waste of time, that Lahiji, by even invoking notions such as the rule of law, had diminished the ultimate sovereignty that resided in the will of the people. While conservative accounts of the revolution whitewash such important debates, emphasizing a ubiquitous religiosity, Lahiji defended legal reasoning. Our revolutionary aim was ethical, moral, and legally sanctioned, he insisted. The Pahlavi state, he argued, had plundered the county and violated the will of the people, a transgression that justified ordinary Iranians' uprising.

Tragically, just as Iran started to undergo a political opening, the revolutionary movement faltered. We sought utopia but found ruins. The left had slowly been eliminated as an organized force—imprisoned, exiled, or worse—and soon enough the sphere of leftist activities was limited to high schools, universities, and subterranean cells. By the 1960s, and certainly by the 1970s, this policy of systematic marginalization rendered the left poorly organized, under-resourced, and unable to communicate its vision to Iranian society, allowing Islamism and clerical activism, a much better supplied alternative, to flourish. Of course, other secular forces, whether liberal or nationalist, were scarcely in a better position. Despite a few notable leaders, they had little in the way of organization or resources. Reluctantly, or at other times with mistaken enthusiasm, some of these groups joined forces with Islamists. This was the apex of the *tajaddod* confusion. The creation, on unequal footing, of a coalition of Khomeinists and leftists, in my mind, gravely damaged the revolution's "spirituality," or the fearless flow of Iranians into the streets in solidarity with fellow Iranians. I was afraid that in the absence of a plurality of voices, the revolution would become curbed and eventually, that we would lose the spirit of hope and creativity that had carried us so far. I did not want the mosques, the only public space left to function in relative freedom until the final hour of the 1978–79 Revolution, to take over the streets.

The growing Islamist movement advanced a vision of Iran's future impervious to the ideals of democracy and legal transparency Lahiji and others upheld. A principal proponent of this Islamist vision was the popular orator Taghi Falsafi. One mass gathering at which he spoke vividly reveals the stakes and profound differences between secular leftists and Islamists. Falsafi stood behind a podium amid a sea of spectators lecturing at length on the Shi'i leadership's goal of the total cultural and moral transformation of Iran. He proclaimed that: "In the name of *taraqqi* [progress] and *tajaddod* [modernity], they have taken away our religion, offering us only the illusion of a better material life . . . We call for the return to our faith and our honorable leader [Khomeini]." By his account, the *tajaddod* confusion could be resolved by rejecting the false promises of modernity—progress, development, women's rights—and returning in pure and simple fashion to our authentic Iranian roots. The glorification of this closed-off Iranian identity sounded the death knell for revolutionary spirituality. Reducing the quintessence of Iranian identity to religion and forwarding Islam as the sole cultural foundation of the nation gravely damaged Iran's national unity, by asking all to conform to one set of values.

Iranians did not consent to the systemic suppression of their civil society. They did not choose to route all political action through the most authoritarian channels, or to eliminate every opportunity for shared dialogue and unified organization. They cannot be blamed for the Pahlavi state's systematic suppression of all self-organizing institutions of civil society nor for the policy of rapid top-down modernization that limited such autonomous spaces in the first place. My account contains ample evidence of the pervasive worry young leftist activists of my generation felt about the perils of ascendant Islamism. Among my circle of friends in the late 1970s lingering reservations persisted about the emergence of a new, revolutionary religious language. Iran's constitutional tradition was being eclipsed by a moralistic turn to culture based on a simulacrum of religion. We recognized that the popularity of the Fedayeen or of Mohammad Mosaddegh had become just that—images without institutional embeddedness. The religious forces, meanwhile, consolidated hegemony through potent revolutionary symbols and organizational tact. We struggled over the public's imagination of Iran until the last hours of the revolution, and the fatal ferocity of this struggle is proven in my near loss of life on that fall day. It still strikes me profoundly to consider that I was targeted not by Pahlavi security forces, but by other revolutionaries simply for not supporting Khomeini.

Yet members of Iran's liberal and left intelligentsia, perhaps under the pressure of political expediency, did in some instances make concessions to the rise of Islamist forces. On one occasion, this was done to shore up unity in the face of growing factional fissures. A major demonstration at the Behesht-e Zahra (Zahra's Paradise) cemetery was underway in 1978; I walked up to a crowd to see the respected Tehran University professor of history, Dr Homa Nategh, putting foreign reporters who had inquired about Islam and its treatment of women in their place. Nategh defended Islam and the role of religious activists in the demonstrations, telling reporters that our revolution recognized no difference between men and women. We were entirely unconcerned, she maintained before them, about the situation for women after the revolution. For Nategh, the Western reporters' questions about women's rights were not only irrelevant but a sign of foreign chauvinism worth publicly chiding. In the end, Nategh would not be not alone in accepting the terms of the Islamist movement as a matter of revolutionary expediency, with tragic costs.

By November of 1978 it was becoming clear that the Pahlavi State was collapsing. The Islamists exerted their leadership over city streets, university campuses, mosques, and most government offices. The institutions that kept the state running were either corroding or defecting to the general strikes, and I knew the regime was bound to fall. I turned my attention to imagining what would replace it, an exciting and confusing prospect. I found myself daily discussing what a post-Pahlavi leadership and future might look like with friends and strangers. Yet I never thought that I would spend several years fighting those who came to power, and from the United States, a place of exile, no less.

Troubled Memories

In the immediate aftermath of the revolution, I struggled to reconcile the image of Iran I had hoped to realize with the reality of oppression and exclusion its ultimately violent transition gave way to. I held on to, despite the rise of a government increasingly hostile to my existence and that of my loved ones, hope for a different Iran. At the same time, I feared that the national imaginary, the very idea and meaning of Iran, was being co-opted by those who had come to power and tasked with violent legitimizations. It is in part because these concerns continue to haunt me that I feel compelled to record these remembrances. Memories are never a complete history of the author's life, but only those aspects of life as "recalled" and remembered. In other words, an autobiography—a partially invented or even fictionalized reconstruction of the personal past—harbors "unthought" or forgotten elements. The recesses of memory, and of the unspoken, are scarcely preserved in written history. It is the possibility of integrating the two that makes autobiographies, which straddle the space between history, memory, and fantasy, potentially productive.

It is only now that I recognize the impossibility of treating autobiography as simply one person's view of their own life. My writing will likely be read as a first-hand account of larger events and historical moments, and I welcome this potential with the hope that it will provide new perspective onto the past. Reading several autobiographies about a period, an event, or a generation can help us attain greater proximity to the objective truth claims that historians make. While I can of course write only about my own experiences, what I have written is about much more than me. It is a story of Iranian life—student, provincial, and metropolitan—during the 1960s and 1970s.

Memoirs invite us to reflect upon how we conceptualize ordinary experiences and spectacular events. These two categories of memories do not often overlap, but they may appear as two accounts of a single event. Memoirs strive to capture the fleeting and ineffable truth of affective and sensuous experience, rather than to appraise the reality of these experiences according to the intelligible concepts of sociology. While other authors, such as Azar Nafisi, have attempted to capture what she calls "the texture of real experience," which played out for her during the revolution in university classrooms and, under the mounting surveillance of an oppressive regime, in secret literature classes inside of the author's home, her milieu of political elites gives a window onto experiences available only to a narrow group.

Here is perhaps the major divergence between my memoir and others of the revolution. I have taken pains to illustrate a different and more popular type of educational experience. My autobiography occurs primarily in the public spaces through which Iranians pursued revolution as the Pahlavi regime crumbled. These experiences of debate and violent struggle range from the sea changes in a young individual's life as he makes reading a daily habit, feasting on the works of Chekhov, Dostoyevsky, Gorky, Hedayat, and Alavi, to the teeming gatherings in working-class Tehran and across the city's university campuses, which were equally formative to my political development and participation in the revolution. Although some occurred in the capital city of Tehran, and others in small towns like Nahavand, there was much connecting these places I thought to be worlds apart. The web holding them together can be understood in terms of the interconnection between *ghorbat*, *tajaddod*, the "spirits" of revolution, and as the betrayal of that "spirituality" by an Islamist ideology and the Shi'i clerics' thirst for power that left me and other strangers to our country once again. Yet, my aim in telling my life story is not to pass judgments of guilt or innocence on people and their ideas I encountered. My hope is that my story will help us to probe the memories, personal and collective, that we leave unspoken.

1

Dorud and Nahavand, 1956–1966

The Pain of *Ghorbat*

I was contemplating the soft strands of hair framing my mother's face when my eyes fell upon her searching gaze. She had called me to the living room, where she sat resting upon a lounge chair, and gently pulled me close to her. She drew my head to her chest as I sat beside her, those same strands of hair now grazing my head, and whispered sorrowfully, "My dear (*azizam*), as it happens, we live in *ghorbat* now, but we have roots in a place where people are brave and generous . . . They live a truly joyous life. They love and help each other endlessly. They are a happy people."

It was around this time that I, only a pre-school-aged child of four or five years old, became aware that whenever my mother slipped into a passing depression, whether because of a squabble with my father, the tiresome habits of her friends and neighbors, or just dismay with the world at large, she would return to this word—*ghorbat*—and pronounce: "I have the pain of *ghorbat* (strangeness) [*dardi-ye ghorbat daram*]." What,

I wondered, was the source of this pain that so profoundly and frequently gripped my mother? *Ghorbat* appeared to capture a feeling of solitude among strangers, the sense that life had unfairly estranged her from all that was familiar to her. My mother had, after all, left her family home in Nahavand to be with my father and would let no one forget this. Perhaps life had been cruel to her, I wondered, or perhaps she simply longed for her hometown and family. The refrain was so routine, such a part of her character, that I came to spend considerable time contemplating the curious idea of *ghorbat* and trying to imagine a life for my mother outside of it. Little did I know then that I would spend my life in *ghorbat* too, in places unfathomably remote to her.

Adding to my confusion about the meaning of *ghorbat* was the fact that my mother would invoke it not only when she was sullen but when she was feeling sentimental too. On these occasions, *ghorbat* captured nostalgia for her roots. Although I understood this, my mother's invocation of the word still perplexed me. Why must she live as a stranger among our neighbors? Are the people here not loving, helpful, or happy as they were in Nahavand? Loving her, I found the idea that others might treat her differently simply because she was from another town unjust. Was I living in *ghorbat* too? What would happen if my friends were to find out that I was not a local but a *gharibeh* (stranger)? Yet I was too young and afraid to probe these questions any further than the moment they jostled before my mind, and never raised them with my mother.

As a person with little real attachment to a specific place, constantly reestablishing roots in other people's towns, setting myself apart from others seemed self-defeating. I attempted instead to define myself by how I lived in the world, that is, through sport teams, educational institutions, reading clubs, and so on. To this day, I have never used the words *gharibeh* or *ghorbat* to describe my life, not when I lived in Iran, moving from one town to another every three or four years, nor when I left Iran to live for two years in the U.K. and another forty years in the U.S. I distanced myself from the term, finding *ghorbat* frightening for reasons beyond my own comprehension. Perhaps I thought admitting to *ghorbat* was tantamount to conceding that essential differences do exist between humans, that there is something fundamentally unknowable about others that no amount of effort, intention, or dialogue can overcome. If this were true, then the friends and people I wanted badly to befriend would have been right to keep me at arm's length as I attempted to make my home among them. Whatever the cause of my bitterness about being marked an "outsider," I knew I desired a different, more generous understanding of culture and identity and of the possibilities for belonging that we afforded others. I held on to the belief that friendship, kindness, and solidarity could, by the grace of time, transform a *gharibeh* into a *khodi* (an insider, one of us). I wished those at home within a culture or region would give me the chance to make a home beside them. But I also recognized that cultural rootedness was a privilege most "insiders" would not extend to others, lest they dilute its power.

Ghorbat, a wandering Arabic word that found a second home for itself in Persian centuries ago, as reflected in my mother's speech, describes an immersive state of being, the aching loneliness of knowing oneself to be a stranger among others. The word carries with it the weight of isolation, alienation, and grief for all that has been lost. Yet it also signifies a will to name, remember, and love what we know, even in its absence: a respect for culture or community, a nostalgia for good days gone by. Given its dual meaning, and as much as I hesitated to describe my own situation as one of *ghorbat*, I developed as a child an ambivalent curiosity for it.

I quietly envied my mother, who proudly remembered her home, culture, and people as good and wholesome, a community I knew not so much through lived membership but passed-down memories. She had countless stories to draw on, figures to reference, and events to narrate to substantiate this conviction. Before settling in Nahavand, a city in the northwestern province of Hamadan, my mother's forebears lived among a Lor tribe in Aleshtar (Lorestan). Their story of settlement is one episode in a larger history of state-led tribal sedentarization and persecution. Reza Shah's military forcibly settled Iran's nomadic tribes, like the Lors, the Qashqais and the Bakhtiaris, in order to remake the country in the mold of

Figure 1.1 Ali Mirsepassi, three years old, Malayer.

an integrated and civilized nation. The tribes were stripped of their autonomy and made to live under the rule of regional government. I was raised on countless stories inherited, memorized, and shared by my beloved grandmother, stories of her youth, of her tribe in its happier days, and of Reza Shah's brutal suppression of their once communal lifestyle.

Batul Khanum

My maternal grandmother, known to all as Batul Khanum, the only grandparent I ever really knew, the other three having passed away before I was born, passed down to me stories of her family's tribal roots. As a boy, I thought Batul Khanum was the prettiest and most fitting name for my dear grandmother, but I did not want to be everybody else and made a point to call her *madar*, an intimate yet reverent word for mother in Persian, signaling the special closeness of our bond. My grandmother lived in a farming complex on the edge of Nahavand with her older brother, Mr Ahmad Esfandiari, a notable figure in town, her son (my uncle) Mohammad Ali Esfandiari, and their families. I lived with my grandmother in Nahavand until

Figure 1.2 My mother and sister, Dorud, early 1960s.

I was school aged, or seven years old. I had not been given notice of our impending separation, and I vividly recall the day my parents took me from her.

I was playing with my cousin Bijan, who was a year younger than me, on our family farm one sticky summer afternoon. We were seated in the shade of a large, majestic walnut tree, enjoying the vast and colorful awning its enormity provided us. We had been rambling around the fruit orchards earlier and towed in our hands the day's haul: a heaping pile of apples, peaches, and pears. I remember comparing the fruits Bijan and I had plucked and marveling in childlike wonder at the color, grandeur, and perfect symmetry of our apple and pear prizes. As we set off to clean and eat the apples, I saw my grandmother emerge from the house. Her characteristically soft and slow steps carried her across the field and in our direction. At her sight, Bijan and I rested our treasure on the ground and waited for my grandmother to join us under the walnut tree. She seemed suddenly to be moving impossibly slow, as if time had stretched to expand each second and footstep. I could hardly stand the anticipation of waiting to hear what she had come to tell us. Finally, she stooped close enough to whisper in my ear, "Your parents are here, Ali dear. Go and see them."

With these words, my grandmother disappeared into the orchards. But the excitement of knowing my parents had come from the neighboring town of Dorud to Nahavand for me pushed all other thoughts out of my mind. The evening passed happily, then the next day a driver came to my grandmother's house. Everyone busied themselves running to and from his car, helping my parents load boxes, bags, and any other trace of me left in my grandmother's house into it. This was no routine visit, so I asked my grandmother, "Am I going back home with my parents? Can you come with me?" My grandmother responded, "You need to go by yourself and get ready to start school." I peeked up at her face and saw tears slowly falling from her eyes.

I leapt from the living room and raced breathlessly to the courtyard and farther still to the street flanking the property. I kept ahead but could hear a crowd of voices rising from behind, yelling, "Stop! Where are you going?" I had not even made it to the street when a family friend snatched me into his arms. He tried to calm me down and kept asking me to stop crying, but I continued wailing, raucously refusing to go home. But the decision had already been made. I would have no choice but to go back to and live with my parents.

My struggle had at least delayed the move by a few hours. By early evening, I had been pacified and came to the sad realization that my time with my grandmother had come to an end. All that was left to do was to accept the reality that I was to go home with my parents and start school as any normal child would.

But I would always carry with me the stories *madar* told me, which, in their half-truths and magic, teleported me to a private world of two. My grandmother was a gentle, kind and caring soul who lavished me in special love and attention. In our time together in Nahavand she always encouraged me to spend my days playing outdoors with the other neighborhood boys. But after dinner at night, we would while the evening away together, my head resting on her lap as she regaled me with the most colorful stories about her family and her travels,

Figure 1.3 My mother, first from left, and her friends, Dorud, early 1960s.

and with tales involving fictitious boys and girls, a genre I felt she invented specially for me. Although I was a little boy who did not always know how to behave, she never let on any irritation with my ways, making my room in that large house a little heaven.

In our time together, my grandmother handed down to me three kinds of stories. When her attention turned to the serious subject of tribes and the government, she always made sure to sprinkle her stories with editorial commentary, reminding me that there was no need to get upset and guiding me toward the moral of the story. Then there were stories, which she most enjoyed telling, of her pilgrimages to Shiʿi shrines in Iraq, places like Karbala, Najaf, and Baghdad.

My grandmother's stories gave me the impression that her youth and just about every moment since had been perfectly preserved in her memories. She described her father, in what appeared to be a political move, marrying her off at sixteen to a man close to Mehr Ali Khan, the brave chief of the Hasanvand tribe in Aleshtar, Lorestan, as if it happened only yesterday.

My grandmother's life after she married and moved from Nahavand to Lorestan was full of adventures and, in my mind, a classic struggle of good against evil. Although theirs was a relationship born of political expediency, over the course of their marriage, my grandmother developed the utmost respect for her husband and for the whole Hasanvand tribe. Over the years, I heard more than a dozen versions of her family history. All variations, however, centered around the life and death of the larger-than-life men Mehr Ali Khan, Reza Shah, and general Amir Ahmadi.

While it was never clear what *madar*'s views on Reza Shah were precisely, it was clear his rule was for her a watershed. The words she used were *doreh-ye* Reza Shah (the time of Reza Shah) and *pas az* Reza Shah (after Reza Shah), all demarcating his rule (1925–1944) as a period of profound transition not just for Iran, but for her family too. Reza Shah's rule set the stage for the single greatest trauma of her life: the brutal suppression of Lorestan's tribal communities. This, for her, outstripped *hamleh-ye Moghol*, or the Mongol invasions. While her feelings about Reza Shah were ambiguous

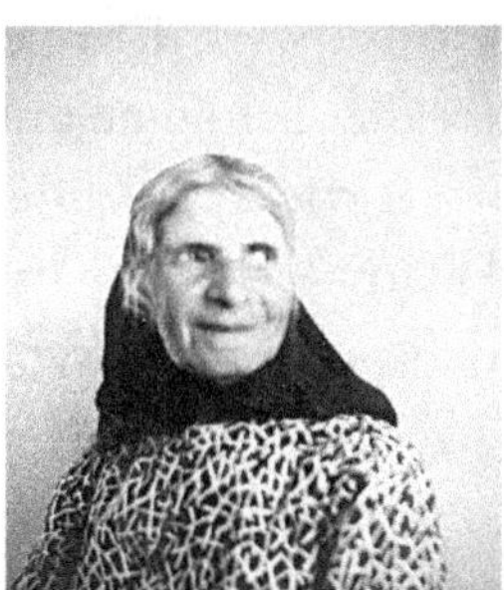

Figure 1.4 My grandmother, Nahavand, early 1960s.

to me, the villain in this tragic family incident was not the king but Sepahbod Amir Ahmadi, the general Reza Shah sent to suppress the tribes in Lorestan. My grandmother, usually nuanced in her storytelling, was absolutely clear and unambiguous on one point: General Amir Ahmadi embodied evil and had no respect for people, life, community or culture, yet pretended to bring peace, security, and progress to Lorestan and its people, particularly to her own tribe, the Hasanvand. The tribe had trusted and collaborated with the general only to be betrayed when he invited the tribal leaders for a lunch and arrested and hanged them all.

Yet my grandmother was supportive of General Amir Ahmadi's mission to disarm the tribes under the control of Iran's central government in Tehran. She was tired of tribal conflicts, the rule of *khan khani* (landlordism) in Lorestan, and all the insecurity they sowed between tribes. Disarmament and sedentarization, for her, had encouraged tribes to get involved in stable economic activities, and, through the introduction of law and dicipline, to treat people in surrounding towns well. My grandmother's inclusion in the Hasanvand tribe was the product of a peace-making marriage, a fact that colored her understanding of tribal ways. I remember her telling me with some dismay that after her home town of Nahavand was attacked by rival tribes, it was agreed, after a series of negotiations, that she would marry Mehr Ali Khan's trusted secretary. While she would have happily done away with this practice of tribal raids, which caught hapless women in their crossfire, she loved being part of a tribe and cherished the sense of solidarity and independence that came with it. Rather than have the state play the role of people's protector, my grandmother thought that we should learn from tribes people how to help and support each other, rather than have the government act as our *qa'im* (guardian and protector).

Yet my grandmother's sense of community exceeded her membership in the Hasanvand tribe to include her identity as a Shi'a Muslim. All the stories she told of her travels to shrines in Baghdad, Kufa, and Karbala were without exception exciting yet affable. She often said in wonder, "Ali dear, God has blessed Arab Iraq with all that is heavenly and all that is worldly. One can see God's reflections in Karbala, Najaf, Kufa, in these places of *'ebadat* [worship], then go and stay in Baghdad, a city blessed with the fruits of human labor and the wonders of so much *abadani* [progress]." I knew she wanted me to learn from these stories that the world, in all its unknowns, was not to be feared. When one travels, she would say, our eyes and minds open to see the wonders of the world and the goodness of people. She narrated her travels to the holy places in a soft tone, stopping after describing an event or a place to give me her own interpretation of it.

Figure 1.5 My grandmother, Nahavand, mid-1960s.

For example, after telling me about her visit to Imam Hossein's shrine in Karbala, she paused to add that the place does not remotely resemble what we in Iran think of Imam Hossein or the scenarios we create for Ashura festivals. Imam Hossein's shrine is not a traveling theater but a spiritual space for thinking and reflecting on our own life. Or whenever she discussed her time in Baghdad, she reminded me not to trust Tehranis' boasts about Tehran, insisting that Baghdad was by far the better city to visit.

Then there were special stories about imaginary boys and girls Madar only told me late at night as I prepared to close my eyes for sleep. Boys and girls in these stories would play together, and sometimes they came to have feelings for one another, but no matter what, the boys in her stories knew to respect the girls and give them space. The main characters in these stories encountered situations in their lives that tested their moral beliefs, desires, and capacity to choose between good and evil. The moral of them was to have courage in the face of life's challenges, especially since living an honorable life requires making hard choices.

Cosmopolitan Tafresh

My father's family history is set in a different Iran, where individuals of means found middle-class prosperity by insinuating themselves into the country's growing government bureaucracy during Reza Shah's rule. His family originally hailed from Tafresh, a small town in central Iran close to the city of Qum and three hours outside Nahavand. His relatives were almost all government employees. I once asked my father why all the men in his family, going back several generations, worked in the finance ministry. He smiled and told me that during the late Reza Shah's rule, it was custom for government officials to hire as many of their relatives in the same institution as they could. In his case, so many individuals with his surname had been hired in his hometown of Tafresh that he was relocated to Nahavand, only to be reappointed again to the nearby town of Malayer. Local backlash to nepotism pushed, according to my father, hiring practices to become over time more centralized and formal.

My father always identified Tafresh as his home town. When he was in a good mood, usually after he had woken from his afternoon nap to a cup of fresh tea, he would beckon me to him. Pausing only for his tea, he passed down family lore, most often about "Mirsepassi-ye Bozorg" (Dr Abdolhossein Mirsepassi, the head of the family), a pioneer of modern psychiatry in Iran. Sipping on his customary afternoon tea, one slender glass after another, my father would look at me with a meditative smile which furtively communicated that he was about to tell me something of great value. He then in rather proper Persian would say, "Please consider carefully what I am about to tell you: Dr Mirsepassi studied in France before anyone else in this country. The doctor wrote the first academic book on psychiatry in Persian. Dr Mirsepassi dedicated his life to Iran's scientific development and opened the first psychiatry hospital in Iran, which he named after his mother, Maymenat." After this, he would stop to scan my face for confirmation that I had absorbed this important piece of family information before abruptly picking up his newspaper again, a habit he kept up for the entire time we lived together.

I was never bored by my father's stories. The way he coupled family stories with Iranian history held my interest. He naturally understood that his memories and the lives of notable personalities in our family were part of the story of the making of modern Iran. Of course, my father, just like my mother, was fiercely proud of his home town. Despite my father's love for Tafresh, which he held in esteem as a place of educated, cultured, and all around important people, I hardly ever heard a word about everyday life there. As far as I remember, my father never visited Tafresh nor made a point to encourage us to do so. All the proud Tafreshis I knew instead had left the town.

My father started his career in Iran's finance ministry, with the help of relatives already working there. Yet my father was a capable man and an industrious civil servant. He was always willing to take on a new position if it meant more social status and mobility, and he was frequently asked to take on assignments in other cities, so our stay in one city was often interrupted by a move to another. I was born in Malayer, in western Iran, and lived most of my adolescence in central and western cities like it. Given the impermanence of our residences, I never felt close to any particular place. Despite the cultural distance separating me from the places we moved through, I did grow attached to some local traditions and friends along the way. More than anything, our family's regular relocations taught me early in life the importance of adaptability. My eyes and ears searched for similarities in all that they came across. As a result, instead of exclusive loyalty to one culture or tradition I developed a tendency to tease out cultural similarities and divergences whereever we went.

Figure 1.6 My father, Nahavand, mid-1960s.

People, I learned, resented disinterest in their "local" rituals, landmarks, and histories. It mattered to them that I take interest in the town's unique traits. I was reminded of this and expected to accept it.

The simultaneous fondness and foreignness I felt for and in my surroundings crept into my home life as well. Although my family did not markedly differ from their middle-class bureaucratic peers, the difference between my parents' backgrounds was huge. My parents' marriage was arranged with affection by my father's older sister, Aghdas Khanum, who had married my mother's uncle, Mr Ahmad Esfandiari. It was not a typical arranged marriage as my parents knew of and were interested in each other before the marriage. My father's family, more modern, educated, and cosmopolitan than my mother's, belonged to a new class of civil servants that staffed the nation's burgeoning public institutions, state offices, and army. Traveling abroad to Europe and the U.S. was not uncommon for my father's milieu, and his family exuded a spirit of learned formality at home and with their social relationships. I admired them for representing a new and modern face of Iran. What distanced me from him and his family was the code of class difference they abided. I chafed against his internalized elitism, a mode of social assessment common among Pahlavi officials. My mother came from a family of landowners, yet they did not observe the same social hierarchies. They did not condescend the workers and farmers around them in keeping with tribal values. I felt closest to my mother's family when they rejected the arrogance of the upper classes. At the same time, their love of the land rung hollow to me, since I never drew sustenance from it as they had.

Over time I came to both admire and resent the lifestyle and worldview of my fathers' relatives, which impacted how I looked at my own life. Their public contributions, committment to higher education, and professional status, and travels outside of Iran guided my ambitions, yet I kept an emotional distance from them in my private life. Today, I fear this distance foreclosed the chance to know them better. My father was a role model for me. He was a self-made man who prided himself on his high work standards, yet he lacked a single shred of arrogance. He treasured education and made a point to study foreign languages throughout his life. From an early age, I watched my father read everyday with utmost joy and wonder. Like clockwork, he would come home from work (at about one in the afternoon), have lunch, then rest for an hour or so. As soon as he woke from his nap and washed, he would return to his study, where my mother served him freshly brewed tea. My father would then pick up the latest issue of *Ettela'at*, a widely circulating Iranian daily and his personal favorite, unfold its oversized pages and commence his reading. As a little boy, I delighted in seeing him tame the unruly pages of the newspaper, which he would diligently work through with a cup of tea at his side. He habitually read at night as well, and to me, his small library cabinet was a precious member of our family. The library had a glass door, and my father always made sure to lock it after he finished reading for the night. While my friends complained of their mothers locking cookies away in our home cookies were left unguarded on the coffee table and it was my father's little library that was locked.

My father also saved a stash of weekly magazines, like *Taraqqi* (Progress) and *Ettela'at-e Haftegi* (Weekly News), which appealed to me at thirteen. They peddled fantastical stories that painted ancient Iran as a gilded civilization tragically plundered by primitive people (the usual roster of Arabs, Mongols, and Turks). Iran, once a proud and creative civilization had been brought to its knees by marauding gangs to whom treasonous and inept rulers turned a blind eye. Tropes of Iran's untimely demise were repeated in our high school textbooks, which picked from the *Shahnameh* (Book of Kings) and other historical texts to confirm the historicity of this narrative of a great civilization unjustly conquered. Soon enough, I found myself believing it.

Reading Classics and American Detective Novels

Having read the entirety of my father's small library by the time I was fourteen years old, I moved on to serialized historical novels, published in *Ettela'at-e Haftegi*. By the time we relocated in 1966 from Dorud to Nahavand, I was about to start my seventh year of school and reading had become a daily habit for me. In the years we lived in Nahavand, I made regular visits to its bookshops to feed my growing appetite for books. There were three to choose from. There was Keshavarzian, the high-end option named after the respected Mr Keshavarzian, a local leader during the oil nationalization movement who was particularly known and respected for his pro-Mosaddegh politics. Then there was Aminian's Bookstore, a stationery shop that carried books, newspapers, and magazines, most of which were published in Tehran. Last but not least was Hedayat Bookshop, my favorite of the three, and yet by far the least attractive. The unassuming store carried a large selection of detective and crime novels, which I then devoured. Best of all, the owner, Mr Hedayat, rented books, which no other bookstore did. Novels could be rented for one rial a night, affordable even on a child's allowance. I almost always read my books in one night, two if the book was especially long, and so stretched the little money I had as a child as far as it would go.

Try as I might to save, the bulk of my money went to renting and buying books from Hedayat Bookshop. I vividly remember receiving crisp new bills, as tradition dictates, on Nowruz (Persian New Year) and impatiently waiting the next day for the bookstores to open. I always wondered how Mr Hedayat, a rather humble person, managed to procure his books. Was our local bookseller a secret authority on American detective novels, I wondered? But my attempts to pry at the histroy of his bookstore were met with the same reaction: Mr Hedayat would politely cut me off by asking what books I was interested in renting.

In Golpayegan, our home after Nahavand and where I attended the last three years of high school between the years

Figure 1.7 Ali Mirsepassi, thirteen years old, Nahavand.

1966 and 1969, the names of the bookstores changed, but my reading habit persisted. At school, I would recount what I had read to my classmates so that the experience might be shared. By high school, my taste had grown more varied. I dabbled in political and philosophical novels, including Sadegh Hedayat's *Zendeh beh Gur* (Buried Alive), *Seh Qatreh Khun* (Three Drops of Blood), and *Buf-e Kur* (The Blind Owl); Sadegh Chubak's *Antari ke Lutish Mordeh bud* (The Monkey whose Master Died), and *Sang-e Sabur* (The Patient Stone); Bozorg Alavi's *Chamedan* (The Suitcase) and *Chashmhayash* (Her Eyes); Jalal Ale Ahmad's *Modir-e Madrese* (The School Principal), *Nun va Qalam* (By the Pen), and *Nefrin bar Zamin* (The Cursing of the Land); Ali Mohammad Afghani's—*Shuhar-e Ahu Khanum* (Mrs Ahu's Husband); some French and British classics; the novels of Russian writers like Chekhov, Dostoyevsky, and Gorky; Arabic non-fiction and fiction (mostly historical works), and translated Turkish novels, by Aziz Nesin in particular. These writers were considered important intellectuals and literary figures I felt I needed to know and read before I could join certain conversations with others.

Figure 1.8 My father, Nahavand, mid-1960s.

My access to books, whether in Golpayegan or Nahavand, was limited by bookshop offerings. State censorship did not permit the luxury of discrimination. So I even cherished encyclopedias as portals into faraway places. One of my favorite hobbies as a child was to memorize encyclopedias and compete in local and, on a few occasions, national trivia competitions. Two or three winners from each town would be selected to participate in the state championship. At one point, I was ranked number one in our town, but my father would not allow me to travel to the capital to compete. As fond as I was of my encyclopedias, it did not slip my attention that they, translations from English and French originals, had barely a word to say about Iran or the Islamic world. The process of translation had not transformed them; no effort had been made to supplement the originals with any information about Asia or Iran. In the end, I decided to treat the books as an excursion to Europe.

If encyclopedias offered a bird's eye view of the (largely European) world, detective novels and crime fiction engrossed me in mundane struggles far outside Iran. While Iranian novelists, like Parviz Ghazi Saeed and M. Ashiri, wrote in the genre of crime novels, even they favored faraway places like Hong Kong or New York City for their settings. Since my family did not have a television either in Nahavand or Golpayegan, detective novels were my only window, and an accurate one I thought too, onto the everyday life of urban Americans. I was fascinated by the detailed descriptions of life in New York City, San Francisco, and Chicago they offered. I learned through these novels to distinguish between cunning and likeable detectives and churlish policemen. The policemen were low-level functionaries, unintelligent and unconcerned with society's best interests, and worryingly trigger-happy, especially when it came to dealing with the poor and society's other outcasts. By contrast, I regarded the detectives as the real protagonists—men willing to think outside the confines of police procedure in their courageous pursuit of the criminally powerful and corrupt.

Of course, one mundane and material reason why detective novels constituted such a large part of my literary diet was their wide availability in the 1960s and 1970s. Not only were

Figure 1.9 Ali Mirsepassi, fourteen years old, Nahavand.

they popular, but they were also, despite their frank depictions of American crime and poverty, too remote from state concerns to warrant censorship. From Persian translations of detective stories by American writers like Mickey Spillane to Iranian originals by Parviz Ghazi Saeed and others pulp fiction was never in short supply. The genre even made its way to radio with the popular program "Yours Truly: Johnny Dollar." Far from being entertainment trifles, detective novels plunged me into new cities (or at the least, Iranian simulations of them) and made me aware of social and racial inequalities in the United States, inequalities that, unbeknownst to me at the time, I would live to experience.

Ghorbat and Nativism

In reading, I found reprieve from my life of *ghorbat*. Despite, or perhaps because of, the failure of my efforts to convince my "local" friends otherwise, over time I came to the conclusion that I could never force them to accept me as one of their own. As a newcomer to the small western and central towns of Nahavand and Golpayegan, I came to understand that the people who had made their homes there were, by virtue of their unstinting loyalty to their locality, the ultimate custodian of its histories and customs, a privilege they guarded and passed down carefully. Their claims to local authenticity and exceptionalism, however, did not trouble me much. I reluctantly came to accept that my friends and neighbors, as *bumi* (local) residents, had cared for these towns for generations and so had the prerogative to speak for them. I was a *mehman*, or guest, in a town that would always be rightly theirs. While I made a good faith effort to respect local attitudes and lifestyles, always bearing in mind the hierarchies of age and place that designated me a young outsider, I expected my hosts in turn to be *mehmanavaz* (hospitable) to us *gharibeh*s (strangers). My expectation was not outside the pale of local norms. Indeed, Nahavandis and Golpayeganis considered *mehmannavazi* integral to their sense of sociability. Yet my hosts persisted in using labels such as *gharibeh* to pronounce on my status. They may not have sensed any inconsistency in referring to a guest as a stranger, but I did.

What I gradually realized and took comfort in, however, was that while my Nahavandi friends and I did not share the bond of place, we did share larger interests. Important aspects of my life, like reading, painting, and playing volleyball and other sports, were identity neutral but still integral to our sense of self. It was around these commonalities that my circle of friends formed, and together we indulged our love of sports, books, and the arts. For once, I felt I was on equal footing with my friends from Nahavand. We were on the same team, members of the same club, and equal participants in an art workshop.

As a transplant to small towns full of home-grown people, I was aware of the disturbances an outsider could have on their well-maintained ecosystems. Sensitive to their hesitance, I developed an appreciation for the place-based identities they harbored and protected. I saw how this relation to place, learning its history and sharing it with others, talking about it with care and personal sentiment, might add genuine purpose and meaning to their world. Yet I reserved special compassion for other *gharibehs*, who lived unmoored from local cultures. Even as I learned more about the impossibility of isolating a culture or a place and branding it as authentic, I still found claims to place-based belonging harmless so long as they expressed an individual's lived experience. This was mainly out of respect for those who were born and grew up in a place and had real human connections to the place they called home.

Yet we should all treat claims to authenticity and place-based identity with a grain of salt. As with most other facets of our identity, assumed or assigned, our attachment to a place and the degree to which it informs shared characteristics is imagined and constructed. Moreover, there is a world of difference between imagined ideas that are reflections of our lived experiences and those that are invented with little connection to everyday reality; that is an artificial authenticity. A troubling and confusing pattern I observed as an adolescent, reading books and magazines and going to the movies was the unreal romanticization, mostly by intellectuals and artists in Tehran, of Iran's small towns and villages. The unspoiled serenity of these fictitious villages would be juxtaposed (for urban audiences, ironically enough), by films like *Swallows Return to Their Nests*, against the hardened horrors of big cities, particularly Tehran.

Swallows Return to Their Nests

The year was 1963. I was thirteen years old and living in Nahavand, when my father came home one afternoon and excitedly told me, "There is an important film I want you to see." He had only read about the film, but had already decided the work was nothing short of a national treasure. There was only one movie theater in Nahavand, which was not screening the film and had no plans to. So the following Friday, my father, brother, and I drove two hours to the nearest theater in Hamadan to see it. Between the commotion it had caused and the fact that it starred Azar Shiva, my favorite Iranian actor, I was almost as excited as my father that day.

We hurried to our theater seats and watched the film totally transfixed. The film animated my father even more than reading about it had. On the drive back to Nahavand he energetically rehashed the film's moral message: patriotic Iranians should stand firmly on the side of progress and welcome into their lives modern technologies and sciences, while treasuring national traditions and *salat-e farhangi* (authentic culture). I had found the movie lackluster at best and was mystified by my father's admiration for it. I always thought of him, the man who on more than one occasion had reminded me that "Reza Shah is the father of modern Iran," as a staunch modernist, not a sentimentalist. How could he fall for such a shallow film about the goodness of rural customs and the wickedness of modern city life? His response—"Ali, this film is not about progress, it is about keeping our treasured culture"—only added to my confusion. How, I kept asking, could one embrace progress and change and go on worshipping at the altar of tradition? My father and I argued about this for many days but reached no resolution.

The only thing, apart from seeing Azar Shiva, I liked about the film was its title, *Parastu-ha beh Laneh bar Migardand* (Swallows Return to Their Nests), which struck me as poetic. The 1963 movie tells the story of a simple hardworking farmer, Ali, and his two sons. Ali's youngest son dies from a lack of basic medical care in the village. Determined to send his remaining son, Jalal, to college, Ali moves his family to Tehran in search of better-paying work. Ali and his wife live a hard life in the city trying to support their family. He spends his days working in construction, and his nights as a street performer. His wife finds back-breaking work cleaning the houses of Tehran's nouveau riche. But their sweat and tears are soon redeemed: After Jalal graduates from university in Tehran, Ali manages to send him to Paris to study medicine. At this point, Ali and his wife return to their home village, blissfully anticipating their eldest son's return.

Back in the village, Ali and his friends work to build a medical clinic. He hastens to have the clinic ready by his son's graduation from medical school, so that Jalal can return, run the clinic, and spare the village another preventable and premature death, like his younger brother's. To his complete shock, Ali one day receives a letter from Jalal declaring his intention to marry and remain in France. After receiving this staggering news, Ali writes a long and emotional letter to his son. He implores Jalal to remember his obligations to his "ancient homeland where thousands of people have sacrifced their lives for the well-being of our beloved nation." He reads the letter at a public gathering in the village—this is not a private affair, after all, but a communal concern. He pours some of the village soil into the envelope to seal his plea and mails his heartfelt letter to Paris. When Jalal takes in his father's words and the sight and scent of his village soil, something in him stirs. He suddenly awakens to his duties to his family and community, and returns at once to his village in a joyous welcome home ceremony.

Watching this drama unfold in the theater, the film's allure disappeared as I realized it was little more than a weepy ode to a fictive past. While I could stomach its sentimentality, what upset me was its debasement of city people. The film, which argued for the honesty and purity of country living by contrasting it to the corruption and degradation of the city, hewed closely to the conventions of the "pastoral" literary and artistic genre. Those struggling to get ahead in modern urban environments must reckon with the painful realities of the Faustian bargain they make. Yet, despite its pastoral world view, the film conceded modernity's benefits, like a developed medical center, but only accepted them if they could be transplanted and re-localized. This way, the "authenticity" of the rural setting is maintained and even strengthened.

Majid Mohseni, the film's director and lead actor, lived the life of a celebrated artist in Tehran. Mohseni, who was born outside the capital but reared there, successfully ensconced himself in Iranian high society. He managed to find success as an actor, filmmaker, and politician, serving in the Iranian parliament for two terms in the 1960s. He traveled the world, collecting national and international awards, including from a Moscow film festival for *The Swallows Return to Their Nests*. It is said that the film moved the Shah and Queen Farah to tears. The Shah was allegedly so touched that he ordered the government to waive a tax traditionally charged movie-makers. All the while, these very same leaders were hard at work modernizing and urbanizing Iranian society, tearing at the fabric of the villages they now held in romantic esteem. Yet their tears, apocryphal or not, suggest Iran's elite was already yearning for a life they were eager to destroy.

Mohseni's image of life in Iran's small towns and villages bore little resemblance to what I knew of small- and middling-town life. While I considered myself an outsider with no direct access to the lived history, hopes, and concerns of rural Iranians, I felt certain that Mohseni's depiction of Ali and his family could only have come from his own fictional romance with rural life. I now know that a preoccupation with the "pastoral" pervaded the thought of mid-century intellectuals and artists all over the world. Ten years after the film's release, in 1973, the Welsh philosopher Raymond Williams wrote *The Country and the City*, explaining the urban elite's preoccupation with "the pastoral mode," which artistically reconstructed rural life. The pastoral mode, he argued, did not realistically represent rural or urban ways of living; it was interested in a world that cannot and did not exist. In the imagination of urban artists and intellectual elites, the desire for a more "authentic" mode of being in the world had taken hold. Rural life was for them synonymous with an organic community unbreakably linked to the ancient past, from which modernity had suddenly and tragically estranged us. Gradual historical change, according to this narrative, was overwhelmed by a single fundamental transformation, and nostalgia for an imagined golden age was the only way to relate to a rapidly receding past against an alien present. The romanticization of "simple" and "innocent" village life involved the construction of a mythology that only tenuously connected to the lived experience of villagers.

The Trouble with Home in *Ghorbat*

As I worked my way through Iranian and world-renowned classics in translation (Balzac, Tolstoy, Gorky, Hesse, Dostoevsky, Kafka, etc.), I developed resentment for my involuntary state of *ghorbat*. While I was excited to learn that writers

Figure 1.10 Ali Mirsepassi (middle), brother Mansour (right), and cousin Bijan (left), Nahavand, mid-1960s.

across the world were concerned with issues like home, cultural birthright, and belonging, with which I was grappling, I found their treatments of place distressing. I kept telling myself, "This is so *ashrafi* (aristocratic). No one should be honored, nor should they be entitled to special status on the basis of their family or place they are born." The more I read, the more determined I was to dispense with the curse of living as an outsider. Whatever my new identity, I only wanted it to be bona fide.

I was alarmed to discover celebrated writers and intellectuals echoing my mother's belief that one can only ever be at home and attain the dignity that comes with it by staying closest to what one knows. I feared what this possibility, if true, might mean for me. As much as I loved my mother and wanted her to feel at home, I recognized that my own destiny was very much unlike hers. I had no home town to imagine returning to. I was a traveler who could not recall where his journey had started and where it would end. In fact, I envied my mother's experience of *ghorbat*, since I thought it was only those privileged with a home who could have originated the idea. For those of us without roots, *ghorbat* was a permanent state of being.

It took some time, but I gradually came to realize that battles over the homeland were coursing through all of Iran. I read stories that picked up on and expounded my mother's longing for her home town. In family gatherings and in class there was talk of Iran becoming too westernized, of Iranians growing scornful of our traditions and culture. I was too young to understand that what was going on was a rushed modernization process. Caught in the grips of something life- and world-altering that they had no control over, people feared the future and sought refuge in the past. But I felt certain that what was going on was too immense to end. The nature of what was transpiring and the powers behind it remained a mystery to me.

On Hospitality and Samad Behrangi

As a teenager, I gravitated toward neighbors, shopkeepers, and classmates who took pride in their home town but who made a point to welcome others into it so that their culture might be shared. I found myself befriending smalltowners or villagers who found dignity in their birthplace. I had several close high-school friends who came from two different villages outside of Nahavand. Everyday they would bike to school and back home. We formed a study group where three of us would meet once a week to discuss books or magazine articles or reports. I would later argue with my Tehrani friends, who regarded "provincials" like them as uniformly narrow-minded and "boring," that these people had been some of my greatest teachers. I always found I could learn from them, steeped as they were in the history, culture, and land of small places like Nahavand or Golpayegan. What made our friendship possible, however, was their unqualified hospitality, a virtue celebrated in the works of a few Iranian writers. One of them was Mohammad Ebrahim Bastani-Parizi, an unassuming scholar and professor of history from the southeastern province of Kerman who wrote extensively about his home town Pariz, especially in a little volume I came to love and read many times.

Bastani-Parizi (1925–2014) completed his early education in Kerman and received a PhD in history from Tehran University in 1963, where he later joined the faculty. After spending a sabbatical in Paris in 1970, he wrote his popular autobiography, *Az Pariz ta Paris* (*From Pariz to Paris*), a love letter to his hometown, but also a statement of open-minded appreciation for the world. During my student days at Tehran University, in 1971 and 1972, I took advantage of every chance I had to attend his talks or classes. After lectures, I often walked with him to his destination, no matter how far it might have been from mine, just to hear him talk. He would walk at a leisurely pace as I asked him about Iranian history and his work. His answers would connect the issues at hand to Kerman or Pariz. I remember once sharing with him the amazement I felt reading one of his books and descriptions of Nishapur. "Last week, my friend, Mohammad Ali and I were discussing reading your book and your wonderful description of Nishapur," I told him. "I wish you had only written more about this city and the culture of tenth-century Khorasan." Dr Parizi held my hand for a moment and started talking about medieval Iranian history, greater Khorasan, and what life in Nishapur was like at the time. I enjoyed his storytelling style and the fact that he had stopped walking to look me in the face before describing a local bit of Iranian history in a lively manner.

Another writer who inspired me was the young country teacher from Azerbaijan Samad Behrangi (1939–68). I learned about Behrangi when I was a high-school student in Golpayegan, mostly through reports and stories about his death. Behrangi drowned on August 31, 1968 in the Aras River in northern Iran while swimming. Some, including Jalal Al-e Ahmad, who wrote a piece on the occasion of his death, believed his death was not an accident but a targeted killing by the Shah's government.

During my first year at Tehran University, I noticed that everyone, no matter the occasion, made reference to Samad Behrangi. As I started reading his books, my affinity for this small town writer grew. I imagined him to be a humble but fierce young man who had managed to attract the attention of Tehrani intellectuals. Behrangi, for me, was a home-grown humanist whose care for the children of Azerbaijan's little villages was palpable. A schoolteacher turned writer, he dedicated his life to capturing and campaigning against the poverty and injustices that affected Azerbaijani children, sharing their stories with all of Iran. Behrangi's hospitality was reflected in his decision, as an Azeri speaker, to write and publish in Persian, a choice that allowed Iranians like me who did not know Turkish a glimpse into his world.

Behrangi's writings brimmed with admiration for country living, which moved him to point out the poverty and neglect provincial Iranians confronted. Behrangi's admiration for his and other neglected provinces did not mean he wanted to preserve their situation but in fact led him to make a strong case for social change. By the late 1950s he began to develop a critique of the state-sponsored modernization and standardization of education. Behrangi was especially critical of the state-produced textbooks used in schools. His well-known 1965 essay "Kandokav dar Masa'el-e Tarbiyati-ye Iran" (A Critical Exploration of Educational Problems in Iran) contested the Tehran-centrism of education design and policy and established Behrangi as a social critic willing to broach an issue that touched the lives of many Iranians. That a few, faraway officials in the Ministry of Education dictated how and what rural schools should teach, he argued, naturally led to poor education outcomes for children. Behrangi envisioned a new educational system in which local communities participated in designing curriculums appropriate to the linguistic, economic, and communal needs of their children.

In the late 1960s and 1970s, when Tehran-centric intellectuals dominated the Iranian cultural scene, Behrangi's was a fresh voice. Even when writing about issues relevant to rural villages or small towns, most other intellectuals tended to contemplate these questions from the vantage point of the capital. Behrangi, an advocate for educational and cultural reform in Iran, proposed an alternative approach to the centralized educational system. Sensitive to the weight of lived experience and local culture, Behrangi appreciated the difficulty rural Iranian children had in understanding school textbooks, whose lessons and characters were remote from their ways of life. Yet Behrangi is most remembered in Iran for his children's stories, which he began writing and translating from Turkish when he was still young. Behrangi's first book, published in 1965, was a collection of several Azeri folk stories translated to Persian. A year later, he published his first children's story, *Ulduz va Kalag-ha* (Ulduz and the Crows), which was met with acclaim and made Behrangi a well-known writer and public figure.

The Little Black Fish

It was not until his premature death at the age of twenty-nine in 1968 that Behrangi, with the publication of his most celebrated book, *Mahi-ye Siyah-e Kuchulu* (The Little Black Fish), became a nationally known writer and social critic.

The Little Black Fish tells the story of a small black fish unhappy with life in its small stream. The fish is one day inspired to defy his isolation and venture beyond the stream he has always known into a wider world. The black fish's story is one of audacity and love, of curiosity and hunger for more. But it is also a story of alienation and injustice. It calls on marginalized people to fight as the little black fish does for a better life and, in this sense, can be read as representing the radicalism of the 1960s. Behrangi's story inspires readers, particularly the children of the poor, to take action to change their circumstances. Many readers have interpreted it as an anti-establishment allegory. While Behrangi did not live to see the influence of his book, it is believed that *The Little Black Fish* was the unofficial manifesto of the Fadaiyan-e Khalq (the People's Fedayeen), a Marxist organization popular among university students and intellectuals which engaged in urban guerrilla activities in the 1970s and which, after the revolution, emerged as a leading leftist organization.

Behrangi himself came from a working-class family in Tabriz, a major Iranian city and the capital of Azerbaijan province. His father, tired of the paltry pay of seasonal work in Azerbaijan, left for the Caucasus never to return. Behrangi grew up in poverty and only completed the minimum education needed to become a teacher at eighteen. After high school, he trained as a teacher and taught in village schools in Azar Shahr district, about 50 km southwest of his home, for eleven years. His concern with uplifting the communities closest to him came from a lifetime among them. Yet Behrangi worked with Iran's national context in mind, publishing and translating many of his works into Persian. Meanwhile, his views were informed by the secular tradition of the Iranian left, which he gave expression to in accessible works such as *The Little Black Fish*. Compared to intellectuals who never set foot outside Tehran, his biography established Behrangi as a genuine representative of Iran's peripheries.

A Wandering Poet: Ahmad Shamlu

My admiration for Samad Behrangi was, on the whole, limited to his ideas. Our lives overlapped little. He was an Azerbaijani who took it upon himself, as his duty by birth, to communicate to the nation the conditions there. Among such a milieu, I was a *gharibeh*. The figure I thought of as my intellectual role model was Ahmad Shamlu (1925–2000). He too lived his early life as a *gharibeh*, a condition he overcame through the cultivation of cosmopolitan sensibilities. I felt at home reciting Shamlu's poetry, listening to his public interviews, and reading the foreign works he translated. His imaginative world was one I wanted as my own. I particularly appreciated the poetic brilliance he brought to ordinary life. This can be seen in poems like "*Sha'ri keh Zendegist*" (The Poetry that is Life):

The theme of the traditional poet
Was not of life.
In the barren expanse of his imagination
He conversed with his mistress and wine
Living in an imaginary world
He was a captive
Held by a beloved's funny tresses.

As for others,
They held, in one hand a cup
In the other
A mistress's tresses
While they distressed
The entire world
With the intoxicating cries
They let loose.

Shamlu's cosmopolitan attitude makes a direct appearance in the latter part of the same poem:

Whereas
I have personally,
With my poems
Fought alongside "Chen Chui" the Korean
Even, at a point
Several years ago,
I strung up "Hamidi the poet"
On the gallows of my verse.

The situation with poetry
Today
Is different altogether . . . (Translated by Iraj Bashiri)

Among Shamlu's political poems, "In This Blind Alley" was the most powerful, which he wrote just after the revolution:

They smell your mouth
Lest you've told someone
'I love you'
They smell your heart!
These are strange times my dear
Love,
they drag out under lampposts
to thrash.
Love must be hid in closets at home.
In the cold of this blind alley
They keep their fire ablaze
burning our anthems and poems.
Do not venture to think.
(Translated by Saya Ovaisy)

The closeness I felt to Ahmad Shamlu had much to do with our family backgrounds. Shamlu was born into a middle-class family from Tehran. His father was an army officer, and because of his duties, Shamlu's family was also itinerant. He was educated in schools across Iran, including Zahedan in the southeast and Mashhad in the northeast. Shamlu, also known by his pen name A. Bamdad, was a prolific writer and would go on to be translated into multiple languages. Drawing on the work of Nima Yushij, the founder of Iranian "new poetry," and a slew of international poets, from the Spanish Federico Garcia Lorca to the Frenchman Paul Éluard and the American Langston Hughes, some of whose works he translated, Shamlu challenged the conventions of classical Persian poetry to pioneer new poetic techniques. Shamlu traveled throughout the United States and Europe in the 1970s and 1980s to lecture, deliver poetry readings, and participate in poetry festivals. For nearly four decades, Shamlu was a prominent voice in Iranian culture. During the 1960s and 1970s he criticized the nativism gaining traction among cultural producers and continued to write in the modernist tradition that he helped pioneer. It was empowering to know that such a towering personality, who never shied away from radicalism, shared something of my upbringing. One area, however, in which our autobiographies differed was our exposure to religious communities, such as Golpayegan, or to religion more broadly. This was perhaps due to the fact that Shamlu was of an earlier generation, for whom political culture was by far more secular.

Although he did not shy away from criticizing its conventions and excesses, Shamlu was a devoted student of his country's cultural traditions. He edited a new collection of the lyrical poems or *ghazals* of the classical poet Hafez, reciting some of them on audio tape. He spent four decades collecting Iranian folklore, which he started publishing his notes and essays on in the literary magazine of *Ketab-e Hafteh* (Book of the Week) in the 1960s. In 1979, Shamlu and his wife, Aida Sarkisian, also published a multi-volume encyclopedia of Iranian proverbs and wisdom called *Ketab-e Kucheh* (The Book of the Alley). A significant contribution to the understanding of Iranian folklore, the encyclopedia touches on traditional beliefs, customs, rituals, proverbs, aphorisms, riddles, laments, curses, prayers, stories, and more. Already spanning fifteen volumes, one of which was published posthumously, it is said that there are nearly 8,000 indexical entries that remain unpublished.

Shamlu's work extended the horizon of artistic possibility for Iranian writers and readers but was rooted in a larger twentieth-century movement. In 2018, as I was conducting research for a book about Taghi Arani, a pioneering Iranian radical, I came to appreciate the ways in which Shamlu was part of a broader tradition of Iranian radicalism. Arani trained abroad as a chemist, but he was in equal measure a Marxist intellectual committed to a cosmopolitan vision of Iran's future. Shamlu too, as a poet and activist, walked the same intellectual path. His poetic works were an affirmation of the secular and humanist tendencies that shaped the Mashruteh and the early Tudeh Party.

I had the good fortune of meeting Shamlu twice in the late 1980s in Manhattan. I probably spent no more than four hours with him and his wife Aida in a small Midtown apartment. However, the short conversation my friends and I shared with Shamlu and Aida confirmed all that I thought about him. He was an uncompromising radical for whom humanism came prior to nationalism. His love for what he called *hamin mardom-e Iran* (ordinary Iranians) embodied his humanism and made the entirety of Iran his home, a sensibility I aspire to.

We are *mehman-navaz*

The only place I could call home without being written off as a *gharibeh* was my mother's home town of Nahavand. My family and I moved there in the summer of 1962. We would stay in Nahavand for nearly four years, until the summer of 1966. I completed my seventh through ninth grades of schooling in that time. For all my hopes of conquering *ghorbat* in my mother's ancestral homeland, my first year in Nahavand was very painful. For the first time in my life, and despite my outsider status elsewhere, I became the object of several students' merciless bullying. Every day that I stepped into school a new terror awaited me.

It all started during my first week of school in early October 1962. A small group of upper-class students, their bodies carried forward by an air of intimidation, approached me during a break. All but one of them stopped a short distance from me. He walked toward me, stopped inches from my face and said in an almost imperceptibly threatening tone, "Our school is not a safe place for you. We don't like outsiders. After Friday, do not come back. Go join the wimps at the other high schools." I had not expected to be presented so bluntly with an ultimatum, and I looked at him silently, hoping to buy enough time to regain my composure. I wanted to tell him that I was not an outsider, that he and his odd group of friends could not intimidate me. But I hesitated, and by the time I had found my nerve, he was already walking back to his friends.

And so, I found myself the only *gharibeh* in a large and unfriendly high school, swarmed by kids who either genuinely hated me or who saw me as the perfect person to bully. In those early days, I did not fully recognize how grave my situation was, choosing to believe I could tolerate the occasional teasing, that it would surely have to end. But after a month or so, I gathered that my bullies had no intention of relenting. For me to bow to their intimidation and transfer to another school, however, was out of the question. Their demand was unjust, and I was determined not to let them succeed. I decided that I would fight rather than live my life in fear. I was of course very naïve, and they continued to make my life terribly unpleasant for the remaining school year.

The most heart-rending part of all this was that not a single student in the entire school came to my rescue. Not once did my classmates try to lend me a hand in fighting these tormentors. So I did what I had to do and kept on. I was determined not to let them break me and decided I would keep fighting them, even though they hurt me each time we did. I soon learned that even the teachers could not help me. Another student relayed that once, some of the school toughs went to the house of a teacher they disliked late at night, broke in, and threatened that if the teacher did not leave them alone, that they would harm his family, all because this teacher supported a rival volleyball team.

One day, after a brawl with these students, I returned to class with a black eye. Although I was bruised, I was happy to have fought back and defended myself with a punch to one of their stomachs. I could tell that everyone in class pitied me, because no one would hold my gaze. At moments like this, I struggled to understand why they did nothing to defend me. The nicest ones would simply beg, "Ali, please transfer, they will kill you." After class that day, the Vice Principal came to me and said, "Ali, this school is not a *gharibeh* friendly place. Tensions are high among the students, and you should really consider transferring to the other high school." By the time I had this conversation, it was May, and I told the Vice Principal that I would not transfer, that I would rather stay and fight the bullies. But the daily dodging and fighting had worn me down to the point that I failed my algebra and chemistry classes. I was told to prepare for the two classes, and that I would have the chance to pass them by taking an exam in August. After studying over the summer, I passed the algebra exam, but my Vice Principal, who was trying to help me finish the seventh grade so that I could transfer to the other school, informed me that I was one point shy of passing the chemistry exam. My chemistry teacher discouraged leniency and told the Vice Principal that he should fail me for fighting with other students all year long. And so I ended my seventh grade with the poorest academic record of my life. Failing the seventh grade devastated me, and I resignedly transferred to the neighboring Ferdowsi High School.

My life, however, soon took on a pleasant, normal rhythm at Ferdowsi. It was not long before I joined the high school's volleyball team and its theater group. For the first time in my life, my paintings had been selected for an annual group exhibition attended by parents, the town's notables, and government officials, including my father. In an ironic way, the bullies were right—I was better off with this new school and all it had to offer me.

I found many new friends at Ferdowsi, but one in particular I was very close to—Said Bayzavi. Said was the captain of our volleyball team and a talented painter and calligrapher. Although I admired Said, I took issue with the ways in which he distinguished me from all our other classmates with subtle comments like, "We Nahavandis . . .," or "I'll live here forever, but, who knows, you may leave next year, and I'll never hear from you again." I felt it was unfair to keep reminding me of these obvious realities, which only generated needless distance between us.

One April day after school, I visited Said at his house to see his new paintings. I told him that I found his new works impressive, but he was critical of them and looked dissatisfied as he stood appraising them. We went outside, and his mood lifted. Realizing that he was in better spirits, I started a conversation about the fact that the differences between us, he a native Nahavandi and me a newcomer to the town, were not so great after all. Yet by the end of that fateful conversation, I had come to accept, if not embrace, my status as a *gharibeh*. Said and I attended grades seven to nine together in the almost four years that my family and I lived in Nahavand. At the time of our conversation, Said and I were fifteen years old. Like me, he loved painting and volleyball, though he was far better at both. Yet for the all the interests we shared, I was an outsider to Said's world. It was during this conversation that I finally worked up the courage to ask why he persisted in walling me off as a stranger to all that he, as a Nahavandi, knew. With one forceful confrontation, I hoped to clear up any confusion about my "roots," a perpetual thorn in our friendship. "It's not as if I'm from some place so far away as Tehran. Now, a Tehrani might think he's better than you or the other Nahavandi boys, but I certainly don't. And let's not forget that my mother was born here, my grandmother married here, and that many of my relatives call the town home." And so began my desperate attempt to convince a friend I admired and considered a role model.

Said, however, was not the least bit swayed by my reasoning. He countered as soon as I had finished, "Ali, you don't have the local accent. You like our ways but don't do many of the things we do [by which I assumed he meant participating in local religious ceremonies, like the Ashura and Nowruz celebrations, a long and elaborate series of events and rituals, including fantastic fireworks that went on for days], and more importantly, you are the only person in Nahavand with your last name." He continued, "It is all about *sabeqeh* [history, background] and *farhang* [culture], and those things are not going to grow overnight."

I eventually recognized that he was dead right. I did not speak with the local accent (although my relatives from Tehran always made fun of me for one), which in fact sounded grating to my ears, and I was one of only five people in town with the surname Mirsepassi. Despite my mother's birth there, I felt no connection to Nahavandi history or culture, only a passing fondness for it. I wanted my friends to accept me as one of their own, but by the end of my time in Nahavand, I had made peace with the fact that my reality would be one of *ghorbat.* And this was the only time in my life that I had a crack at becoming a part of a community and calling it home. My friends in Nahavand, however, did not mind much that I was *gharibeh,* and at times I was given favorable treatment because they considered me the object of their special hospitality.

One much happier occasion, which took place in Said's house, perhaps tempered my tendency to search for home in places I was not a native of. It was the first time I visited Said's home in June 1963. Said had invited three of us to his house for fresh grapes his family had grown on their well-known winery,

Figure 1.11 My mother, second on the left, and relatives, Nahavand, mid-1960s.

which sat just outside of town. When I arrived, Said and the other two friends were playing soccer in the yard, but, as I entered the house, Said's mother came out, asked them to stop, and told them to wash up. She then walked toward me and welcomed me into their home after offering a very pleasant greeting. I was then guided to the guest room, a simple room clearly decorated with care and attention to detail. A red rug covered most of the floor and several cushions decorated in tribal patterns rested against the wall for guests to sit on and use for their backs. A large beautiful round table neatly set up with cookies and fruits occupied the center of the room, and a tea pot rested next to them. One of his two friends, who had been to Said's house before, seemed to be surprised by the arrangement and jokingly asked Said's mom, "Why are you treating Ali like a *shahzadeh* (prince)? Are you *gharibeh-parast* (a xenophile)?"

Said's mom did not stop what she was doing to look at the child and simply acted as if she had not heard him. She asked us to sit and started pouring tea in golden rimmed teacups for us.

She then turned to face the friend who had questioned her and said, "I want to tell you this one time. We are *mehman-navaz* [hospitable]. Never, ever, forget this." She then turned to me and said, "You are our *mehman* in Nahavand, and we always

Figure 1.12 My father (back left), uncle (back right), brother Mansour (first on left), myself (second on left), cousin Bijan (third from left), and cousin Farhang (first from right), Tagh-e Bostan, Kermanshah, mid-1960s.

Figure 1.13 My mother (back left), my brother Masoud (back middle), myself (front right), my brother Mansour (back right), and my sister Susan (front left), Nahavand, mid-1960s.

treat our guests from out of town with the utmost respect, so that they feel at home." I keenly listened to her as I looked at her sincere face. I almost wanted to thank her for thinking of me as a *mehman* and not a *gharibeh*, but decided it would be rude to say so.

Thanks in no small part to some of these experiences, I never came to consider Nahavand my "home town," although I had been taught by my mother to think of it as such. While I loved living so close to my grandmother, the town was *ghorbat* for me, albeit of the benign kind. I wanted my friends to think of me as one of their own, but outside of my family no one recognized me as a local Nahavandi. Instead, my friends and schoolteachers inquired about my family's Nowruz customs, wedding traditions, and food preferences, certain that as a *gharibeh* my culture was distinct from theirs. My response was always the same: With a sad face, I'd say, "We don't have any noteworthy traditions; we do as others do in the towns we live in." I did not mind being a *gharibeh* as much as I badly desired to be accepted by the locals and particularly by my good friends, who, despite their overall kindness and respect, never spoke of me as one of their own. This was my real dilemma. Tacitly barred from commenting on "local" matters, my friends only solicited my opinion about the town to get an outsider's perspective. I lived almost always evading any discussion about who I was and where I came from. That was until that conversation with Said, after which I learned that, as the son of a wandering civil servant and a mother sick for small-town comforts, *ghorbat* was the life I was born to inhabit, putting to rest my desire to fix an identity for myself outside of it.

2

Golpayegan, 1966–1970

An Olive Branch with a Cardboard Cover

The book I was hiding in my jacket was cloaked in an unassuming light brown dust jacket. It was late fall 1969, I was eighteen, and the anonymous volume tucked in my pocket had just been given to me by Mr Eshraghi and Mr Amjadi, my high school literature teachers in Golpayegan. The young teachers had lent me the book on the strict condition that I refrain from so much as mentioning it or the transaction that brought it to my pocket to anyone. They had approached me in the hallway earlier that day to ask that I join them in the teacher's lounge during our lunch hour. All of our teachers shared the one large room as their office. The space was almost always empty during the long lunch break, as most teachers returned home to have lunch and rest. Although the two Tehran transplants had arrived to Golpayegan only three months earlier, they had quickly made an impression on us students for their refusal to disavow, even in the face of our small-town strictures, their Marxist convictions. In both history and Persian literature classes, they offered what they called a materialist analysis of texts, events, and Iran's political and cultural elite. No other teacher in Golpayegan dared use a term like materialism, except perhaps to characterize an excessive desire for wealth and lack of spirituality. Eager to enter their orbit, and despite my ambivalence about their being from Tehran, I had approached Mr Eshraghi and Mr Amjadi not long before the encounter that brought the book to my jacket to share an unsolicited five-page statement professing my fondness for the leftist Iranian writer Bozorg Alavi and his latest novel, *Chasmhayash*. Once we had gathered in the lounge, Mr Amjadi and Mr Eshraghi dispensed with all niceties and spared no words in telling me they found Alavi's romantic storytelling puerile and my appreciation for his work misplaced. At the end of this excoriation, however, was an olive branch. Mr Amjadi and Mr Eshraghi asked if I would care to read a short book of their choice, a proposal I immediately accepted. They slipped me a slim, brown-covered book, noting that I needed a proper political education. This mysterious little book, I surmised, must then be my guide. I discreetly tucked the volume into my coat pocket, thanked the two teachers, and left for my afternoon class. Suspense ate at me the rest of that day. What lay beyond the book's cardboard-colored cover? Class could not end any sooner, and the moment it did at 4.40 in the afternoon, I bolted home, where I pried the cover from the book as soon as my bedroom door hit the frame. Two lines of text rested on the cover: a three-word title and the author's name. The cover felt spartan, even crude, though its minimalism gave it an air of quiet dignity.

I thought the book's title, *Dowlat va Enqelab* (State and Revolution), was not particularly attractive. But I recognized its author's name, Vladimir Lenin, from time spent listening to Radio Berlin. This resonance piqued my interest, and I forged ahead. What I read, however, was worlds away from what I had expected my two teachers to share with me. I had walked away from their attack on Alavi thinking they had lent me their own favorite Iranian novel. Thinking back to their parting remarks about my lack of a political education, I pushed aside my creeping disappointment and contented myself with the opportunity to read proper Marxist theory for the first time in my life.

I spent that night and perhaps ten others trying to understand *State and Revolution*, failing miserably to make it past the first few pages each time. The writing was impenetrable; it was tough, technical, and simply impossible for me to decipher at seventeen. After wrestling with the book for hours, I sat in my room and imagined Lenin debating a roomful of Russians as I sat in a corner clueless as to the conversation around me. Yet I found Lenin's polemical style oddly endearing. His analytical attacks were measured but energetic, and I imagined they left his detractors absolutely cowed and confounded. I felt ill suited, however, for such a model of intellectual interaction, since I thought of my primary intellectual interlocutors, schoolteachers like Mr Eshraghi and Mr Amjadi, not as enemies, but as mentors. It is hard to attack your adversaries as Lenin does when you most want them to affirm you. I decided that Lenin, a radical versed in the practice of politics, and I, a political fledging at only seventeen, were simply constituted differently.

After absorbing as much as I could of the book's lessons in revolutionary rhetoric and argumentation, I decided to return the slim volume to its owners. I told my teachers that just as the bourgeois protagonist of *Chashmhayash,* Farangis, could recognize, but not alter, the regrettable reality of her parasitic class status, I could consume Alavi's beautiful novel in one night but could not read Lenin even if it might make my mentors happy.

If the goal of debate is understood to be the decimation of an enemy's view, then even demagoguery and disinformation can be marshalled toward that end. This, however, assumes that one side possesses the truth, while the other trades in falsehoods that ought to be eliminated. Intimidation and ad hominem attack, within this paradigm, are scarcely out of the question. Looking back and comparing Alavi's views to the polemical stance in Lenin's *State and Revolution*, which professes a certain pathos of inevitability, *Chashmhayash* clearly proposes a different understanding of dialogue and its possibilities. In hindsight, Mr Eshraghi and Mr Amjadi's understanding of Marxism and literature seems unforgivingly rigid. The acuity of a text's class analysis was for them one and the same as its artistic value.

Yet today I also appreciate the disparity in my teachers' political perspectives and interests as proof that there was no shortage of discussion about world events happening in Golpayegan. The perspectives coloring these informal debates could not be reduced to the confines of official Pahlavi discourse. The world was being reimagined across Iran in the 1960s and 1970s, and cities and provinces beyond Tehran offered competing conceptions of *jahan*, or the "new world." Local voices in Golpayegan, however covertly, challenged the Pahlavi regime as out of step with the world, undermining its claims to universalism while proposing alternate roads for making Iran an international nation. In this light, Tehran-centrism is its own form of provincialism, since activism was proliferating across Iran. The story of Golpayegan is but one of many of Iran's smaller, overlooked centers of activism.

Making Home in *Ghorbat*

My family's move to Golpayegan two years earlier had been sudden and unexpected. It was June 1965, summer was just around the corner, and I was days away from completing the ninth grade and starting a new chapter of my education. I was set to begin my second cycle (*sikl-e dovom*) of high school at a new school in Nahavand, Ebn-e Sina High School. Iran's education system in the 1960s required students, upon completing ninth grade, to declare one of three concentrations: mathematics, natural sciences, or literature. I made the controversial choice of concentrating in literature (*reshteh-ye adabi*), and it was this decision that set my transfer to Ebn-e Sina High School in motion. Nahavand's Pahlavi High School, where I had finished my ninth-grade studies, only offered a concentration in natural sciences (that is, biology and other life sciences). Ebn-e Sina High School, however, offered specialized instruction in mathematics and literature. Iranians, then and now, consider literature, which did little in terms of promising a path to vertical mobility or social prestige, an unusual aspiration for a student with a strong academic profile. Compared with the privileges of being a *doktor* or *mohandes* (engineer), literature conferred little status on those who studied it, and so it was assumed that those who did had no other choice. I gravitated, however, toward history, languages, and literature, so it seemed only natural that I should major in literature. The choice was anything but natural to my father, who reproached me for what he considered to be my bad judgment. He believed I had what it took to pursue a "more serious" track in the sciences, that my talents would be wasted concentrating on something so insubstantial. Although he treasured literature, history, and Arabic, my father considered himself a *tajaddod-zadeh* person (a modern man), a staunch supporter of Reza Shah's vision of national progress through economic industrialization and political rationalization. My father, a devotee of the wonders of technology, had little doubt, as he would say, that "the future belongs to the sciences." For him, *adabiyat* (literature) was trivial, an extracurricular pursuit at best. One could read and commit the classics to heart without instruction, as a favorite rejoinder of his, "Hafez and Sa'di never went to university," argued.

I put it plainly to my father, who had inspired my interest in literature, that I was determined to pursue my studies and ambitions to be a scholar. Like Ali in *Swallows Return to Their Nests*, my father never had the chance to attend college, so

Figure 2.1 High School teachers, Golpayegan, 1966.

sending me, his first-born son, to university was the realization of his deferred dreams. My father lost his father when he was in sixth grade and was thrust into the world of work, ending his chance of a college education. He hoped that I would be able to fulfill his dream and attend college. I worked his soft spot for academics, invoking the memory of my psychiatrist grandfather and others who had shaped society by means other than the immediately tangible, until he, against his own objection, allowed me to pursue the literature track. My father's work in the finance ministry was a game of numbers at which he excelled, but I always knew that his real love was history and literature.

But one late afternoon, all that I had planned was ruined. My sister, brother, and I had returned from school when my father summoned us to join him and my mother in his study, not a routine gathering for my family. Anticipation hung over the room like a thick fog, and I could sense they were about to announce something big. Yet all of this was happening without notice, and I had no time to brace myself for the news. My father glanced at us. He took a long pause and looked us over once more to confirm he had our full attention. He then announced that he had been offered a position as the head of the Finance Office in Golpayegan. We were to pack and within a month leave Nahavand for Golpayegan. He preempted any negative reaction on our parts with the explanation that this was a promotion for him and that we ought to be happy.

Grief and resignation washed over me. Life felt like a story scripted with little regard for my feelings or desires. I was simply to go through motions already chosen for me. And then fear set in. My initial fears, however, had little to do with myself. I worried what moving from Nahavand would mean for our family. After all, Nahavand was my mother's birthplace and the comfort of having her relatives nearby had eased the loneliness she had felt in Dorud. Nahavand was the only place in the world where my mother's Persian accent was perfectly understandable. She was being compelled to leave her home for *ghorbat* again. Yet that day, my mother seemed rather content with the news. Perhaps after living years away from Nahavand, the prospect of leaving her mother and brother for an unfamiliar place was not so daunting.

I knew little about Golpayegan at the time, aside from the fact that it was a short distance from the grand old city of Isfahan. As the news settled in, and the more I focused on our future proximity to Isfahan, the less our move seemed worth grieving. My family, including my grandmother, had visited Isfahan for Nowruz or New Year holidays, and I had delighted in all the city had to offer. With its great many cinemas, bookstores, architectural wonders, and centuries of history inscribed in its streets, Isfahan was a majestic place. I quickly started rationalizing our abrupt departure from Nahavand and the interruption in my schooling by imagining the good life awaiting us in Golpayegan.

Land of Tulips

The word Golpayegan means "land of tulips," and the city, located northwest of Isfahan, lives up to the pastoral intonations of its name, producing heaps of wheat, cotton, barley, apricots, cherries, and cucumbers each year. In addition to its agricultural plenty, Golpayegan boasts a rich history of animal husbandry, carpet weaving, and woodcarving. Bordered by mountains and cut through by the Ghebla River, Golpayegan is home to roving jackals, foxes, and wolves. I spent four years in Golpayegan, including the formative year in which I finished high school. My life there was a stark departure from my three years in Nahavand. In the eyes of society, I was by then an adult. When we settled there, I was about sixteen years old, too old to any longer be considered a boy. Life suddenly took on the flavor of a challenge. I felt life was sizing me up, and to prove my mettle, I doubled down on my commitment to ideas, institutions, and beliefs, which I thought would make a coherent identity out of my inchoate youth. I was of course a confused teenager, but I was also working in earnest to find a cause worthy of a life-long commitment. In a way, my time in Golpayegan was one prolonged search for a life worth living, a life of purpose.

My life in Golpayegan also coincided with the worldwide political reckoning of the 1960s. Movements for national independence and political liberation transpiring thousands of miles away seeped into small towns like it, catalyzing an intellectual and political awakening that stretched into the 1970s. In high school classrooms, bookshops and other public places of intellectual production and consumption, my generation assembled to discuss, debate, and draw inspiration from ideas articulated around the world, from Nehru's independent India to the Palestinian struggle for dignity in autonomy. Our ideal of the Iranian nation resembled these distant examples more than any image conjured by the mythology of the Pahlavi state and its modernization program.

My family was nonetheless the product of Pahlavi modernization, a fact with which we had reconciled. Conversations

Figure 2.2 High School teachers, in front of my high school, Golpayegan, 1966.

between my father, already a taciturn man, and I were marked by a studied avoidance of politics, a quality I today attribute to his fear that I might get involved in politics and to the government's general de-politicization of the country. Within this climate, my father's involvement in politics was limited to attending annual commemorations, like the Shah's birthday, held on the fourth of Aban, and the anniversary of the 1946 liberation of Azerbaijan. Yet my father reserved special admiration for the efforts of the first Pahlavi monarch, Reza Shah, a point he often communicated to me with reminders like, "I and everything I believe in are the result of Reza Shah's labors."

Although he spoke to me little about his memories of the 1950s oil nationalization struggle, I was aware that my father had sided with the royalists and opposed nationalizing prime minister Mohammad Mosaddegh. My father was a purist in his assessment of Mosaddegh's commitment to democracy and blamed him for not following the letter of the law during his premiership. However, when it came to his view of the Shah, my father argued that geopolitics and the limitations of Iranian society made it premature to attempt democratic governance. Although he opposed the leftist Tudeh Party, my father was also wary of growing clerical interference in politics. Their defense of tradition threatened all that he stood for—modernization and the prioritization of national interests and government above parochial religious matters. Yet my father was a man of faith, with his own nationalistic interpretation of Shiʿism, and despite his professions of admiration for the late Pahlavi monarch, he declined to join any pro-Shah party, such as the royalist New Iran Party or the People's Party. While he never divulged why he abstained from politics, he most likely did not believe in political competition between royalist parties, which, after all, differed little from one another. That his admiration for the Shah's modernizing vision did not translate into political action, then, was not a curiosity but a consequence of the very narrowing of politics the Pahlavi state engineered.

For the most part, I shared my father's commitment to modernizing Iran and sympathies for Shiʿism. I felt uncomfortable, however, with the elitism of his government peers, with their open contempt for poor and provincial Iranians, which parroted the condescension of the Pahlavi state toward the Iranian masses. In Golpayegan, as in Nahavand, many of my friends traced their roots generations back to the town or its nearby villages. Yet my family felt duty-bound to chastise me for socializing with, in their view, country bumpkins, or *dahati*s. As I grew older and more confident in my views, I challenged my father's nationalism. I would ask, "Why is it that in your nationalism most regular Iranians have no place?" Never liking this, he would respond: "Regular people don't know what is good for them. I admire our leaders, who know what is good for the country and make it happen." Within my father's clipped rationale and understanding of Iranian history, our nation had declined, losing its sovereignty and prestige under feeble Qajar rule, but had rebuilt its lost glory thanks to the uncompromising and visionary leadership of Reza Shah. What enthusiasm he lacked for contemporary political issues, my father made up for with his love of memorizing Iran's past victories and miseries. He handed down these stories to me, and in all of them, Iran was framed as a nation tragically besieged by lesser peoples.

Although I shared my father's respect for our country, I was little interested in recounting ancient Iran's fabled greatness. Nor did I share his unforgiving view of Arabs, Turks, and others who had contributed, through conquest and collaboration, to the multicolored mosaic of Iran's history. In my view, history was a chain of mistreatment and resistance that spared no nation or ethnicity, so it made no sense to grieve the historic injustices Iran suffered, since we too had played the role of adversary. Nor was I interested in the many stories I heard from my father, teachers, and state radio broadcasters about the shameful ineptitude of Qajar rulers. Despite the little knowledge I had about eighteenth- and nineteenth-century Persia, I concluded that it had been a time of material privation I had no interest in revisiting. Iran had simply lacked the military might to overcome the great powers' game of encroachment. The past was not a series of moral failings or successes, as I saw it, so there was little use in mourning it.

At the same time, during my high school years and against, or perhaps in spite of, the condescension of my middle-class milieu's worldview, my love for regular people deepened. I, who slipped from town to town, yearned for the kind of community I perceived the many ordinary Iranians in Golpayegan enjoyed. I was moved by the way the everyday men and women in my midst spoke of their kin and community, as if the earth they trod upon and cultivated was life's greatest treasure. The connectedness I perceived among them was all the more striking since, outside of my immediate family, I felt no genuine connection to any group of people. No matter where we relocated, locals always designated me an outsider. While a sense of community and belonging evaded my early adolescence, I found solidarity in the small intellectual world and path of political activism I followed as a high school student, which in my daily life took the form of small activities, like joining reading groups, exchanging news and ideas the state prohibited, and indulging in banned books.

The intellectual roamers I counted as my tribe represented a generation of Iranians, many of whom would participate in the revolution, who still aspired to the democratic ideals of the Mashruteh, or constitutional, project, which peaked in the initial years of the twentieth century. We understood this project to mean the realization of a modern Iran that invited its citizens to participate actively in the country's affairs. With an appreciation for Iran's political past and its connection to contemporary struggles near and far, we in Golpayegan and countless other small towns like it did not experience politics from a limited, local view. Instead, young high school students marshaled a far richer assortment of evidence as they passionately debated and interacted with events, ideas, and actors from Tehran, the West, and across the global south.

Islam and Marxism in our Town

If wonderstruck lust for all things modern was the defining feature of Pahlavi Iran, then Golpayegan was a mid-century anomaly. At the time of my adolescence, in the late 1960s, the mundane markers of modern life were hardly discernible there. The town lacked a movie theater, alcoholic beverages were prohibited for sale or consumption, men, including students at the two men's high schools, were expected to grow their beards, and women seldom appeared in public without a chador (although the hijab was not mandatory at the one women's high school in town). My father once told me that the high-ranking cleric Grand Ayatollah Golpayegani beseeched the Shah to guard Golpayegan, near which he was born, as his name suggests, from these indecencies, to which the Shah agreed. To taste what was in Golpayegan taboo, we would escape to neighboring towns like Khansar and Khomein, where there were new hotels and movie theaters to enjoy. Although Golpayegan outsized these towns, its inhabitants continued to make a living, as many before them had, by cultivating the land, caring for livestock, and performing religious rituals. Stubbornly insular, Golpayegan may have been an ideal place to conduct anthropological fieldwork, but it was not the most happening place for a teenage boy. The religiosity of its citizens found outlet in the pervasive proprieties of everyday life. Men greeted each other with Quranic proverbs; listening to radio courted controversy; modesty was deemed a virtue; and public life was marked by the symbolism of Shi'i ceremonies and collective rituals, like the call for prayers (*Azan*), Ashura festivals, Eid-e Qorban celebrations, and so on. In my first year of school, I learned that the overwhelming majority of my classmates knew so many Arabic words that they spoke almost a mix of Persian and Arabic. Iran today, where public displays of religion are enforced from on high but practiced only skin deep, offers a marked contrast to the Golpayegan of my adolescence. A visitor to it would immediately observe the town's transparent affection for land, cattle, and God.

Flush with the vigor of youth, I and so many others of my generation were eager to embrace new ways of being and living. Yet the pace and authoritarian nature of the modernizing changes unfolding around us precluded us from participating in them. Where I sought opportunities to captain change, I found confusion and closed doors. Change was a thing happening to Iran rather than being brought about by Iranians, with the Pahlavi state offering its citizens no opportunity to own these transformations. Neither our thoughts nor our initiatives could guide a modernization process that treated us with benevolent paternalism at best and brutal indifference at worst. It was the disjuncture between design and implementation that rendered modernization such a violent and frightening process, devoid of liberatory potential for so many. My generation's hunger for community was cavernous, and the alienation we endured helps explains our intense affinity for religious and leftist politics. We found a sense of belonging in a shared struggle over the Iran of tomorrow.

Practicing anti-authoritarian politics in Golpayegan, where public interactions were more suffused with religion than any other place I had encountered in Iran, posed a unique set of problems. While it was there that I began taking up radical politics, I remained fond of the towns people, even if I chafed at the expectation that I should adhere to their religious norms. This confusion was hard to overcome. Religion and public performances of religiosity for most people in Golpayegan were not ideologically motivated. Golpayeganis did not become religious to make a political statement or express their resentments toward Iranian modernization. A more politically motivated Islam did come to Golpayegan later and mostly from Tehran. This was a critical development one needs to consider in explaining the rise and dominance of political Islam in Iran.

How do we explain the political trajectory in Golpayegan and across Iran from public piety to ideological calls for a "return to the self"? This shift cannot be explained as a reaction to the modern erosion of religious sensibilities. The dynamic between public and political professions of faith is instead relational. Both ordinary Muslims and their modernist counterparts, who drew inspiration from Ali Shari'ati and others, resisted the state's narrowing of religion. However, the latter presented piety as a transformative ideology for national change, whereas the former appeared more interested in showing what people already believed and practiced.

Yet Golpayegan should not be taken as a microcosm of mid-century Iran either. The town differed greatly from what I encountered in Nahavand, perhaps most markedly in terms of how each town's inhabitants situated themselves relative to the world. In Nahavand, people situated themselves in time and space with reference to the broader sweep of the history of Iran and the tribes of Lorestan. Nahavand, I was often told, had been the last battleground, in 642, before the Sasanian Empire fell to conquering Muslim Arabs. The town of Nahavand was marked by the symbolism of "nabard Nahavand" (Nahavand's defeat), with the Qaleh-ye Nahavand (Castle of Nahavand) hovering above the town's horizon.

In contrast, Golpayegan struck me as a bounded psychocultural place. While its inhabitants demonstrated keen interest in a few places beyond the town, such as Khansar and Khomein, I hardly heard anyone talk about Golpayegan in terms of the Iranian nation. People were more interested in the culture and politics of the Middle East and the world at large. The Arab-Israeli conflict, Gamal Abdel Nasser's pan-Arabism, and the Vietnam War loomed large in the political deliberations of my teachers and of other local intellectuals, including bookstore owners and some government employees. This is not to mention political goings-on in Tehran, which neighborhood thinkers dissected with dexterous care. That Golpayeganis looked abroad to think through local politics gives further substance to the idea that knowing the world is genealogically prior to knowing the nation. To better apprehend this relationship between the world and nation, we ought to look at grassroots nationalism, which emerged out of high school classrooms, bookstore gatherings, and other public thoroughfares, not the "official nationalism" forced from above. As contradictory as it then may seem, Golpayeganis, in contrast to people of Nahavand, were at once more interested in their own humble town and in the history and cultures of the larger world. I can say based on my years of living in these two towns in the 1960s, that Nahavand, with its movie theater, liquor stores, and Jewish quarter, was a more modern and secular place than Golpayegan. Nahavandis were religious but not to the same extent as Golpayeganis and not so publicly. Nahavandis did have a sense of regionalism, though, through their close interactions with Kurdistan and Lorestan, for example. On the other hand, the residents of Golpayegan, a town with almost no crime, and where education, art, and culture were taken seriously, lived a civic life. Still, for Golpayeganis, civic commitment did not include religious minorities or even other Muslims whose lifestyles differed from Golpayegan's mainstream.

Perhaps this, the internal cohesion of Golpayegan, explains how such a tame town had such a robust cultural life of its own. The two all-male high schools in town, Ebn-e Sina and Pahlavi, were for teachers and youth alike centers of culture and politics. Based on my sister's reports, the one girls' high school welcomed women's activities. But as far as I can remember, only men attended public events in Golpayegan. It was there that aspiring activists, such as myself, encountered politically seasoned teachers, who participated in cultural and (mostly, though not exclusively, religious) political activities. I took as a model of inspiration our teacher Mr Jafar Tavakol. He was a slender man in his late thirties, and he always came to school dressed in a dark suit and white shirt.

To me, Mr Tavakol was unbelievably learned and an exemplar in matters of personal and professional conduct. Although I thought he approached perfection, I could not identify with his lifestyle or even contemplate friendship with him. He resembled a personality out of our religious textbooks: ideal in all respects, but too pure to be real or relatable. Why did I feel this way? Perhaps it was the anti-hero, whose imperfection at least made him multidimensional, to whom I really gravitated. Or perhaps I simply desired a more open and diverse lifestyle, since to me Mr Tavakol led a rather one-dimensional existence, judging everything, his students and colleagues, philosophers, and world events, from his religious perspective. Other small worlds orbited our high school. Mr Amjadi and Mr Eshraghi, the two young teachers of social studies, geography, and history who extended to me an olive branch in the form of Lenin's cloaked *State and Revolution*, would introduce me to another such world. They were new to the town unlike most of our teachers, who were either native Golpayeganis or from nearby Isfahan. They had both graduated from Tehran's Teacher College, and their year in Golpayegan was their first working as teachers.

Misters Amjadi and Eshraghi had yet to learn to couch their political polemics and provocations in the euphemisms common to activists at the time. Instead, their Marxism announced itself as soon as they opened their mouths to speak with you. They did not hesitate to stop and correct us students for neglecting to mention class in our analysis of current events or history, which, they reminded us, had its own laws of motion. They were also adamant that literature should not be analyzed according to its formal qualities alone, since it reflected its author's attitude toward *tabaqat-e ejtema'i* (social classes).

As much as I took umbrage at them for assuming that any student with an interest in politics was sympathetic to Marxism, bulldozing ahead with their references to Samad Behrangi, Maxim Gorky, Latin American revolutionaries and taboo others, and for taking the liberty to tell students that they did not think properly, their perspective was refreshing. Knowledge, I had so far thought, rested on the accumulation

Figure 2.3 High school teachers in a classroom, Golpayegan, late 1960s.

of information, but they revealed to me that just as critical to amassing information is the way one approaches it. Their political directness was also striking, since at the time, those of us who wanted to learn about Marxism and other revolutionary thought had few places to turn to other than literature or radio stations broadcasting outside of Iran.

Chashmhayash (Her Eyes)

I had one particularly impassioned discussion with Mr Eshraghi and Mr Amjadi. It was late fall 1968 and I had just completed reading Bozorg Alavi's splendid novel *Chashmhayash* (Her Eyes). At the time, I was seventeen and found it the most inspiring and realistic piece of political literature I had ever encountered. I felt lucky just to have read it, since it had been banned and was unavailable at bookstores. I was only able to access it through a classmate, who himself had borrowed it from his uncle, a former member of the Tudeh Party who had spent several years in prison for his political activities.

Figure 2.4 High School teachers and students, Golpayegan, 1966.

Chashmhayash traps its reader in a web. At the center of this web is a painting immortalizing a woman and her beguiling eyes, the inspiration behind the book's title. The web spins a story around her eyes, extending outward to show that Iranian society is ensnared in the same terror and turmoil frozen in the woman's gaze. Ostensibly about a painter named Ostad Makan, the novel builds nesting domes of meaning around Makan's life and work. The enigmatic eyes of the woman in the portrait evade fixed interpretation and instead present the viewer with a swirl of mixed messages. We can never trust what we see, for reality varies moment to moment:

> The woman was very beautiful but what amazed the beholder was not the beauty of her face. It was rather the riddle and mystery of the eyes themselves . . . At times you looked at the painting and were moved to tears. Other times, on the contrary, you imagined a woman who was torturing the painter with her look. Then you experienced a wave of revulsion. But none of the painter's friends or

> relatives believed a woman had ever played an important role in his life.[1]

The book's web widens and contracts, and the inscrutable stare at the narrative's center represents the confusion gripping a society where information is censored and conflicting. The mystery is not just in the woman's eyes, but in Iranian society:

> Journalists brought forth incredible incidents from their repertoire of lies and deceit . . . Fortunately, these stories have subsided little by little and now the moment is drawing near when someone might take a deeper look into the career of Ostad during the period of the dictatorship and clean up the mystery that shrouds his life.[2]

The mystery surrounding the life of Ostad Makan transports the reader to the heart of Pahlavi society:

> The events do not form an unbroken sequence, and yet, there seems to be a mysterious thread running through them . . . From the first day that the idea occurred to write the history of Iran's great painter, I realized that if I didn't find the unknown woman whose eyes appear in the painting, all I could write was what had been published in the newspapers. I'd read the police documents too. But there were no clues in them either.[3]

We too must venture beyond the official world of state-run newspapers and police records if we are to glimpse the spirit

[1] Alavi, 11.
[2] Ibid., 14.
[3] Ibid., 21.

of ordinary Iranians. Without the subtle tension of this aesthetic stratagem, it is difficult to imagine the novel's powerful epiphany (of seeking and finding Farangis) having the same impact on the reader.

I was keen to share my thoughts with Mr Eshraghi and Mr Amjadi, who I thought would appreciate the social critique latent to Alavi's writing. When disagreement arose between us in the past, they had always managed to express their criticisms tactfully. So I wrote a summary of my thoughts about the novel, which I quietly handed to the two teachers after class one day. Weeks passed, until they summoned me to talk with them in the teacher's lounge. There they plainly told me that my estimation of the work's political and artistic merits had been guided by naivety and sentimentalism. They argued that *Chashmhayash* was too romantic, its narrative style passé, and its representation of class relations under Reza Shah's reign unrealistic. It would not, they charged, reach the rank of an important literary work bestowed on other Iranian political novels. They urged me to read what they considered more important literary works, pointing me to writers like the celebrated dramatist Gholamhossein Sa'edi and others I no longer recall.

I replied, once I had overcome my initial shock and upset, that any judgment so unequivocal had to be unfair and one-sided. I had to admit, however, that I lacked their literary expertise, and that, as my teachers, I had no choice but to respect their views. At the conversation's end, sealed in secrecy and stamped with peace by their offering of what turned out to be a copy of Lenin's *State and Revolution* to me, I announced that I planned to reflect further on my reaction to the book and write a response defending my affection for it.

They approved of my attitude, however misguided they must have found the notion that I could change their minds, and looked forward to reading my defense. As we prepared to part ways, they commented that they hoped to change my mind and help me "find the right path" (*beh rah-ye rast biya'id*). The right path (*rah-ye rast*), I replied, coincided with the straight path (*rah-ye mustaqim*), a favorite religious expression of Mr Tavakol, and as Marxists they had already erred in choosing not the right but the "left" path to truth. We all laughed, but I walked away with a weight on my shoulders: I was to defend a book I adored to two men I held in esteem. I spent a full week drafting and redrafting my defense, convinced that with enough care and precision I could convince my teachers of what I knew to be true.

Today, only a cloudy impression remains of what I wrote to them. My recollections might suggest a brighter defense than what I really mounted, since the substance of my defense is not as clear today as are the feelings that swelled in me as I debated my two teachers. Why this exchange remains alive in my mind, their faces appearing before my mind's eye as if captured in a photograph, evades me. Perhaps it is because of the acute awareness of my limitations with which I entered the debate. I was a teenager full of admiration and gratitude for those who, like my teachers, took my opinions seriously. While Mr Eshraghi and Mr Amjadi were kind to engage me on issues I found important, they were years my seniors and far better versed in the matters at hand.

After about seven days, I asked the two teachers if they would allow me to read my written response to them and they kindly agreed. I prefaced my comments, which I read aloud, with the admission that it was difficult to debate two men who routinely and seamlessly finished each other's thoughts. I asked them to bear these disadvantages in mind. In the past, I had almost always hesitated to challenge them, either changing the subject, staying silent, or stopping the conversation. The closest I had ever come to challenging them was when Mr Eshraghi commented that Mosaddegh was a member of the Qajar aristocracy. "He cannot be our political role model; we need an Iranian version of Egypt's Nasser," he argued. I was tempted to respond that Nasser himself had said he was inspired by Mosaddegh's movement to do away with British control of Iranian oil. On this occasion, however, I chose to speak truthfully, because I felt they had failed to recognize what was clearly right.

And so, I began my defense by confessing that their refusal to acknowledge the merits of this novel and its author bewildered me. My admiration for *Chashmhayash*, I argued, was on solid ground from both a literary and political perspective. Alavi belonged to the Tudeh Party, had spent time imprisoned as a member of the famous "group of 53," a cohort of Iranians summarily tried and jailed in the late 1930s for promoting "collectivist ideology," prohibited by Reza Shah's draconian national security law, and was now living in East Germany in exile. Alavi had written other important books, many of them political: *Chamedan* (The Suitcase, 1934), *Varaq Pareh-ha-ye Zendan* (Scrap Papers from Prison, 1941), *Panjah-o Seh Nafar* (Fifty-Three Persons, 1942), and *Nameh-ha va Dastan-ha-ye Digar* (Letters and Other Stories, 1952). Given the scale of his output and the price he had paid for his politics, how could they fail to consider Alavi a leading Iranian writer or call into question his leftist credentials? I did my best to argue that *Chashmhayash* was a powerful and inspiring novel, the politics of its author aside. In my view, only Sadegh Hedayat was a superior writer to Alavi. I was more familiar with Hedayat's work, having read many of his books, including *Zendeh be Gur* (Buried Alive, 1930), *Seh Qatreh Khun* (Three Drops of Blood, 1932), and his magnum opus *Buf-e Kur* (The Blind Owl,1936), when we lived in Nahavand.

As a piece of literature, *Chashmhayash* was not juvenile, as they had suggested, but thematically and structurally complex. On the most immediate level, the novel, which also doubles as a police detective story, analyzes the abuse of power and reconstructs from fragments collective political memory. Dread for the police state, the paranoia caused by neighbors spying on each other, and the secrecy of 1930s transnational surveillance pervade the emotional frame of the novel. Second, *Chashmhayash* also treads existential questions concerning the fundamental opacity of inner motivation, as its narrator, Farangis, finds herself constantly uncertain about her own motivations and identity. This existential theme corresponds to its third strength: the power of its sociological analysis. Farangis' ambivalence about herself stems from the complexity of the modern world, where incommensurable worldviews and interests work to conceal the consequences of our and others' actions.

Fourth and finally, the work offers a Marxist analysis of contemporary Iranian class relations. Farangis painfully discovers that her upper-class standing, which has shielded her from the indignities of labor, rests upon the violent exploitation of the Iranian masses. This realization sets in during an encounter with Iranians exiled in Paris, including with the son of a gardener who is lifted by the revolutionary leadership of Ostad, but nonetheless doomed to an early death because of his poverty and poor health. Mental anguish haunts Farangis as she contemplates her lifetime of material ease and unlimited possibilities.

Yet *Chashmhayash* is not a work of cold social realism, nor a polemical condemnation of the Iranian upper class, but an intimate exploration of the mutual transformation that occurs as classes that lived together but apart in a stratified society come into contact. I explained to my teachers that the novel laid bare the desolation of the Reza Shah period with passages like the following:

> A death-like silence reigned over the whole country. Everybody made believe he was content. The newspapers published nothing but eulogies on behalf of the dictator. People were starved for news and secretly circulated fantastic lies. Who would dare say publicly that anything was wrong? Was it possible anything could be wrong in the land of the King of Kings?[4]

Most importantly, unlike the uninspiring fictions broadcast by state media, the novel offered an image of a world, one in which individuals, despite state censorship and their victimization by ruling classes, endeavored to do good, that for once corresponded to my experience of reality.

> Ostad Makan was a great painter and was certain that through the art of painting he could fight against injustice

[4] Alavi, 7.

> and oppression. Ostad was more than just a painter; he was a great artist because as a human being he felt compassion for the suffering of others. For him painting was a means of combating tyranny; his pursuit of art had a social and humanitarian dimension. Ostad wanted to render service to his fellow man. This is what painting meant to him and for precisely that reason his art moved people.[5]

I explained to Mr Eshraghi and Mr Amjadi that Ostad Makan represented to me the well-known Iranian painter Kamalolmolk (1848–1940), born Mohamad Ghaffari, who had helped plant in me the idea that I should study painting at the Tehran's University Art Faculty. My nascent hopes of studying painting, however, were put to rest by my father, who wanted me to attend medical school. After many heated arguments, we eventually struck a compromise: I agreed to apply to law school and shelve my artistic ambitions in exchange for his permission to specialize in literature after the ninth grade. Nonetheless, my love of painting made Kamalolmolk an almost mythical figure in my eyes. Kamalolmolk had in his lifetime traveled to Europe, where he honed his artistic techniques, and still found time to spare to participate in the Constitutional Revolution after growingly increasingly disaffected with Qajar rule. Despite Reza Shah's attempts to lure him into his political circle, Kamalolmolk refused this temptation too. He eventually grew so critical of Reza Shah's tyrannical rule that he resigned as director of his art school and left Tehran in 1928 to live in exile in Nishapur until his death in 1940. It so happened

[5] Ibid., 28.

that the year Kamalolmolk died, Alavi was freed from prison following Reza Shah's forced abdication and exile.

Kamalolmolk's courage, who preferred exile to state cooptation, explains in part why *Chashmhayash* impacted readers like me. The narrator's quest to unravel the mystery of Ostad's well-concealed life, which ends with his exile and death in the provinces, by tracking down the mysterious subject of Ostad's painting, thinking she holds the key to decoding Ostad's life, resurrects for readers the life of Kamalolmolk. Piecing together the secrets of his life, the narrator hopes to restore narrative order and meaning to a fractured Iranian nation, to banish the ghostly, enigmatic fragments haunting it.

But rather than advance this existential rationale, I thought I would be better off appealing to the didactic leanings of my Marxist schoolteachers and so argued that *Chashmhayash* was an instructive political novel. In my view, it posited Ostad as a radical worth emulating. Dedicated foremost to the well-being of his people and nation and inspired by a heightened sense of honor, Makan rejects the allure of power and wealth. Alavi, I continued, found heroism in his principal female character too. Farangis rises above personal and political circumstance to follow her own desires. Ostad and Farangis shared a rare personal quality: each hewed closely to their convictions and never confused the good for the convenient. And so Ostad rejected the state's temptation of wealth and prestige, while Farangis forsook the comforts of her class to pursue her love, Ostad Makan.

Yet Alavi did more than construct characters worthy of his readers' emulation. He provided a powerful antidote to nostalgia for the first Pahlavi monarchy. Reza Shah may have been a devout modernizer, but his tyranny inhibited the ability of progressive Iranians, such as Ostad Makan, to contribute to the development of Iran and its people. I referred my teachers to the first paragraph of the book, where Alavi brilliantly sketches the claustrophobic mood his rule fostered:

> Tehran is suffocating. Nobody is breathing. Everybody is afraid of another person. Families are afraid of each other. Children fear their teachers; the teacher fears the janitor and the janitor fears the hairdresser. Everybody is afraid of himself and his shadow. The people can see the shadow of the government thugs everywhere: in their house, in the mosque, behind the shop counter, in the school, in the university and in the bathhouse. When the royal anthem is played in the cinema the people watch their neighbors lest a crazy fellow should forget to rise and create problems for the audience. A deadly silence prevails all over the country. Everybody pretends to be happy. The papers had nothing to write but to praise the dictator.[6]

I concluded my defense of Alavi with an affirmation of his political and emotional sensibilities about 1930s Iran. It was too convenient for my teachers, I added, to strike a contrarian pose and dismiss what the novel had to offer. It was more radical to fight on behalf of what is good and useful, as *Chashmhayash* did. They sat there silently, subtle smiles resting like secrets on their faces, until I finished, at which point they simply responded, "There is a lot we need to talk with you about."

[6] Alavi, *Her Eyes*, 1.

With my comments concluded, I handed my notes over, when I thought to add as a postscript, "I don't know much, but I have tried my best to explain my interest in this book thoughtfully and clearly. I hope you as my teachers and mentors will consider what I have to say." A few days later, Mr Eshraghi and Mr Amjadi asked me after class to visit them in the teacher's lounge during our lunch hour. While I usually spent lunch playing volleyball, I skipped the game that day. I made my way to the teacher's lounge, where my teachers and I exchanged a few short pleasantries, after which they quickly cut to the chase. My defense had not moved them one bit. In fact, reading it they thought I was behaving like a "child" (*bacheh*) enthralled by Alavi's romantic storytelling. I sat shocked by the coldness of their response. What had happened to the considerate if uncompromising teachers I had known?

They urged me to look beyond the pretty pose of *Chashmhayash*, so that I might see the puerility lurking beneath. I rejoinded that I struggled to understand how two Marxists could so loathe *Chashmhayash*, and with this, their comments took a turn for the dismissive. Their patience for a stubborn student had run out, and they insisted that Alavi's literary style in *Chashmhayash* was influenced by the romantic *ashrafi* (aristocratic) genre of 1940s Iran. "Alavi's no more a Marxist than Mohammad Hejazi," a writer and statesmen whose characters reflected his upper-class milieu. "If you think otherwise, just read Hejazi's *Homa* to see how *Chashmhayash* replicates the cheap sentimentalism of bourgeois literature." They also named Hosseingholi Mosta'an (1904–1983), a writer and journalist known for his popular historical novels and his translation of Victor Hugo's *Les Misérables* (Binavayan), and Javad Fazel (1914–1961), a popular serial writer known for his religiously inspired stories, as novelists with similar styles.

I endured their criticisms in studied silence. Responding, I thought, would only make things worse when I must have already crossed my teachers to warrant such severity. So it remained unsaid that I had already read all of Hejazi's novels, about which I felt wholly indifferent, since his characters often reminded me of the self-satisfied state functionaries with whom my family associated. The sad look I wore upon my face as I listened perhaps encouraged a happier end to the debate. One of the teachers amiably offered an olive branch, asking if I would care to read a small book of their choice. Relieved not to lose their friendship, I accepted. He handed me a book with a plain brown dust jacket and asked that I hide it in my coat and refrain from sharing or mentioning it to anyone. They noted as they passed me the book that literature could only do so much to help us understand social relations, and beyond that, I needed to read proper political texts if I were to complete my education. I thanked them and left for my afternoon class.

As I reflect on this and our other encounters, I am struck by the conviction with which Mr Eshraghi and Mr Amjadi identified class, not form, ethics, or culture, as the key to understanding social reality. They scorned Jalal Al-e Ahmad and other novelists we students liked, including the dearly beloved Sadegh Hedayat, whose social analyses, they reasoned, were diminished by the defeatism of their generation. Against the nihilism of so many Iranian intellectuals, they urged us students to tide the present and embrace the future with optimism. So, while we often argued, I found their unstinting demands for a better world refreshing and more human than the religious fatalism of Mr Tavakol, and regarded them as a part of my generation. They were agents of the future, so I countenanced even their reservations about Al-e Ahmad and Hedayat.

Al-e Ahmad, of course, was a Marxist whose writings were radical. It was his disillusionment with the Soviet Union and the leftist Tudeh Party that led Al-e Ahmad to seek a political alternative in a "return to our roots" ideology. An examination of Al-e Ahmad's writings helps us understand how organic bonds of religious solidarity transformed into a state politics of official religion. Al-e Ahmad idealized the harmony of religious life and developed it into a modern ideology of popular mobilization. It is a difficult trajectory to trace, but something goes tragically astray along the way. Looking back on Al-e Ahmad today, Mr Eshraghi and Mr Amjadi appear right in a way: Al-e Ahmad did express a kind of defeatism and a mistaken vision for the nation. What my teachers failed to see was that Al-e Ahmad was redrawing the boundaries of politics to accommodate a new Iranian middle class who no longer fully believed in the religious rituals of old but yearned to defend their homeland and traditions from being trampled underfoot by the West.

Despite my teachers' critiques of him, they were just as critical of the West as Al-e Ahmad was. But where they invoked America's catastrophic military interventions in Vietnam and its support for murderous regimes from Israel to Latin America to account for their position, the religiously inclined, like my teacher Mr Tavakol, focused their ire on the corrosive effects of Western culture. Mr Tavakol powerfully condemned the corruption eating away at the Iranian state, peoples' growing alienation from their history, and the hazards of materialist consumerism in Iranian society, a trend concentrated among the elites of Tehran. In his mind, Tehran embodied all that was wrong with Iran. His notion that communal virtue and solidarity were most stifled precisely where Western lifestyles had most taken root was at once shocking and sensible to me. My conclusion as a teenage activist was that this was all the fault of the Shah. He was debasing our culture and turning Iran into a hell. This gives us some insight into Al-e Ahmad's growing appeal and how he unknowingly cleared the way for the transformation of organic religious sensibilities in small towns like Golpayegan into an Islamist ideology the revolutionary state promised to export the world over to cure the planet of modern scourges. This, too, reflects the unthought, for it is unlikely that Al-e Ahmad, who died in 1969, envisioned that he and his critique of *gharbzadegi* (Westoxification) would help galvanize a movement for religious rule. Nor did most of the population of Golpayegan. It is like the famous line at the end of the Wong Kar-wai film *In the Mood for Love:* "In the beginning I wanted to understand how everything began. Now I know. Things happen without us realizing."

I now realize that while my teachers, classmates, and I sincerely desired a prosperous future for our country, our thinking was steeped in the past. We never stopped to question our radical credentials. We whiled away months, even years, dreaming of a free future we had no idea how to build. Although I came to suspect this during my university years, at the time, our attention and energy were absorbed not by strategic reflection or action but mundane exercises in politics: reading, debating, and following national and international news. We did not dwell much on the consequences of our actions. "Consequentialism" is still lacking in leftist thought, and this is a complex problem going back to dialectics among other things. Even as a youth sympathetic to religion, I was more concerned with belonging to a community in the here and now than with how life in heaven would transpire. The pervasive desire to belong explains a great deal about politics, including some of its worst aspects.

On the crucial question of the ideal society, my teachers strongly disagreed with each other. Mr Tavakol mined the wisdom of Persian poets and historians to imagine the virtuous person, community, and society. He never tired of sharing with us his synthetic vision of Persian morality, adorned with beautiful images from the tenth-century poet Rudaki's verses, of Rumi's musings on life's mysteries, and of Imam Hossein's passion for justice and good. Yet Mr Tavakol was not necessarily a nationalist. He was quick to recommend exemplary works by Arab and Muslim thinkers. He had traveled across the Middle East and shared with us the sublime awe that filled him during his pilgrimage in Mecca, spoke positively of Iraq, Iran's geopolitical rival, and, in coded language, told us stories of the unflagging courage of Palestinian resistance fighters. He had a library of materials on Palestine and played audio recordings about the struggle there for his students. The dedication that sustained the Palestinian fight for liberation amazed me. Given the wealth of rare and politically risky books, journals, and audio recordings he possessed, I suspected that Mr Tavakol was part of a network of politically minded individuals.

How he obtained these materials, however, remained a secret to our class.

Mr Tavakol spoke with such conviction about our obligations to our neighboring brethren in Palestine and the wonders of Mecca that I decided at the end of my tenth grade, at seventeen years old, to switch from studying English as a foreign language to Arabic with great seriousness. After school, I let the sounds of Arabic radio fill our house, and it was easy to do so, since our radio received Arabic stations more clearly than it did Iranian stations. My brother, Masoud, and sister, Susan, visibly annoyed, pressed me on my newfound interest in Arabic. We only had one radio in our house, and they preferred listening to music. These discussions, the full extent of my family's conversations about "transnationalism," led them to question why they found spoken Arabic harsh but sung Arabic to be pleasant and joyful.

God in our Classroom

In my last two years of high school, Mr Tavakol turned into something of a disciplinarian. He had always been a fastidious teacher, but the way he obsessed over classroom organization in those final years quietly worried me. Class consisted of almost literal readings of our textbook, and he prohibited us from asking questions that were not covered in the book. Even when discussion was allowed we were to draw our talking points strictly from what was in the textbook. At the same time, he became fussier about students' appearances, making comments about some of us who had long hair or shaved beards.

At the same time as these changes, Mr Tavakol started playing tape-recorded speeches of a well-known Tehrani cleric in class. I was surprised and amused to see our well-respected teacher deviate from protocol. Perhaps, I thought to myself, our teacher has realized that there's more to life and learning than memorizing Persian poetry, Arabic grammar, and Iranian history. It was not in Mr Tavakol's character—the confidence he projected made all his judgments seem judicious—to explain his teaching decisions, and the same habit applied here.

For two years across almost thirty classes we listened to the lectures of one man: Mohammad Taghi Falsafi (1908–1998), a well-known, rabble-rousing Shi'i cleric. In June 1951, during the oil nationalization crisis, Falsafi was known in religious circles as "one of Iran's most influential younger mullahs" whose lectures had led to riots and stoked ill will against the U.K., U.S., and U.S.S.R. Despite his contempt for the U.S., a CIA operation called BEDAMN sought to prop up Falsafi as an alternative to the pro-nationalizing Ayatollah Kashani during the oil crisis. I was acquainted with his name and, thanks to my political friends, knew Falsafi to be an anti-regime cleric

Figure 2.5 High School teachers, Golpayegan, 1966.

and something of a transnational preacher, traveling from Pakistan to the Persian Gulf and across the Arab world to make his movement for Islamic revival known. Despite being barred from public preaching or speaking, he continued, at the invitation of patrons, to preach in private homes and religious ceremonies, sermons which attracted hundreds of people and circulated to thousands more on cassette tapes, about the errors of the Pahlavi state and official Shiʿi policies.

Falsafi added to the chorus of voices I encountered in Golpayegan about Iranian nationhood. I initially listened to the cassettes Mr Tavakol played sitting at the edge of my seat, absorbing every word, knowing this opportunity would not be available at home or elsewhere. This was the first time that we, a group of about thirty students, listened collectively and publicly to a well-known opposition figure. The effect of mass political action—even if this action was merely listening and limited to a class of thirty—was exhilarating. I was so thrilled by the experience, by Falsafi's enchanting voice and rhetorical power, that I hardly stopped to process the content of his lectures at first. Most of my acts of protest, such as reading banned books or listening to opposition radio, had until then been solitary. I dreamed of sharing my political sentiments with my peers, family members, and community, so I was grateful to Mr Tavakol for providing this shared listening space and, with it, an outlet for my first act of public rebellion against the state. I felt older and wiser because of it.

But Mr Tavakol practiced prudence even in his transgressions. He stood taciturn as the cassettes played, never providing commentary on Falsafi's speeches, or asking us questions about them. This did not stop us students, of course, from discussing our views on Falsafi outside of class. The electrifying power of his orations, whether we agreed with his message or not, testifies to the fact that anti-Pahlavi radicalism was not the exclusive domain of the left. Islamists had critiques of their own which expanded the contours of radical dissent.

After weeks of careful listening, however, Falsafi's novelty began to fade. He appeared as he was—another man of my father's generation who had little more to offer than moral rebuke. For Falsafi, the crisis facing Iran's youth was a moral one traceable to the Iranian government. Under the influence of the Pahlavi state, he argued, members of my generation had grown detached from tradition and even disinterested in religion. As evidence of rising immorality, he pointed to the prevalence of Westoxicated behaviors, like dresses for girls, long hair for boys, and growing disrespect for parents. Falsafi's moralizing made clear that we had opposite aspirations for Iran. The problem to be overcome in my mind was not the deviancy of younger Iranians but the cultural constraints and political oppression that limited our thought and action. Where Falsafi believed the government's moral laxity had corrupted younger generations, I felt the state and its representatives were constantly telling us what to do, while never giving us the freedom to express our thoughts or aspirations.

There was only one teacher in our high school who did not brook his colleagues' *sonnat-gera'i* (traditionalism), and that was Mr Esmaili, our physics teacher. Born and raised in Golpayegan, Mr Esmaili too was a religious person, but he felt teachers like Mr Tavakol who used the classroom as a captive audience had overstepped their bounds. Once in a private conversation, he confided to me, only half-jokingly, "Most of my colleagues here would be more comfortable living in the Middle Ages." Mr Esmaili was a rather quiet and soft-spoken man, but he sometimes surprised me with his critical comments and observations about the town and our school. Impressed by his frankness, I thought he would be a good source for learning more about Falsafi's background. So one day, I laid out my questions, Mr Esmaili all the while only slyly smiling, until I finished and he said, "Falsafi is Satan himself. The man is virulently anti-Baha'i and is connected to the likes of Ayatollah Khomeini." News of his anti-Bahaism upset me, and I was apprehensive about his connection to Khomeini too. Although I admired Khomeini's courage for standing up to the Shah in 1963, which ultimately resulted in his exile to Iraq, several of his speeches broadcast by Radio Baghdad left me unimpressed. I felt there was a serious generational gap between the language he used and the concerns of a teenage student like me.

The following year, 1969, was my last year of high school. I had lost my tolerance for Falsafi's speeches and even developed a nostalgia of sorts for the dry lectures Mr Tavakol used to deliver. Still, I admired my teacher and did not want to upset him by raising any negative comments in class. For some time, I struggled with what to do, wanting neither to stay silent nor to speak. Eventually I hit upon a plan. One day after class I approached Mr Tavakol and asked in almost a whisper: "I have some private thoughts and a few questions that I would like to share with you. Would you mind if I wrote them down and gave them to you, so that you might kindly read them and share with me your reflections?" He gave me a gentle but inquiring look, before replying, "Yes, of course, I am your teacher. That is what I do, in or outside of class." That night tested me. Putting my questions, which sprang from my disappointment, into words was a difficult and emotional task. I sat at my bedside table long into the night writing questions only to discard them and start over. I was unable to conceive of any question without preemptively imagining Mr Tavakol's anger at my indiscretion. I finally decided the best course of action would be to write my questions in the most straightforward style possible. I would frame my dissatisfaction, moreover, not as a shortcoming on Mr Tavakol's part, but in terms of the dissonance between his insistence on valuing knowledge, rational reflection, and intellectual independence and the irrationality of Falsafi's views.

My letter opened by declaring how much I valued Mr Tavakol and his mentorship. I went so far as to apologize: "I know I am not from Golpayegan but a *gharibeh* to this town. I know that as head of the city's finance office, my father is considered a high official and that I carry the privileges accruing to his status. I am very sorry for this. I hope you understand that we do not choose the family we are from. I have tried to follow your advice and be a good person. I hope this essay will not change your view of me." I then raised three crucial inconsistencies, asking him to clarify how he reconciled them: First, I wrote, how can you implore us to fear God while pushing us to study hard, learn as much as possible, and think independently? If we ought to think for ourselves, then how could fear be a valuable motivator? If we love God yet fear his wrath, then why learn about Islam or the Prophet? I considered myself a good Muslim, as I tried to be an ethical person and meet my religious duties. Yet I had difficulty coming to terms with certain notions integral to the tradition, such as the afterlife and heaven, which seemed to me like fantasy. Mr Tavakol believed firmly in these dogmas, so I dared not ask him questions about the Qur'an. Instead, I concluded this section by asking him to consider my questions in the spirit of open inquiry he had encouraged his students to pursue.

I ventured my second question: Is Islam in your view the only source of ethical instruction? If there are non-religious sources we ought to consult to cultivate our intellectual, physical, and ethical faculties ourselves, why do they never figure into our class discussions? I gestured here to my involvement in theater, painting, and sports, which I took as seriously and found as fortifying as my religious studies. How was I to sustain motivation for these activities when I heard only negative comments about artists and athletes from men like Falsafi? I noted that Islamic civilization owed much to artists, poets, architects, and other cultural pioneers. Limiting our understanding of the Islamic past and ways of living to the teachings of preachers and jurists denied the civilization its broader horizons.

I saved my most pressing question for last: Why, I pressed with discernible disappointment, did he present Falsafi to

Figure 2.6 Ali Mirsepassi, eleventh grade, Golpayegan, late 1960s.

students as a figure worth emulating? Falsafi's thought was limited to moral tropes, while his outdated understanding of modern Iran was unrecognizable to most young Iranians. He spoke from the perspective of the ulama and would have happily had Iranians rearrange their lives to the satisfaction of clerics. I asked him kindly and simply to explain his rationale for devoting so much class time to Falsafi.

By the end of that night, I had written over thirty pages full of references to Falsafi's most objectionable ideas. Working up the courage and piecing together the evidence to challenge credibly Mr Tavakol's authority, however humbly, was a monumental task for me, but I was pleased with its result. Although this did little to quell my anxiety at how it would be received. I worried Mr Tavakol would interpret the first two questions as declarations of diminished faith. In truth, at that time, I was undecided about God. Yet this was not an especially important issue for me.

I approached Mr Tavakol after class the following day with my written questions. He was at his large, wooden desk, which stood at the head of the classroom and gave him a commanding view of the room. With my head bowed, I explained that these handwritten pages contained my questions for him. He took the bundle of pages from my hands and thanked me. I walked out of the classroom, and a week passed before he asked to see me. I followed him after class that day to the teacher's lounge, a large rectangular room tucked away in the back corner of the second floor. I had often seen teachers crossing its threshold, and here I was entering it for the first time. It was a simple room, containing two rows of chairs that ran down either side of a long, plain table. As always, Mr Tavakol was wearing a dark brown suit and a white shirt buttoned all the way to his neck. Although I got the sense that he was avoiding my gaze, he managed to be perfectly polite. He asked me to sit next to him, pointing to the chair closest to his, before telling me that he appreciated the care that had gone into writing my essay. "You gave me a book," he joked, "when I was expecting a single page of questions. However," he continued, "I'm pleased that one of my students has the courage to raise these important issues with me." He then removed an envelope from his jacket, which he handed to me and explained contained his responses to my questions. I took the envelope, thanked him for his time, then hurried to the schoolyard to read his response.

His reply was brief, no more than three or four pages, but addressed nearly every issue I had raised. Responding to my first set of questions about education, he wrote, "I remind you that this world's existence is not an accident of nature. Our life and being, resulting from Divine Creation, exists for a sacred purpose. We must strive to live a purposeful life according to God's teachings and our faith. But we can only live according to the principle of right action by using our hearts and minds. We therefore need two different kinds of knowledge: (1) *'elm-e dini*, religious knowledge; and (2) *'elm-e in-jahani,* life sciences." He saw no tension between belief in this cosmology and the pursuit of worldly knowledge. "Achieving worldly knowledge," he wrote, "gratifies God and abides by the wise path of the Prophet. However, worldly knowledge is always partial in reach and substance. Sciences are neutral on matters of life's ultimate meaning and even other matters where much is unknown. Where science does not or cannot help us know, we must depend on faith." He concluded his response to my first question by saying: "If something in your studies is not in accordance with religious teachings, lose neither your faith nor your love of science. Find others with whom to discuss the issue. One must remain open to discussion and debate." He reminded me of "a long and rich history of debate in religious seminaries," saying we needed "more of this today."

While Mr Tavakol had not ceded any ground to me, it was comforting to know his arguments were rational, not dogmatic. His clear-minded patience with my skepticism emboldened me, and I regretted not having raised specific points of contradiction between science and our religious teachings.

His response to my second question was brief. My view of Islam, which distinguished philosophy and the arts from the religious sciences, he insisted, was mistakenly limited and resembled a Christian, rather than Islamic, understanding of religion. Muslims writers, artists, architects, and engineers, he acknowledged, are part of the Islamic tradition, not outside it. He ended this section by reiterating that Islam values the humanistic sciences, but if some artists or philosophers do not care for Islam, their problem is as it would be for any other person.

Regarding my criticism of Falsafi, Mr Tavakol was adamant that I was mistaken, politically inexperienced, and perhaps even misguided. Falsafi, he argued, was a respected religious leader and a learned man, the kind of man Iranians should be proud to call their own. I simply needed to listen to him more carefully to understand the truth of his message.

My memories of Mr Tavakol remain to this day fond. Despite our many differences, I owe who I am partly to him and his devotion to his students. He was a formal, serious-minded teacher whose nature left little room for fun or spontaneity in our conversations. However, I admired his command of Persian and Arabic literature and his commitment to rigorous yet stimulating teaching. After graduating from high school and moving to Tehran, I sadly lost contact with him. While writing this I reached out to several people from Golpayegan who I thought might offer clues into his whereabouts, but I have struggled to learn what happened to this dear teacher of mine after the revolution. I did learn that someone from Golpayegan with the same name, Jafar Tavakol, was elected to the first Majlis after the revolution in 1980. However, the election was contested, and voting irregularities ultimately voided the results and prevented him from sitting as a member of parliament. Printed alongside one local newspaper report about the election's outcome was a picture of a man who closely resembled my teacher. The report also mentioned that this Jafar Tavakol visited the war fronts during the Iran–Iraq War to provide comfort and assistance to soldiers from Golpayegan. Whether this man was my teacher, however, I may never know.

Picturing Iran

As a teenager undergoing political upheavals of his own, I thought Iranian society was in transition. My generation and our forebears were still steeped in the immediacy of local culture and the daily intimacies of family life, but we also reached for connections to wider happenings. We faithfully imbibed the literature and politics of distant worlds. Although the ties of home and family bound us to Golpayegan we were also developing a new global consciousness. For us, the late

1960s and 1970s were a "place," and the whole world had a seat at this great table. Evidence of synchronous change was everywhere: in the youth movements of Europe, resistance movements unfolding in Vietnam and across the Third World, the Palestinian cause, and other dramatic changes reported by state radio about the Arab world. The radicalism of the era manifested itself even in music, with bands like the Beatles championing humanistic change to pop melodies. We came to feel certain that a worldwide movement against old dominations was coalescing around us, and this feeling, along with the flurry of books, films, and radio programs flooding us with information, helped connect our struggle in Iran to those happening elsewhere and across several dramatic decades. Translations of European and Arabic texts were critical sources of information, since novels, short stories, histories, and religious texts that passed the scrutiny of state censors were available to us in Persian. Works from abroad helped compensate for the fact that censors restricted writings on domestic politics and Iranian history to a trickle. We dreamed within an informational world of translations and traces. Despite the restrictions on what state media deemed permissible, we avidly read Iranian magazines and newspapers, like the weekly *Ferdowsi*.

The Pahlavi state guarded against our yearnings for international resistance with its own idea of Iran, which we were exposed to whenever we listened to Radio Iran and which thoroughly permeated politics. The state-sanctioned Iran Novin Party (New Iran Party) controlled both the parliament and the cabinet. For routine celebrations of the Shah's birthday on October 27, students from all parts of Iran were forced to present themselves to their city's main sports stadium. There, under obligation, we celebrated the Shah as a leader gifted to us by God, listening to speeches in which he proclaimed himself the embodiment of the Iranian nation. Foreign dignitaries and Iranian state officials abided this command, addressing the Shah as the very personification of Iran.

The image of Iran the state put forward and demanded our allegiance to was burdened with tedious rituals demonstrating nothing other than the Shah's power. We participated in these rituals under duress, and given the compulsion involved, these displays of kingly grandeur stirred nothing in my heart. I saw only a giant bureaucratic machine at the head of which stood the Shah. Without him, it could not survive. The regime's image of Iran conflated the country with the monarchy, narrating its present as the sum of the Shah's achievements and its past as the mythology of Persian kingship. Both images reaffirmed my view that the Shah's Iran was a fictive country I had no ties to.

Despite the propaganda saturating our lives, which conflated the Shah with the nation, and the state with the will of the people, our eyes remained fixed on a completely different Iran. Nurtured in our hearts was a political and emotional affinity with faraway places like Vietnam, Palestine, Cuba, and India. On several occasions I met college students who were back home visiting Golpayegan, and they explained to me what they were discussing with other, more experienced and older leftists. More than once, these college students referenced Jawaharlal Nehru's *Discovery of India.* Contemplating India's push for independence, I recognized that the ghosts of empire still haunted Iran in the form of outsized U.S. influence in its affairs. Yet the Pahlavi state, rather than defend Iranian sovereignty, was party to this game of geopolitics, and in many ways, a direct outcome of America's freshest violation of our national independence. Many discussions among students and older activists focused on U.S. involvement in the 1953 *coup d'état.* I felt that all of Iran's woes could be traced to foreign intervention. It was the lasting trauma of this history that depended my interest in the anti-imperial struggles of other countries, such as Vietnam. Yet why this emotional affinity? What caused Iranians in Golpayegan to identify with the national experience of Cuba more than with contemporary Pahlavi Iran? What made us envision Iran's future in terms of the international?

Perhaps it was because we felt that our everyday realities and our experiences were absent in official imaginings of Iran. This absence, or "space" (since absences too occupy space) encompassed a tangle of histories and ideas. Within it, we imagined Iran as an idea in emergence, a possibility pushed to the surface by international upheavals. On one hand, then, Iran was a point on the horizon that resembled Nehru's India, Castro's Cuba, Lenin's Soviet Union, and the country earlier Iranian constitutionalists had envisioned. On the other, however, the Iran we imagined was distinctly Persian, a tapestry woven of the lyricism of Hafez, Sa'di, and Rumi; the philosophy of Farabi, Avicenna, and Suhrawardi; the political legacy of constitutionalists, like Sattar Khan, Bagher Khan, Dehkhoda, and Mosaddegh; and the free verses of Ahmad Shamlu, Mehdi Akhavan Sales, and Forough Farrokhzad. Thus, while we admired Japanese, Indian, and European achievements, we still considered ourselves stewards of a distinct cultural heritage. This sense of cultural difference did not vitiate the fact that, as

Iranians, we were committed to the liberation of impoverished countries the world over.

In the context of these considerations, we might argue that nationalism involves a tripartite temporality. Its past, present, and future together form a unified structure. And the piecing together of this structure is part of the "unthought" I have been seeking through these recollections. First, there is the past: the latent consciousness of the youth of Golpayegan developed within a historically conditioned cultural space. Then there is the present: Iran as an idea in emergence, as a fledgling potentiality looking to India, Japan, Central Asia, Europe, and the Soviet Union as its guide. From this perspective, we notice a striking and counterintuitive detail: the act of imagining the world precedes nationalism genealogically. And finally there is the future: a future in which Iran would learn from and come to look like Nehru's India, Castro's Cuba, and Lenin's Soviet Union.

This future was creative and contradictory. We simultaneously idealized the Soviet Union and Nehru's India as two struggles for justice for the poor. Yet their similarities were only nominal. These two regimes harbored conflicting political and economic logics, the dire consequences of which cannot be dispelled by any amount of utopian enthusiasm. But we are describing an emergent consciousness among youth in a country facing an uncertain future. Contradictions should therefore scarcely surprise us.

Small Town, Grand *Donya*

However tentative and ambiguous our understandings of the "national" or "global" were, one consistency persisted, and that was our use of the words *donya* and sometimes *jahan* to articulate our perspectives on the world. Both words literally mean "world" in English. Yet they contain greater differences than this translation suggests. *Donya* refers to an integrated and inter-related world. Usually used by Islamic theologians and theorists to refer to the material world of human corporeality, it also carries a normative quality. *Jahan* more closely approximates the idea of the global or the cosmopolitan. For those of us sympathetic to Marxism, we preferred *donya* and spoke readily of the *donya-ye gharb* (the Western world) or *donya-ye kommunist* (the communist world). More religious-leaning friends, including Mr Tavakol, tended to opt for *jahan*. Mr Tavakol often used *donya* in a negative way. For example, *donya bi arzesh ast* (this world is worthless), or *beh donya del naband* (do not attach yourself to *donya*). My sense was that for him *donya* signified the material world, a diversion from a more meaningful spiritual universe.

An intellectual might describe Persian literature in terms of *adabiyat-e jahani* (world literature). They spoke of *jahan-e 'arab* (the Arab world), and we all used the term *jahan-e sevvom* (the Third World). Mr Eshraghi and Mr Amjadi proudly informed us that the first Marxist journal published in Iran was *Donya*, the brainchild of the German-educated Iranian chemist, Taghi Arani. The journal *Jahan-e Islam* was a popular religious publication read by everyone in our town.

During my years in Golpayegan, I participated in a number of small reading and study groups, which, despite their differences, offered us students a space to grapple with Iran's relation to the world. We would meet regularly in the summer and during the school year on Fridays, our day off. I often gathered with classmates and family friends to memorize trivia from world encyclopedias. We mainly focused on memorizing capitals of countries and the dates of world events from antiquity to the present. Those of us who were more experienced worked on committing to memory information about world famous authors, political figures, inventors and their inventions, and of course, facts about movies, directors, actors, and so on.

Then there were study groups in which we met to discuss a book or article we had all read or a political movement that interested us. No matter which group, and however elliptically, these discussions often returned to the question of Iran's place in the world.

For me, *donya* was something aspirational, my own imaginative remaking of the world. *Jahan*, by contrast, referred to the empirical world "out there". In this respect, Iran at that time was not a part of *donya* but an odd part of *jahan*. Conversely, the Pahlavi state in the late 1960s and 1970s sought to make Iran a pivot of regional and world affairs. The Shah's Iran would be distinct from and superior to the wider world while existing at its very center. In my imagination, Iran had insulated itself from the larger world and lost sight of what it had been and should be. This situation was challenging and potentially destructive. I did not think of myself as a citizen of Iran, since I was never permitted to contribute to its well-being in any practical way. This, of course, was what the government desired: for young Iranians to remain uninvolved in political affairs, acting only as pliant cheerleaders for the Shah. But I loved my country and its people, and the only space available for a young person like me was oppositional politics.

In these complex and confusing times, it was liberating to think of Iran in terms of the *donya* I had invented, a constellation of transnational ideas and cultural exchanges. I thought of Iran as a space in which Iranian and world cultures mingled as equals, although emotionally, Iran remained the axis of this world (*donya*) as I knew it. The struggle over national consciousness was no small matter, since it was through this imaginative and collective process that we participated in making the nation. In my thinking, contemporary Iran was owned by the Shah, so why should we limit our imaginations to national borders? The two options that presented themselves before us were either to look for inspiration in historical Iran or to project onto the future a new world (*donya*). Although much of my thinking was oriented toward the future, the Shah's supposed resurrection of the glories of pre-Islamic Iran and religious writers' converse insistence on situating Iran within the Islamic world fed my preoccupation with the history and culture of Iran. I did my best to read all I could and make sense of both the pre- and post-Islamic periods, but was overwhelmed by so many competing accounts of the past. Instead it was the present *donya* that could be seized as our domain; it was this space that millions of young people all over the world had already marked on our behalf. Student movements in Europe, the anti-war movement in the U.S., and struggles for national liberation across Palestine, Africa, and Latin America all symbolized our young hearts' hopes and desires.

We fed our curiosity about the world by listening to English, Arabic, and Persian radio stations based in East Berlin, Baghdad, London, and Beijing. We tapped our contacts in Tehran to acquire copies of *Time* magazine and

Newsweek. Our English teacher, Mr Nurbakhsh, was especially helpful in facilitating our access to English-language magazines, although we suspected that he was pro-Western and used these magazines to sway us. I imagined Golpayegan was a lonely place for him at times, but outside of teaching he was content with working his land. We also made sure to put ample time and effort into learning foreign languages, like English and Arabic, and into conversing with the few non-Iranians who crossed our paths. Yet my friends and I made limited headway into improving our English. It was only with the help of Mr Nurbakhsh that we could read an English atlas. Arabic, however, was a different story. There was a vibrant culture of teaching and learning Arabic in Golpayegan at the time, and it was not unusual for my high school classmates to read Arabic literature, poetry, religious scholarship, and newspapers. I myself was able to read some Arabic books and journals dealing with contemporary politics, religion, and historical matters.

Contact with non-Iranians was, however, limited in Golpayegan. The only chance I had to interact with foreigners was when a young American couple was assigned to our town as Peace Corps volunteers. Despite their strange insistence on teaching us carpentry, I found them likeable. So I visited the workshop they set up at our high school, sneaking in questions between instruction in hopes of learning about the U.S. and improving my English. Yet their hapless attempts to "cultivate" us through carpentry classes struck me as odd, especially since the most important handicraft in Golpayegan was woodworking, a higher skill, I thought, than the crude carpentry they thought us. Of course, eager as I was to learn of different people and places, exercise my English skills, and learn about the U.S., I decided sawing and sanding wood was a cost worth paying. I most wanted to learn what our young Americans visitors had to say about U.S. culture and politics, but they were reticent to talk about themselves or their country. Instead, they lived a rather guarded life, refraining from mixing more than was necessary with the locals.

In Golpayegan, I formed for the first time what I believed to be an intellectually sophisticated understanding of myself and the world. Two worldviews became anathema to what I could tolerate: anti-intellectualism, or *bifarhangi*, and provincialism, or *mahaligera'i.* My friends and I erected these rather vague categories to distinguish ourselves from those we viewed as reactionaries. While we sought to transcend parochial concerns, we did not consider ourselves nationalists or even *tajaddodgera* (modernizers), outdated and meaningless terms we considered part of the regime's rhetoric. While I wanted my politics to embrace the whole world, I did not scorn the appreciation Golpayeganis felt for their town, or their tendency to reminisce about their lives. I always treasured these moments of generational exchange, eager to learn about local cultures and lifestyles. If anything, I had little tolerance for those, mainly from Tehran, who visited our town without showing interest in its people and culture, judging us inferior because we lacked theaters and other metropolitan amenities. For so many Tehranis, beyond Iran's capital lay nothing of interest but the simple-minded innocence of provincials. Both Tehran-centrism and *mahaligera'i* (provincialism) were to me two sides of the same dogma, too narrow to see beyond their own immediate surroundings.

Yet I distinguished "localism" from provincialism and traditionalism. Local mannerisms reflected patterns of social interaction and cultural transmission. Meditating on them was itself a lesson in historical thinking. In a way, I was somewhat of a traditionalist, but not a *mahaligera* (provincialist). I was interested in Iranian history, culture, and religion, and for me, *farhang* (culture) was key to defining myself and the world. Yet culture for me was not divisible into modern and traditional camps, but "good" and "bad" ones. I embraced the views of my peers who were interested in reading, knowing, and being broadly open to the world, a condition of intellectual openness we named *bafarhang* (cultured). Those who were only interested in the received habits and customs of Golpayegan we called *bifarhang* (uncultured).

Golpayegan's experience presents a window onto the hopes and horizons of local Iranians during global decades. It puts us beyond official narratives and those accounts that peer at Iran and the world exclusively from Tehran's vantage point. The local is not pure, simple, or small, but as complex as life gets. It is deeply interwoven with and evolves alongside Tehran, Iran, and the world. The emergence of political Islam and new forms of Marxism were the fruits of complex national and transnational processes, which do not in the least fit a universal/local dichotomy but were instead dynamized by the circulatory movements of people and ideas.

Evil Averted

My relationship with Mr Tavakol grew distant and cloudy by the end of my high school studies. I continued to respect him as a teacher, but my disappointment after the Falsafi episode created an emotional barrier between us. Confused and lonely, I connected with another religious teacher in Golpayegan after a chance encounter. I was on a bus headed to Tehran in late October of my senior high school year, when I noticed that our science teacher, Mr Safi, from Ebn Sina High School was sitting next to me. We started a conversation, and he casually asked if I was involved in any extracurricular activities. I replied that I practiced painting and sports with a group of students and teachers, but in such a religious town, I still felt isolated from the community. "Are you seriously interested in religious activities?" he asked, to which I answered, "I'm open to meeting anyone critical of the regime." Smiling, he proposed to introduce me to someone he thought I might like. He gave me the man's name and told me to mention that Mr Safi had recommended I join the Anjoman (association or society).

I returned from Tehran to Golpayegan less than a week later. As soon as I did, I retrieved the piece of paper on which Mr Safi had written his friend's name, who turned out to be the owner of a stationery shop in town. I called him up, and he put me in contact with a high school student I already knew. He was a mathematics major active in various extracurricular activities at the high school. This student and I met one day after school, and he accompanied me to my first Anjoman meeting. The Anjoman, I learned, was a sort of secret operation. There was no formal procedure for becoming a member, nor was there a particular place or even a regular time set for their meetings. Some of the meetings took place in the high school, others at the homes of students or teachers who were members.

During these clandestine meetings, an older man talked to us about Islam and particularly about the Baha'i faith. Together we read a few original Baha'i writings. I was curious why the group acted so secretively, since they were effectively little more than a glorified study group. They were critical of the Shah but practiced more caution when expressing these views. While it soon became apparent that I was in the midst of anti-Baha'i crusaders, I convinced myself I could set this unsavory aspect aside. Membership in the group was a "privilege" I was not ready to give up. It was mostly students and teachers who attended their meetings, so there was a scholarly aura to the Anjoman that I found very appealing.

Two months progressed like this, until one day, as I was leaving a meeting at the other high school, a teacher present there, who I understood to be one of the Anjoman leaders, approached me and asked to speak to me privately. He was in his early forties, brown haired, and I remember that he wore a checkered blazer. We walked away from the high school building. He looked over his shoulder, making sure no one was close to us, then, in his most complimentary tone, said that I was a very "special" person. "Because of your father's position in the Ministry of Finance," he said, "we can involve you in important tasks without fear for your safety." He then asked if I would be willing to be part of an important religious mission. Flattered, I told him I would. Overcome with excitement and anxiety about my new role, I did not stop to ask about the nature of the mission.

I would not have to wait long to learn more of my secret assignment, however. As it happened, the man organizing the mission requested that we meet the following day after school. I was instructed to meet another student, someone I was not friends with but who I knew to be a mathematics major at the other high school, at the bazaar. From there, I followed him to where we were to meet the others. We walked through the bazaar, me trailing behind my silent guide, until we abruptly cut across a narrow alleyway. At the end of the alley, we stopped. My companion knocked on a blue door, which a friendly older man unlocked in short order to offer us warm greetings. The door opened onto a courtyard lined with colorful roses and lush plants, and at its center stood a pool filled with crystal-clear water. The house was not particularly big, but it had the gleam of a newer construction.

We followed the man who had opened the door up a few steps, with me all the while assuming that this was his house. But at the stairway's end, he pointed to the last room on the left. The older man said Mr Safi is waiting for you in the guest room, then disappeared to the other side of the house. Upon entering the room, I encountered four other students and a man of about thirty years old seated silently. I was expecting Mr Safi to be waiting for us, but he was nowhere in sight. The adult among us appeared agitated; an inauspicious sign, I thought. Mr Safi was a soft-spoken yet confident person, while this man was anything but calm. His attempt at a hushed voice barely concealed his frayed nerves. He began by explaining that we had been entrusted with an important and sensitive undertaking. A long lecture followed on the importance of secrecy and absolute allegiance to the Anjoman. He informed us of the best ways to disavow involvement should we be called for questioning by high school officials or the police. Anxiety gnawed at me. I suddenly and forcefully realized that I disliked and distrusted this man. That an adult should entrust children with an admittedly dangerous mission struck me as callous and reckless. This tension, however, is part of the mysterious allure of political activism. One feels a new sense of agency in actively engaging and even endangering one's life. Yet in becoming part of collective action and a secret operation, one also feels powerless and carried along helplessly by a larger current. This issue became even more significant for me later in my life when I grew more seriously engaged in politics, both during the Iranian Revolution and in the U.S. working with the Confederation of Iranian Students.

My misgivings were confirmed when the man announced that late one night the following week we would be sent to "disrupt" a Baha'i home and terrify the family into "voluntarily" leaving Golpayegan. He then attempted to comfort us, insisting no one would be hurt nor would anyone find out about it. Even in the odd event that the police discovered our involvement, he reasoned they would look the other way, since they resented the influence of Baha'is in Golpayegan too. He explained that the targeted homeowner was a high school teacher, whose name and address would only be revealed to us closer to the date of the "disruption." If others found out about our deed, we would say we had retaliated after the teacher pressured us to abandon Islam and convert to Baha'ism. Everything had been planned and accounted for, he proudly concluded.

The news sent shockwaves through my body, devastating me and my thought process. I tried to look at the man, who appeared to me like Norman Bates from Alfred Hitchcock's *Psycho*, except he lacked Bates's boy-next-door look. He was, in short, a creep, but I was too confused to mount a challenge, and he at any rate appeared too domineering to be challenged.

Five high school students including myself sat before him, but I was so unsettled that the others faded from my vision. I cannot remember what the other students said or how they reacted. I felt I was trapped alone with the older man. Completely at a loss and with no place to turn, I started sobbing violently. I lacked the nerve to tell this man that he was a monster, or that his plans were an affront to human decency, making him worse than SAVAK. He grew furious at my tears. He gestured with his hand toward the door and yelled, "You are too weak-willed, go home and never return to the Anjoman." I apologized as I left the house. In that instant, his name-calling did not bother me since I was happy to be free from his gaze. I was saddened and wounded for other reasons, however. In searching for an activist religious model, I chose the Anjoman and rejected the kind Mr Tavakol, who I felt demurred from political action. I was mistaken to think the Anjoman offered a viable alternative. Later that night I felt furious at myself. Why, I asked myself, had I apologized to that man? What happened to the other kids? And what was to befall that Baha'i family?

This experience planted a lasting curiosity about the Anjoman-e Hojjatiyeh in me. At Tehran University, I heard nothing about them, which only added to their mystery. During my compulsory military service, many cadets bonded over their admiration for Taghi Falsafi and played audiotapes of his lectures during their breaks. One day an officer I knew well came to me and said, "I have exciting news: Mr Falsafi is giving a lecture in Qasr-e Shririn (a city in Kermanshah province) this Wednesday night. Would you like to go?" "No thanks," I responded, "I got my fill of him when I was in high school. Now I would like to move on." Word of Falsafi's presence and lecture, however, spread all over the military camp. That Wednesday night, in April 1976, many of the military personnel attended his lecture, giving him a full hero's welcome. It was during this time that I was told that Falsafi was a member of Anjoman.

We now know that the Hojjatiyeh is a conservative anti-Bahai and anti-Marxist religious group with a major presence in the security forces of the Islamic Republic. It is a cruel irony that, searching for a utopia and a kinder humanity, I was recruited by this appalling organization. Now I am tainted with a two- or three-month history as a member of Anjoman-e Hojjatiyeh. Our life, as we have lived it, is sometimes more "unreal" than we are willing to disclose. Today, as I write these words, I find myself still lost in a void with respect to these early life events. I have grown so estranged from them that it feels like I am telling the story of another person's life. Is this me, as I have known myself for all these years? And then I think of the "unthought," our failure to recall the parts of our life we lack the audacity to either retell or even remember.

Remembering what I have tried to forget, however, helps us understand how well-intentioned and sensible people can,

Figure 2.7 Ali Mirsepassi (second from left), Golpayegan, late 1960s.

Figure 2.8 Ali Mirsepassi (first from left) with friends, Golpayegan, late 1960s.

in extraordinary times, become embroiled in senseless acts of violence. My experience with the Hojjatiyeh in Golpayegan hints at the unspoken perils of unreflective political mobilization. In moments of collective action, ordinary participants lend their will to a supra-individual force which carries out in their name acts, sometimes against the most marginalized, that they may otherwise reject as downright unconscionable. I am a living testimony to this as are the other poor students who participated in the act.

Figure 2.9 Ali Mirsepassi (third from right) with high school students and vice principal (fourth from left), Golpayegan, late 1960s.

3

Tehran University, 1970–1974

A Tale of Global Radicalism

I was only a few months into my time as a student at the Faculty of Law and Political Science at Tehran University when, on December 7, 1970, student protests and police attacks rocked the campus. I had long imagined myself performing the rites of political initiation expected of all student activists, like demonstrating in annual commemoration of the three university students, Mostafa Bozorgnia, Ahmad Ghandchi, and Mehdi Shariatrazavi, fatally shot by police on December 7, 1953, for protesting, in the wake of the 1953 *coup d'état*, Vice President Nixon's impending visit to Tehran. In their memory, this day was marked Student Day (*ruz-e daneshju*).

The Student Day protests of 1970 spilled beyond the usual commemoration of the three protestors when a group of students decided to seize and occupy the university's most centrally located buildings, bringing instruction to a complete halt. With classes suspended and so many halls occupied, the whole university had been transformed into an open-air protest and joining was as simple as stepping outside my dorm. I had recently turned eighteen and was teeming with excitement at the prospect of finally breaking free from the small-town tedium of Golpayegan to join in the political life of Tehran University, a center of intellectual and dissident activity in 1960s and 1970s Iran. Even before I had received my notice of admission, I had decided that no matter what, I would be in Tehran come fall. I refused to entertain the possibility of pursuing the other options available to me after high school, which were either to begin compulsory military service at once or leave Iran to study abroad. After years of floating from one small town to another, I had decided early in my adolescence that I would taste the charms of urban life, and there was no better place to do so than Tehran. I had even attempted to put this plan into action earlier by applying to Dar al-Fonun high school, initially founded in 1851 by reformist prime minister Amir Kabir as Iran's first modern college but which, given the growing number of specialized colleges, the education reforms of the 1920s converted to a secondary school. I was accepted to Dar al-Fonun in 1969, and, with the support of my parents, made the leap to leave Golpayegan after eleventh grade to finish my last year of secondary school in Tehran. But before the end of my first week at Dar al-Fonun, I was so overwhelmed by the relentless complexities of life in Tehran—a long commute, not knowing anyone, living in a room by myself—that I returned to Golpayegan and continued my senior year there.

Only a year later, I found myself back in Tehran. I braced myself for its crowds and noises, confident that, this time, I would not be cowed by its urban infelicities. It did not take more than a month, however, until the fear that I lacked the constitution to make it in the city came crawling back to me. The city's labyrinthine streets seemed impenetrable. Every other place I had called home existed for me as a series of bounded spaces—farms, houses, high schools, bookstores, bazaars, and familiar streets. I knew people not as individuals but as members of an extended family, whose house I most likely knew the location of and had perhaps even visited. Tehran's streets, however, resisted any attempt I might make to know them, instead swallowing space whole.

The people I met in Tehran seemed to have been dropped there from faraway places I would never visit. How could I ever know them as fully as I knew my peers in Golpayegan? My knowledge of the people around me always felt partial, especially given the tenuous link between people's public appearances and their so-called private lives. The idea of being a *gharibeh* took on new meaning in this city of transplants and itinerants. I was not a *gharibeh* but, as most newcomers to Tehran were called, a *shahrestani* (provincial). What did it mean to live anonymously where everyone and no one was a stranger?

In Tehran, it was not the fact of being an outsider to the city or other Tehranis that sapped one's sense of self. It was the gradual process of growing *gharibeh* to myself as the city worked relentlessly to seize my body and soul. In Tehran, as elsewhere, politics provided a temporary respite from and productive outlet for feelings of alienation, and I seized on that December 1970 protest to make my first foray into the campus' political scene, despite my initial trepidation. I was inside the Faculty of Law hall discussing with a few other students the possibility of forming a theater group. Hamid, a humble and talented artist also new to Tehran, proposed the idea of organizing a playwriting workshop. The audacity of a bunch of first-year students forming a theater workshop to perform the German playwright Bertolt Brecht's plays both excited and intimidated me. As Hamid explained his workshop plan, I heard a crowd chanting from beyond the building. Suddenly a woman student yelled, "The demonstrators are coming! Hide!" Students who did not support the protesters or were disinterested in politics usually avoided being in the same space as them.

I looked to Hamid and the rest of our group, our eyes scanning the other's for an answer to what to do: run or join ranks. Hamid answered the question when he suddenly walked to the center of the hall and yelled, "Free all political prisoners!" Minutes later the demonstrators outside entered the building. Our two groups fused, and we walked together to each classroom, asking professors to stop teaching and inviting students to join us in solidarity with our peers who had been unfairly arrested and jailed. It took no more than two minutes for us to make this declaration at the door of every inhabited room, bringing all the classes to a close as professors left for their offices and as students, except for the approximately fifteen that joined us, emptied the building.

Near the end of the first day of action, we gathered outside the central library. An older student took to the microphone and addressed the crowd for ten minutes. The man, a stranger to me at the time, was a confident and natural leader.

He clearly and directly stated the demands the students had drafted: respect for free speech on campus and the immediate release of all imprisoned students were among them. He ended by declaring, on behalf of all students supporters of freedom and justice at home and abroad, solidarity with the Palestinian struggle for a homeland, and condemnation of U.S. interventions in the Third World. I stood there spellbound, and within ten minutes of first hearing him speak, I felt ready to place my trust in him. Just as the idea formed in my mind to approach him afterwards to learn who he was, word spread from one protestor to another that police had entered the campus and were preparing an imminent attack on the crowd. Within what felt like seconds, the concentrated mass of people that had formed before the library dispersed, bodies darting in all directions. I looked behind me as I ran and, seeing nothing but an empty lectern where the man had moments earlier stood, knew that I had lost my chance to speak with him.

The next day I had lunch in the Faculty of Sciences cafeteria with my friend Bahman, a math major from Astara in northern Iran. We rehashed the previous day's events, effusing about its unexpected success and the great many students who joined us by the day's end. Bahman was one year my senior and lived in the student dorms, where he had the chance to socialize more than I did with other political students. So I thought he might know something about yesterday's mystery man: "Do you know who the speaker was?" I asked, "I was very impressed with him." He was a senior engineering student and a well-known activist three or four years our senior, according to Bahman. "I don't know him well, but I know he goes by Musa." I learned that Musa had spent time in prison for his political activities and was an active member of the Goruh-ye Felestin (Palestine Group), a group formed in 1968 by mainly college-aged members of the National Front. Members of the group, Bahman informed me, had traveled to Palestine in a show of solidarity and, more practically, to train alongside guerrillas in armed resistance. My next question, which came almost instinctively, was whether the Palestine Group was religious or Marxist in its orientation. "They're Marxists," Bahman replied. With this discovery, I began to try on the idea of identifying as a Marxist, a prospect I felt from that day forth surprisingly at ease with. Tired of vacillating between religious radicalism and leftist activism and eager to distance myself from small-town life, I was primed to resolve my political confusion and to take, once and for all, a stand and join the secular left. But while my inner conflict was long in the making and hungry for resolution, I was genuinely inspired by Musa's proclamation of worldwide solidarity with those suffering from foreign domination and oppressive dictatorships, whether in Latin America, Africa, Palestine or nearby Iraq. His sense of perspective and desire to uplift those trampled underfoot near and far made him seem to me like a giant among men, and I aimed to follow his example. Yet my decision to commit to Marxism did not bring my interaction with Muslim intellectuals and activists to a halt. In fact, over the next three years, the individuals who most influenced me—an older student of law, a beloved Persian professor, and my political science mentor—were religious intellectuals whose Marxist sympathies attest to the global nature of Iranian politics during the long 1970s and challenge the narrative of Islamism as the essence of Iranian "authenticity."

In Golpayegan, resistance had been for me a largely private affair: listening to opposition radio, reading the occasional political polemic clandestinely exchanged among friends, and sometimes venturing to discuss the ideas in it with them and our teachers. Excited as I was to be participating in public political action, the thought of exposing myself as an anti-Shah activist gave me chills. Even today, after so many years, the stress of police scrutiny still hangs heavy over my memories. I overcame my fear of participating in demonstrations against the government as I realized the rationality of our actions and demands: almost every demonstration had an aim I supported. And of course, seeing the "spirit" of a crowd of students bravely calling for justice and freedom, was emotionally so powerful that the consequences of joining the demonstrators receded from my considerations.

In the early days of my university education, student activism and political discussions were diffuse, our concerns and strategies alternating from one topic to another depending on the political struggle of the day. Demonstrations could be set off by a new wave of arbitrary police detention of students, fresh news of the mistreatment of political prisoners, or the anniversary of an important event. Whatever the stimulus, more experienced students were key to spreading the word and disseminating information about the names and profiles of the detainees and prisoners we rallied behind. We discussed the exact mechanisms police used to locate and arrest them, the nature of the charges brought against them, and their conditions in jail. On other occasions, when the significance of the issue at hand outstripped university politics (for instance, the mass arrest of political opponents of the Shah, or the execution of well-known oppositional leaders), a student leader would climb the steps of some building or ascend to the top of the soccer stadium and deliver a brief lecture. Students of various political currents, whether they supported the Fedayeen and Mujahedin, the Tudeh Party, or Maoist factions, would congregate and listen, closing each demonstration with slogans of solidarity for revolutionaries in Palestine, Vietnam, Yemen, and sometimes Latin America. The demonstrations, then, were a mixture of convention and innovation. I had heard many chants, like "student prisoners must be free," in high school on opposition radio and seen them printed on political flyers. But protest leaders also tweaked them each time to fit the particular cause we protested for.

For all the grandeur of mass protest, most of my education as an activist happened in the company of a smaller group of friends. Some of these friends were affiliated with underground political organizations, like the Fedayeen and Mujahedin. Others had ties to older and more experienced political activists who facilitated our access to banned books and censored news about imprisoned or exiled dissidents. This band of friends and I most often met after protests to discuss and dissect the day's goings-on. Perhaps for their own safety, experienced political activists who often organized demonstrations seldom participated in these gatherings, while a few students I never saw at demonstrations always attended the smaller discussions. It was in this setting that we ventured to discuss the thoughts of radicals like Herbert Marcuse, Jean-Paul Sartre, Bertolt Brecht, and Friedrich Nietzsche.

Politics as Lifestyle

Most of the students in my circle of friends identified as Marxists or radicals, and despite the initial confusion life in Tehran threw me into, I felt at ease in their presence. For so much of my life, I had abided by the code of religious conduct I learned in Golpayegan, not out of faith but because of a desire to be accepted as a member of the community. In Golpayegan, Islam was not just a religion but a way of being. So the fact that my new Marxist friends did not care for religious niceties helped liberate me to live life as I wanted. This is not to say, however, that things were always simpatico between us.

The comfort I felt in the company of my new friends was tempered by their tendency to use (and so compel others to use) only what they judged to be acceptable terms, ideas, and books. For them, as with my teachers Mr Eshraghi and

Figure 3.1 Ali Mirsepassi, Tehran, 1971.

Mr Amjadi, an author's class status determined in large part the political acuity of his or her work. By college, I had read a fair number of Sadegh Hedayat's novels and wished to discuss them with my well-read newfound friends, but they simply advised me to stop squandering my time on him. Hedayat, they declared, was a self-obsessed and anti-social writer. They were equally derisive of Fereydoun Adamiyat, a prolific historian of Iran's Constitutional Revolution. I had found one of Adamiyat's books, a 1961 study entitled *Fekr-e Azadi va Moqaddameh-ye Nehzat-e Mashrutiyat-e Iran* (The Concept of Liberty and the Beginnings of the Constitutional Movement in Iran) in my father's little library in Nahavand. No other book so vividly brought that forgotten chapter of Iranian history to life for me, so I made sure to acquire and read every other book of his for sale. His 1967 and 1970 intellectual biographies of Mirza Aqa Khan Kermani and Mirza Fath Ali Akhundzadeh, two nineteenth-century nationalist authors who developed an idealized image of pre-Islamic Iran, opened my eyes to radical criticisms of Islam and religion in general. Although I was fascinated by Adamiyat's histories of the constitutional movement, many of my Marxist friends considered him woefully bourgeois and had little interest in discussing his works with me.

What to read, how to read it, and where to stand on contemporary events were matters not of debate but right and wrong, and I learned that my friends were quite willing to instruct me on the "correct" interpretation of these matters. While my love for literature led me to read almost any novel I could get my hands on, my Marxist friends were keen to discourage me from reading "inappropriate" or "worthless" pieces of fiction, like American detective stories, even though I enjoyed them. This act of self-denial made no sense to me, as we had few reading choices at that time. The government had already forbidden us from so many books. Why should we forbid one another from reading the scant works that remained?

My friends extended their class analysis of novelists and scholars to Iranian history and culture. On this matter I was of two minds. Their critical reading of Iranian history was a refreshing break from the self-congratulatory and nationalistic interpretations of Iran's past touted in our textbooks and on media. Their reconstruction of history also taught me that representations of the past are not value neutral but serve specific interests. Yet I felt one could be critical of their nation's history and culture and still harbor a positive intellectual and emotional affinity for it, whereas some of the Marxists I befriended were reluctant to express an attachment to Iran. Two well-known Marxists I liked in this respect were Khosrow Rouzbeh, the chief of the Tudeh Party's military wing until his execution in 1958, and Mehdi Akhavan-Sales, a mid-century poet and fellow member of the Tudeh Party; their works inspired critical care, not antipathy, for Iran in youth like me.

In my first weeks at the university I was drawn to a few older and self-confident student activists. The side of campus facing a major street was like Hyde Park after demonstrations. Students gathered there to debate particular issues, and it was there that I was introduced to many of my friends. One day, a man I had seen debate others several times invited me to join him for a gathering at a nearby tea house. I agreed and found myself seated with him and five or six other students in their usual haunt one early afternoon. The conversation had turned to the subject of *az khod biganegi* (alienation), a term I had noticed was in vogue among more affluent students, often from Tehran. I understood alienation as a posh spin on my mother's idea of *ghorbat*. I sat silently, curious to see where the discussion would go, since, as a young "country boy" in Tehran, I certainly experienced my own life as one of alienation. To my disappointment, that afternoon's tea house discussion turned into a tedious exercise in intellectual showmanship.

As soon as we had all taken seats and been served tea, the students launched into a tiresome debate, jumping from Hegel and Marcuse to the situation of Western youth to the nature of modern technology. The student who had invited me judged Hamid Enayat's most recent essay on alienation, "Ensan az Khod Bigane" (The Alienated Man, 1967), to be worthless, simply tut-tutting, "If one does not know Sartre well, one cannot speak about alienation."

A long digression about Friedrich Nietzsche followed. I struggled to stay afloat amidst a deluge of references, thinking instead to myself, "How is Nietzsche's critique of modern man and notion of the superman relevant to contemporary Iranian intellectual and political concerns?" I had not anticipated the intellectual axis of Tehran to be so firmly rooted in Europe. Although I had made a point to familiarize myself with European history and literature in the past, I found the preoccupation with Western ideas and propensity for name-dropping on display that day off-putting and arrogant. This tendency came out with great force among students of philosophy, whose rapid-fire invocation of towering figures, like Hegel or Nietzsche, and ceaseless citations of Marcuse,

Nietzsche, and Sartre, intimidated me. Still, I admired them for their keen interest in the world and partly blamed myself for being too much of a *shahrestani* to be familiar with the likes of Hegel, Heidegger, and Junger, who Al-e Ahmad referenced in *Gharbzadegi*.

Just as the gathering seemed to be nearing its end, a first-year student, more an activist than an intellectual, from Sanandaj, the capital of Iranian Kurdistan, decided to challenge the cavalier dismissal of Enayat. "Marx," he proclaimed, "wrote about alienation a hundred years before Sartre, and well after Hegel. You don't know what you're talking about." The student who had just been challenged turned his back to my Kurdish friend and said with a sneer, "I don't have time to respond to the insult of a country boy (*bacheh dahati*)." The discussion degenerated into effrontery. I left the gathering thinking I would never go back. Awash in nostalgia for my Golpayegan days, I felt suddenly out of step with the city's intellectual life. All around me were books, articles, and translations of Western philosophers who my teachers and classmates in Golpayegan and Nahavand had never mentioned. The more I learned about Tehran's thinkers and their world, the more I understood that this student was not alone in his infatuation with the West. Many university students showed little interest in Persian classics or even in modern Iranian literature. Those who did were more conservative students I shared little else in common with. Despite our intellectual differences, I continued socializing with this crowd of student activists, not least because their friendship afforded me entry into the political life of the university.

The French, American, and British in our Faculty

After sampling an assortment of classes on offer across the law, social science, and humanities departments, I came to the realization that the faculty at Tehran University were not unlike the students whose orbit I had entered. The intellectual debates and ethical questions that most concerned them derived not from Iranian society but the, mostly European, countries in which they had sojourned and studied. This was the case with my law and political theory classes. As a student and political activist, I was inspired by contemporary anti-colonial and Third-Worldist ideas. Yet, as much as I aspired to know about world struggles and the ideas motivating them, I harbored a particular attachment to Iranian culture. The idea that an Iranian scholar might remain indebted to a foreign intellectual tradition, even well after returning to Iran to research and teach, was new to me. While university students drew inspiration from schools of thought originating in France, Germany, the Middle East, or Latin America, they did so through readerly engagement with certain thinkers.

My university days introduced me to a new kind of Iranian intellectual, one with French, British, or American sensibilities I had never encountered in high school. Despite the number of foreign-educated intellectuals populating the campus' classrooms and walkways, the academic life of the Faculty of Law and Political Science in the 1970s was rather dull. As Abbas Amanat, a historian of Iran at Yale University and former student at Tehran University in the 1960s, put it in an interview I conducted with him: "Tehran University lacked any meaningful dialogue between students and professors . . . It was often a dry and uninspiring environment."

The university was an especially destitute place for a student of political science. Many of the department's professors held key government positions and designated only a few hours of their day to delivering lectures they had recycled for years without any pretense of interest in the class of students to which they were delivered. Students, in turn, paid little attention to class lectures. After my first year of studies, I learned classes, save for the determinative days of final examination, could be skipped with little loss or consequence.

While several faculty members did take teaching seriously, their efforts were consistently constrained by what state censors permitted them to teach. We were students of political science at Iran's premier university, many of us interested in modern Iranian politics and history, yet no faculty member in our department dared to lecture meaningfully on those subjects. All class discussions geared toward modern politics took as their terminus the Mashruteh movement. For the Pahlavi state, the Mashruteh movement, which marked the end of Qajar Iran and the start of a modern Iran (*Iran-e novin*), was at a safe enough remove from the ongoing operation of and opposition to Pahlavi state control to be an acceptable subject of study.

The global influence of the 1960s and 1970s penetrated university life and Iranian political culture, as the cosmopolitan credentials of some of my professors attests to. In 1971, I began my second year of studies and enrolled in one of Dr Hamid Behzadi's classes. Behzadi was a political scientist trained at Columbia University, specializing in nationalism, the first and only American-educated professor I had. He offered a class on comparative nationalism, which I signed up for without reservation. Over the course of the semester, the professor introduced us to theories of nationalism and to the ideological origins of nationalist movements in Africa, the Middle East, and Asia. Dr Behzadi was fond of the American political scientist Hans Joachim Morgenthau, and referenced him no matter the topic he discussed in the class. Yet he did not have a word to dispense about Iranian nationalism or the mid-century movement to nationalize Iran's oil industry. Mohammad Mosaddegh's name was never mentioned in lectures or readings. This was the norm in most classes, which simply carried on as if the Iran we lived in had no worldly existence. The interaction between global politics and the political culture of 1970s Iran was, in other words, not studied but systemically silenced.

Often this silence was inflicted not from without but within. One of the most bizarre experiences I had was a 1972 class instructed by a young professor, Jamshid Nabavi, who had recently earned his doctorate in political theory from the University of Brussels, in Belgium. I registered for his class at the encouragement of a friend, who described Nabavi, then a third-year faculty member, as a young professor interested in conversing with students, whose comments and interventions he welcomed in class. It did not hurt, my friend added, that he was an expert in Marxism and the political affairs of China and the Soviet Union.

Nabavi was certainly pleasant in person, and his interest in exchanging ideas with his students genuine. His lectures, however, turned out to be informal commentaries on current affairs, lacking much scholarly or intellectual depth. Odder yet, he assiduously avoided his supposed area of expertise, Marxism, and dared not discuss how Marxist and other radical political parties had historically interacted with nationalism in Iran or anywhere else for that matter. Despite his utter silence on Iranian Marxism, he would periodically let comments about Belgian Marxism slip. He intimated that Belgian students were almost all Marxists and that, having been coerced by his advisors to study Marxism, he chose instead to debunk it. This professor, however, loved Belgium, to the point that we called him Jamshid Beljiki, to which he did not object.

Good natured though Nabavi was, it turned out, according to a friend's report, that our instructor was a virulently anti-Marxist conservative. He understood his job as our instructor to be to reveal the depravities of Marxism, without offering either evidence or discussion, and illuminating the felicities of modernization theory and modern political institutions. We were meant to trust his authority, since he had written his dissertation on the subject. Nabavi, I later learned from a fellow student who had grown close to him, had used his university position to open the door for himself to government jobs; his ultimate aim was to be appointed to a high government position. And his wish appears to have come true, as he was soon named one of the heads of the Ministry of Information and Tourism.

I recently tried to find out what happened to my old professor. I learned that he continued to teach at Tehran University until 1980, that is, at the start of the "cultural revolution," during which the Islamic Republic closed down universities and conducted a mass purge of "undesirable" academics who had not demonstrated their loyalty to the new government clearly enough. He must, I imagine, have been let go during this purge.

Perhaps it is unfair to blame our professors for the impoverished state of their teaching and scholarship. The Pahlavi state mobilized its considerable political and cultural resources to suppress meaningful discussion of pressing political issues and their historical antecedents. They succeeded at this, intellectually stifling the university, including its political science department. While the same mechanisms of surveillance applied outside of the university, state control attenuated there, and more interesting conversations were to be found in the public sphere.

Nativism of the Metropolis

Although my skepticism for romanticizing Iranian tradition first surfaced in Nahavand and Golpayegan, it was only once I got to university that I fully appreciated the extent to which *bumi gera'i* (nativism) pervaded the attitudes of Tehrani intellectuals, artists, and political elites. I watched in disbelief as those who had lived their whole lives in urban Iran extolled the virtues of local or *bumi* tradition and heaped contempt on modern life in writing, films, and paintings. They were infatuated with a fictive image of "traditional" village communities and cultures. After all, their way of life and fame was rooted in the metropolitan cities of Iran, Europe, and America. One may argue that Majid Mohseni, the director of *The Swallows Return to Their Nests*, the film my father was so smitten with, in his capacity as a filmmaker and artist, had license to embellish since he may have been engaged in creative entertainment, not political polemic. While it would be fair to point this out about Mohseni, this excuse does not quite work in the case of the sociologist Ehsan Naraghi.

Naraghi (1926–2012) split his adult life between Tehran, Geneva, and Paris. Yet his idea of Iran, articulated in his lectures and writings, was a society untouched by modern ideas, institutions, and cultural mores, where peasants worked hard, and paternalistic landlords were wise and caring. There was no connection between his own life and the pastoral world for which he so assiduously advocated.

Naraghi was born in Kashan, a city in central Iran, into a prominent clerical family with a history of intellectual achievement. His parents together established the first secular school for girls in Kashan. When his family moved to Tehran in 1944, Naraghi enrolled in the prestigious Dar al-Fonun High School. Naraghi matriculated at Tehran University's Faculty of Law and Political Science in 1946, where he became involved with the Tudeh Party. In May 1947, he left Iran for Switzerland, where he continued his education. In December 1954, he was granted a scholarship from the Cultural Association of Iran and France to pursue a PhD at the Sorbonne.

In Paris, Naraghi cultivated connections with influential scholars, including Jean Piaget, Georges Balandier, Georges Gurvitch, and Louis Massignon. It was also there that he started a lifelong association with UNESCO, whose Youth Division he directed from 1969 until 1975.

While expanding his international network of contacts, Naraghi established the Institute for Social Studies and Research at Tehran University. He successfully secured funding for the Institute not from the university, as was traditionally done, but directly from the government. His political career continued to grow throughout the 1960s and 1970s, until he enjoyed close connections to Farah Pahlavi, prime minister Amir-Abbas Hoveyda, and Hassan Pakravan, the head of SAVAK. When Naraghi, now a figure of international stature, returned to Iran in 1975, the Shah immediately appointed him the head of one of Iran's premier institutes, the Institute for Educational and Scientific Research and Planning. Naraghi was quietly satisfied with the power he found in his new high-ranking position, admitting, "Most of the time I had more power than a minister had . . . Besides his [Amir-Abbas Hoveyda's] direct support, I had Farah [Pahlavi]'s support. On different occasions, Farah asked me to leave UNESCO and return to Iran."[1] During the final three years of the Pahlavi state, 1975–8, Naraghi, a decorated member of many state-sponsored institutions and an advisor to leading politicians, achieved his dream of publicly presiding over the political life of the state and its institutions.

Despite his role staffing the modernizing Pahlavi state, Naraghi was an intellectual whose writings embraced cultural nativism and critiqued the perceived Westoxification of the 1960s and 1970s. His books advocated anti-modernism and, in some cases, bore the influence of the Heideggerian philosophy of radical nativist Ahmad Fardid. With the advent of the twentieth century, Naraghi contended, the West had entered a spiritual and moral crisis of unchecked individualism and

[1] Tabarra'ian, *Soft Like a Sponge*, Jeld-e Avval, 464

technological domination.[2] Naraghi identified "scientism," or the worship of science (*'elm parasti*), and the technologization of life as the root cause of an existential crisis in the West. "Given this situation [the domination of man by machines]," he warned, "we, as Easterners, should beware of losing our civilization and culture against the onslaught of Western industry."[3]

Naraghi's career was spent theorizing a way of rendering the social sciences amenable to supposedly traditional Iranian values. As he set out to pave this path, Naraghi intoned the virtues of the local like European pastoralists before him. His approach to Iranian and Islamic history and culture, however, inverted the French revolutionary triad of "liberty, equality, fraternity" to privilege the transcendent collective spirituality of "traditional culture":

> Our traditional culture does not speak of "liberty, equality, fraternity." It states "fraternity, equality, liberty." This indicates that, in our traditional culture, "justice" has priority over personal "freedom." One of the aspects of "justice" is "equality." Our traditional culture, merged with Shi'ism, considers "justice" the most important social value.[4]

Naraghi's arguments were mostly statements of beliefs that, at times, resembled a manifesto against the modern West:

> The foundation of Western philosophy rests upon "individualism" and egoism. Meanwhile, "Eastern freedom" means

2 Naraghi, *Ancheh Khod Dasht*, 17.

3 Ibid.

4 Ehsan Naraghi, *Azadi, Haq va 'Edalat: Munazara Esma'il Khui ba Ehsan Naraghi* (Freedom, Right, and Justice: A Talk between Esma'il Khui and Ehsan Naraghi) (Tehran: Javidan, 1976), 199.

> being free of "ego." If one can be free of ego, one cannot be cruel. This is the Eastern point of view on "freedom." Of course, at any time in history when this way of thinking has weakened, cruelty has gained prevalence.[5]

Following this and similar observations, Naraghi rejected the utility of a legal system of rights for Iranian society. He argued that societies like Iran, with their rich moral and cultural traditions, did not need recourse to a codified system of rights to ensure social harmony as Western societies did. Iranians had simply to abide by the values and judgments to which their "souls" predisposed them:

> Westernized Iranians . . . sacrificed "chivalry," "justice," "right," "fraternity," "equality," and all values rooted in our people's soul, which motivated all the turbaned men [*kolah namadi-ha*] and veiled women, in favor of an image of "government," "freedom," and "law" that was "abstract" and Western. This had no connection with our historical, social, and cultural background.[6]

As director of the Institute for Social Studies and Research, Naraghi supported ethnographic fieldwork in rural Iran, whose findings he collectively called the Institute's "Eastern insight" against positivism. By his own admission, Naraghi's approach to sociology changed following a period of introspection on the West during his time at UNESCO:

[5] Naraghi, *Freedom, Right, and Justice*, 117

[6] Naraghi, *Freedom, Right, and Justice*, 208.

> In the beginning, I was fond of Western scientific progress too, like all youth at that time. My colleagues and I at the Institute for Social Studies and Research attempted to employ the "scientific" methods in our social research. We wished to see sociology expanded in Iran as a science. However, after years of living again in Europe, I clearly realized the inadequacy of these methods.[7]

After the 1979 Revolution, Naraghi's status as a government insider brought him fresh scrutiny. The revolutionary government accused him of working with SAVAK and arrested and jailed him for about two years, although he was eventually found not guilty and released from prison in September 1983. Naraghi left Iran for France the following year and rejoined UNESCO as an advisor to its secretary-director general from 1984 to 1999, when he retired. During this time, he cultivated friendly relations with the Islamic Republic, using his UNESCO position to ameliorate relations between the organization and the new Iranian government. Naraghi died in 2012 and was buried in Tehran.

As the son of small towns, I had intimately observed village life and struggled to understand the romance with rural Iran that saturated the writings of intellectuals like Naraghi in the 1960s and 1970s. Although I admired the unpretentious wisdom of the villagers I met, the poverty and scarcity that made for their daily struggles pained me. Some Iranian modernists, however, adopted not a fetish for but an air of superiority toward their rural and provincial compatriots. Yet

[7] Naraghi, *Freedom, Right, and Justice*, 208.

these individuals too either generated (as did Ahmad Fardid, Daryush Shayegan, and so on) or promoted (as did Naraghi) anti-Western and anti-modern discourses.

There is a fine line between caring for one's home and mythologizing one's roots. The former suggests a willingness to forego personal interests for the sake of joining our hopes to those of a larger community. The latter is defined instead by contempt for those who fall outside a prized community. Myths can be imaginative vehicles, yet when we stretch them to cover more than they can, like the whole of our identities or reality itself, we risk breaking their fragile skin. Nativist ideologies that rest on fictive pasts vacillate between self-confident claims of superiority and anxious fear of others. Once we distinguish these two outlooks on belonging, place, and authenticity, nationalism begins to take on different, subtler shades and those political ideologies that claim to own local legitimacy lose their credibility.

The Good Scholar

It was in that same year as a student at the Faculty of Law and Political Science that I began to study the social sciences in earnest. As stimulating as I had found the study of Persian literature in high school, I realized my real academic interests lay elsewhere. Iran was fortunate to have so many scholars of literature studying its long and remarkable literary tradition. However, the social sciences were still new to the country, and for Iran to achieve its place in the world, I thought it was imperative that we pay serious attention to them. For this reason, I considered Dr Hamid Enayat (1932–82) my scholarly role model. That Enayat was not a radical, that he prohibited the discussion of politics in his classroom, and that he had an admittedly lackluster teaching style made him an odd choice for a role model. But I was taken by his ability to engage students in a manner that was at once serious and kind. Enayat was nothing like the self-aggrandizing professors and intellectuals college had accustomed me to. He generously made himself available to students for hours outside of class. We disagreed on nearly every occasion we spoke in his office, yet I cannot remember a time my comments rankled him or his me. He cared for his students too; whenever we spoke, before parting, he would take a moment to express his worry about where my public political statements might land me, and kindly asked me to be careful about making such comments in class. He would end our conversations with compassionate words of caution: "Take care of yourself, our nation needs people like you."

I did not think Enayat, of course, was unimpeachable. One instance cemented this reality for me. He was lecturing for his graduate class on Islamic political thought on Muhammad Iqbal, or as he was known in Iran, Iqbal Lahouri. Enayat spent all of class extolling the virtues of this original Muslim thinker. Eventually I raised my hand and commented that the professor's choice of subject was rather selective. "As we speak, the flames of protest blaze across Palestine, Yemen, and all the Middle East. Are there no intellectuals leading these movements? Is it too much for us students of political science to count on you, our esteemed professor, to inform us about what is happening today? Instead, you dwell on Iqbal who died too long ago to understand the struggle we face." Enayat's response was polite but pointedly terse. In his typically pleasant manner, he knowingly smiled, then said, "The ideas I speak of should matter to you. A discussion of Iqbal is indeed relevant to today's world." While his response did not satisfy me, I was thankful not to have been dismissed outright. When class ended, Enayat asked me to walk with him to his office, where he confided that he feared my comments would land me in trouble with SAVAK: "You know, you are too radical to be in this class. I am worried about you." His tone was sympathetic, and the sincerity of his concern made me feel almost more comforted than alarmed.

Enayat was the chair of the Faculty of Law and Political Sciences in the 1970s and a luminary among his peers, considered by faculty and students to be exceptionally learned. Although the depth and breadth of his knowledge was impressive, I learned more from his writings than his classes. His teaching style did not differ markedly from others and was perhaps even less inspired. In a normal session he would enter the classroom, proceed to lecture in a monotonous tone until the end of class, then abruptly leave. If questioned or challenged by students, he respectfully, but reluctantly, made brief comments, always resisting their attempts to draw him out into an open debate.

Enayat offered classes in his areas of specialization, European and Islamic political thought and theory. He took great care in his class on European political thought to introduce students to canonical texts using his own survey study, *Andisheh-ye Siyasi dar Gharb* (Political Thought in the West), in which he overviewed the intellectual history of classical European political theorists. Despite being a colorless lecturer, he was a focused and well-prepared teacher, and I learned a great deal from this class.

While Enayat's class on Islamic thought, which opened with the struggles over political succession culminating in the Sunni-Shi'i split and ended with an overview of Islamic modernism, was also valuable, his instruction struck me as defensively partisan. He devoted several classes to critiquing Soviet scholarship on Islam, focusing on the economic determinism of Marxism and its failure to apprehend accurately the role of culture, and particularly religion, in social life. His case study was the University of Leningrad professor Ilya Pavlovich Petrushevsky's (1898–1977) 1966 work *Islam in Iran*.

When my friend and a senior student at the university, Abuzar Vardasbi, published a book of the same title as Petrushevsky's, I realized that he and Enayat shared similar views. They both were critical of a Marxist materialist approach to the study of Islam, an impulse that led some to questions its origins and historical evolution. Vardasbi's book aimed to offer an interpretation of Islam and its history beyond past or present social and political realities. He seemed to be using the pretext of Soviet Marxism to make the larger point that Islam ought to be understood on its own terms. I struggled to understand where this reactionary impulse came from. Based on our long friendship, I knew Vardasbi was a committed religious activist and faithful Muslim. I knew little about Enayat's personal or family life, but his sensibilities felt more British than anything. It took me years to learn that he was a member of the Tudeh Party in his youth and one of the founding members of the Confederation of Iranian Students Abroad. Yet I also learned that he, with time, grew closer to the thinkers Ayatollah Motahhari and Ahmad Fardid, who drew inspiration from Islam, than anyone in the Tudeh Party. Ahmad Fardid, an anti-western crusader known as the Heidegger of Iran in the 1960s and 1970s and who coined the term *gharbzadegi*, or Westoxification, went so far as to proclaim himself to be the philosophical spokesperson of the Islamic Republic.

Today Enayat is known to have been a regular member of the Fardidiyeh, a philosophical circle that met weekly in the 1960s and 1970s and at the center of which was the eponymous Fardid. Earlier in life, I blamed Golpayegan's insular cultural environment for producing the tendencies toward parochialism I disliked in my literature teacher, Mr Tavakol. Enayat, however, had studied at the London School of Economics and the School of Oriental and African Studies. How, then, could I explain the many similarities between him and my Golpayegani teacher, whose ambitions and experiences had been so much more limited? After decades of teaching in American and European institutions, where skepticism of political Islam is often taken as criticism of Islam, I know that the rarefied intellectual environments of the West can be less amenable to critically assessing the thought of Islamic intellectuals like Mohamad Iqbal or Ali Shari'ati than those in Iran.

One of my last encounters with Dr Enayat was in 1974. I had excitedly asked to meet with him in his office to share an idea about Hegel I had come across the night before in an intellectual circle. He patiently listened to me explain why I thought Hegel's philosophy of history provided an intellectual base for European colonialism and why Iranian intellectuals were mistaken to write about Hegel as a non-political thinker, before saying something I will never forget:

> You should not pay much attention to the intellectual debates and personalities in our country. Iranian intellectuals project an aura of self-importance, but they are shallow, their minds occupied with trivial matters. They speak of East and West, philosophy, and literature, but what do they know about these subjects? In today's world, no one should claim to be a scholar or intellectual without knowing one or two world languages. One should have serious knowledge of critical texts in those languages. You should go to Europe and study.

I was stunned to learn that beneath Enayat's serene demeanor festered frustrations with Iranian scholarly and intellectual life. I never expected him to so directly tell me not to waste my time in Iran, to study instead in Europe. Of course, I ended up doing precisely this. I left Iran for London, where I had memorable encounters with Iranian activists, a story about the Iranian opposition abroad to save, hopefully, for another day. I was, however, only to return two years later to participate in the 1978–79 Revolution.

Islam and Mistaken Marxism

Before coming to Tehran I had spent the better part of my adolescence shuttling ideologically back and forth between religious activism and secular radicalism, leaving me sympathetic to both. In Golpayegan, I counted as my friends and mentors other students and teachers, like Mr Tavakol. Staying in Nahavand, where my family spent most summers, offered me the chance to be among a few friends and relatives who were influenced by Marxist ideas. By the time I entered the twelfth grade, I felt I had oscillated enough from one camp to another and that I ought to commit finally to one of the two. Why I felt the need to choose one over the other, I do not know. Perhaps I had grown wary of living in between the two worlds. The decision then was political, but it was also about resolving my own identity. As I mulled over the matter I reflected on the fact that although my religious friends were perfectly polite, I had no memory of being invited to their homes or meeting their parents, and whenever I invited them to my house, they tactfully declined. They seemed to want to maintain a safe measure of distance from me. This in a town of very hospitable people was unusual.

My other friends, who were either beginning to identify as Marxists or were not observant Muslims, however, were different. They eagerly invited me to their homes, freely introduced me to their families, and routinely visited me at home. This sense of chivalry, combined with the electrifying speech of the Palestine Group member, cemented my decision to become a Marxist.

Having a group of Marxist friends in the 1970s, I felt I belonged at last to a community of admirable men and women committed to the public good. Yet the political and intellectual environment of Iran in those years was muddled. Anyone with a notion of themselves as political was in dialogue with Marxism—our *beljiki* professor; Dr Enayat; national talking heads like Ahmad Fardid and Ehsan Naraghi; Islamic radicals like Ali Shari'ati; and liberal scholars like Fereydoun Adamiyat. I read underground leaflets, listened to Radio Moscow, Berlin, and Peking, and invariably I was left, even when writers and journalists rejected Marxism, better educated about it. As a university student recently converted to Marxism, life was exciting but perplexing. I expected I would spend my days socializing with other Marxists and sparring with religious intellectuals and activists, but this notion turned out to be illusory. Factionalism hampered our efforts to organize. Yet I appreciated that all these factions were in a way a catalog of various transnational Marxist ideas. The Marxism, for instance, I gravitated toward bore the imprint of Latin American movements and intellectuals, whereas some of my friends sympathetic to the Tudeh Party were fond of Soviet culture and arts. I was at peace with these currents and understood each had its own ideas to contribute to the movement. My peace, I would come to learn, was rooted in the naïve hope that political ambiguity was unique to Golpayegan and that in Tehran, there would be no confusing Marxists with Islamists.

In my four years at Tehran University, three individuals in particular shaped my thinking, either as I strove to emulate them or as I reflected on our disagreements. There was my political science professor and mentor, Dr Hamid Enayat, whose lectures I dutifully attended and in whose office we spent many hours talking. Then there was Dr Shafi'i Kadkani, my Persian literature professor. Finally, there was the older student and experienced political activist, Abuzar Vardasbi, who took me under his wing and introduced me to seasoned radicals. Vardasbi was well known and admired at the university for his fearlessness. Yet he was also the epitome of the political and ideological confusion we all endured at the transnational crossroads of the long 1970s, perhaps then only as the "unthought."

Vardasbi was a member of the Mujahedin-e Khalq, a group founded in 1965 by leftist religious students and activists who drew inspiration from Third World guerrilla movements and Ali Shariʿati's Islamic liberation theology. He had been arrested and imprisoned on several occasions, and during his time in state custody, he was repeatedly tortured yet resisted confession. On one occasion, as he was escaping arrest, he was hit by a car that injured his foot, leaving him with a limp for the rest of his life. Vardasbi was sympathetic to Marxism, and, in both his writing and speech, he borrowed generously from Marxist critiques of capitalist production, class domination, and imperialism to articulate his own views. Still, Vardasbi could not endorse the materialism at the heart of Marxism.

Over the course of our many conversations, Vardasbi expressed disbelief at the Marxist notion that religion, including Islam, had historically served to buttress class oppression. In his view, "true" Islam provided a path to a utopic, classless society. Despite his objection to some aspects of Marxism, Vardasbi had amassed a substantial collection of banned Marxist books and regularly lent me works to read. He introduced me to the world of cultural Marxism through gatherings at publishing houses and bookstores opposite the university. Despite his Marxist sympathies, Vardasbi was a pious man whose radicalism sprang from faith. Nonetheless, he was willing and happy to mentor me, a young Marxist activist, without prodding me to embrace Islamic activism or return to religion. I felt privileged to know him.

Due to a nationwide shortage in qualified schoolteachers, Tehran University, through an arrangement with the government, paid undergraduate students a monthly stipend to teach in the city's schools. I applied, and for one year, I was a part-time teacher at the same elementary school as Vardasbi in the working-class neighborhood of Tehran-now, or New Tehran. Many of the schoolteachers there personally knew Vardasbi and were themselves involved in dissident politics so, after the school day, we often attended political gatherings at different neighborhood houses. It became apparent with time that the schoolteachers believed in a rather conservative interpretation of Islam; their commitment to orthodoxy, particularly on issues of gender and sexuality, outstripped anything I had encountered in Golpayegan. When I raised this issue with Vardasbi, asking him how he could maintain ties with uncompromising conservatives, he simply replied that there was nothing wrong with them. Just like his Marxist friends, he explained, these religious men were fine people, radical and good hearted in their own right. Not wanting to cast their intentions or his judgment in doubt, I kept quiet and we moved on, keeping up our attendance at these meetings. I felt so out of place at every gathering that I scarcely said a word, choosing to instead listen as the others reported on the usual subjects, like Palestine and the escalating Arab-Israeli conflict. Despite my continual discomfort, I learned much from the working-class men of Tehran-now. Their long list of reading recommendations infused fresh complexity into my understanding of the Arab Middle East. And, in a way, these house gatherings reminded me of Golpayegan. Although Tehran outwardly differed from this provincial town, the two were not so different in their political culture, which amalgamated elements of Islamic and secular radicalisms.

Vardasbi was equally at ease debating with the schoolteachers of Tehran-now as he was in the presence of luminaries like Ali Shari'ati, who he knew personally. He insisted more than once on taking me to see Shari'ati lecture, coaxing me with the promise that I would have the opportunity to meet him, but I refused every time. Not only did I feel I shared little with Shari'ati and his vision for Iran, but I also worried about his growing popularity among middle-class Iranians, whose sensibilities he sought to realign with a modern reading of Islam. He was an effective spokesman, but I never detected much substance to his views, which were to me a cherry-picked amalgamation of ideas from Islam and Marxism used to serve his own political objective.

My misgivings about Shari'ati were shaped by my introduction in Golpayegan to a language of resistance steeped in the symbols and stories of Shi'i Islam. I initially found an overtly political reading of Islam a suitable vernacular for mobilizing Iranians. My thinking, however, changed as I learned more about political Islam and particularly after my experience with the Hojjatiyeh, the first political trauma I endured. That Shari'ati reminded me of my Golpayegan years frightened me, since I thought I had put them behind me.

I was more influenced by Al-e Ahmad's critique of the West than by Shari'ati's moralizing anti-Westernism, to which he posed Islam as an indigenous alternative. I was afraid that Shari'ati's Iran would look more like Golpayegan. My opposition to the Shah's regime was not rooted in the supposed moral decay he was causing but in high-level decisions that stifled Iranian civil society and the material wellbeing of the masses.

I had read Al-e Ahmad's *Westoxification* in Golpayegan and felt ambivalent at best about it, although, as I told one of my Marxist teachers, I was struck by how well he captured the authoritarianism of Iran's school system in his novel *Modir-e Madrasa* [The School Principal]. I was not certain what Al-e Ahmad's vision of Iran, should it be realized, would look like, so I filled in this blank space worrying that he and his supporters wanted to take life as I had known in it Golpayegan and impose it on the nation.

Westoxification was an apt diagnosis for the habitus of the Pahlavi elite and even of lay Iranians fascinated with all that was Western, but I was careful to use the term, since conservative Iranian writers had lodged it against leftists too. Even I had been accused of being *gharbzadeh* (Westoxified). Nonetheless, in contrast to Shari'ati, I identified with Al-e Ahmad's lifestyle, radicalism, and intellectual heterodoxy. To me, Shari'ati was a mistaken modernist. He aimed to craft a new, alternative Iranian modernity outside what Iran had achieved since the Mashruteh. Shari'ati's interests, moreover, skewed toward Marxism and western intellectual, leaving him scarcely engaged with Iranian intellectuals and their thoughts.

My skepticism of Shari'ati was also influenced by the suspicion, harbored by me as well as my Marxist friends, that he was something of an intellectual opportunist. His Marxism, my friends, who were sympathetic to the Mujahedin-e Khalq, maintained, was a mixture of messianic Shi'ism and mistaken Marxism (*marksism-e ghalat*). We harbored conflicting feelings about his ease of access to public platforms, suspecting the Pahlavi state was clandestinely bolstering his public profile to undermine the spread of secular and radical ideas and movements. I questioned why Marxist intellectuals, such as Amir Hossein Arianpour, or Baqer Momeni, were not allowed to lecture in public while Shari'ati was.

Vardasbi was both more Marxist and more religious in his inclinations than Shari'ati was. He openly referenced Marxist classics, if only to deconstruct them, while his religious mannerisms resembled those of my Golpayegani literature teacher. Ideologically, Vardasbi was, to use today's language, an Islamist. He was devoted to combating Soviet Marxism and discrediting, in his opinion, ill-informed and propagandistic writings on Iran and Islam. Vardasbi's preoccupation with Soviet historiography of Iran and Islam was shared, as the reader might remember, by my instructor Enayat. University students and Iranian intellectuals of different political orientations found insights worth refuting or rehabilitating in Soviet scholarship. So it made sense that Vardasbi took on the task of writing a book-length refutation of a cornerstone in Soviet Islamic studies. I remember him delivering me a copy, pride illuminating his eyes, of his study *Tarikh-e Jazmiyat-e Hezbi* (History of Dogmatic Partisans), when it was first published. He later asked for my thoughts on the book, and I explained that while I found his argument that histories of Islam and Shi'ism written by Soviet scholars, like Petrushevsky, were ideologically colored convincing, his expectation that materialist scholars should think like his "Doctor" (his sobriquet for Shari'ati) substituted one dogma for another. He smiled and thanked me for reading his work. For all the years I knew him, Vardasbi only became angry with me once. In a fit of pragmatism, I said, "Palestinians are mistaken if they think Israel will one day disappear from the earth." To which he angrily responded, "You should stop saying such nonsense."

A Radical Poet from Khorasan

Dr Shafi'i Kadkani, born in 1939, was a young professor of Persian literature when I met him. He was a man of grace and principle, sympathetic to Marxism and leftist groups like the Fedayeen and Mujahedin and perhaps to some kind of Marxism, but he was also committed to exposing his students to a full spectrum of perspectives. Many years later, as a graduate student of sociology in the U.S., I read Max Weber's "Science as Vocation," and Kadkani immediately came to mind. For our professor, teaching Iranian literature was truly a vocation. The classroom was for him not a place to peddle his own political views but to equip students with the knowledge needed to clarify their own questions with as much precision as possible.

I had the good fortune of participating in his class during my first semester in the fall of 1970. It would be the most joyous class of my four years at Tehran University. As a teacher, Kadkani took the time to listen to our political readings of Persian literature before kindly inviting us to approach literature as a scholarly enterprise. He encouraged us to appreciate its creative qualities as readers rather than political critics. Kadkani was also unique in the deliberate effort he made to show female students respect during class discussions. The effect did not go unnoticed; one woman once told me, "I feel much smarter in Dr Kadkani's class." In matters of lifestyle, I thought Kadkani was a secular person, so I was surprised one day when he revealed that he had once upon time been a seminary student. Of course, this discovery made him even more popular with students, since we felt it took courage to leave the seminary against the expectations of your family and teachers.

Kadkani was above all a learned scholar and a proud Khorasani from the historical city of Nishapur. He made a point to introduce us to the splendid culture of this province, which had contributed more to Iran's history than I had previously known. Khorasan, he explained, had been a distinctive center of literary and cultural production, with unique philosophical schools of thought. For him, this particularity was the glue that held together greater Khorasan, a term long ago used to refer to a region that included parts of contemporary Afghanistan and Central Asia. These civilizational and cultural tendencies, he maintained, had not expired but extended into the modern period in the form of new, free verse poetry, being penned by the likes of Mehdi Akhavan-Sales. I appreciated Dr Kadkani's unusual approach, since almost every other professor I studied with privileged Tehran, Europe, or America in his teaching, and since I personally felt no particular attachment to any single region of Iran.

Dr Kadkani's identification with Khorasan and its history and culture did not isolate him as a *gharibeh* in Tehran. He presented himself not as a man shorn of identity but as the embodiment of Khorasan's culture. I often pondered on his ability to draw Tehrani students into appreciating the cultural achievements of his province. My conundrum was that I, an itinerant son, had no claim to a celebrated cultural tradition. The tendency to overlook the way unrooted persons, like myself, related to culture was perhaps a problem with Kadkani's localizing worldview, but I decided it was nothing to be upset about. A friend of mine from Iranian Kurdistan, however, disagreed. Kadkani's privileged positioning of himself, he argued, was detrimental to Iranian Kurds, Lors, Azeris, and Arabs, and others for whom Persian was not their primary language and who could therefore not claim membership in the Iranian nation by virtue of a shared literary heritage.

Kadkani loved Persian literature, but he was more of a modernist than his present reputation in Iran as a scholar of classical Persian literature suggests. He analyzed Persian literature with theoretical sophistication, freely importing modes of criticism developed in conversation with other literary canons, a tendency I ascribed to a Marxist influence, but this is speculation, since I cannot recall Kadkani ever mentioning Marxism in class. In either case, it was not his politics but his command of the vast sweep of Persian literature that amazed me.

I was also taken by the cosmopolitanism of Kadkani's thinking. His broad vision embodied the best of the transregional political culture of 1970s Iran. He closely considered the historical context in which classical Persian poetry was produced, convincingly arguing that classical poetry was not of our time or social condition. I learned much from him about the urgency of acquiring new modes of writing and thinking and wished that my beloved teachers from Golpayegan could meet and learn from him. If only all religious, or perhaps even secular, Iranians could be like him, I thought. His small book of poetry, *Dar Kucheh-ye*

Baghi-ye Neyshabur (In the Garden Alleys of Nishapur), grounded his representation of the political and cultural life of 1970s Iran in the richness of the Khorasani poetic tradition. Many of the poems in the book took inspiration from the guerrilla movement at the time. This was one of my favourite passages:

> «... من با زبان مرده‌ی نسلی / که هر کتیبه‌اش / زیر هزارخروار خاکستر دروغ / مدفون شده است، با که بگویم / طفلان ما به لهجه‌ی تاتار / تاریخ «پُرشکوه» نیاکان را می‌آموزند؟ / اهل کدام ساحل خشکی / ای قاصد محبت باران». [۳۵]

> How could I say, in the dead language of an entire generation, a language whose inscriptions lie buried under a heavy debris of falsehood, that innocent children parrot the "Glorious History" of our ancestors, with a Tatar accent? O, kind messenger of the rain, which barren shores are you arriving from?

As a young university student coming from the provinces and majoring in Persian literature, poetry was a cultural tradition I was well acquainted with and appreciated. I was particularly inspired by new poets from Khorasan and considered Akhavan Sales's poetry to be precisely of my time and generation. The fact that Kadkani was a student of Akhavan Sales affirmed my belief that the poetry of Khorasan exemplified the Iranian cosmopolitan imagination, yet remained grounded in Iranian history and produced for our time. I now realize how naïve and perhaps narrow-minded my idea of cosmopolitanism and Iranian history and culture was then. Iranian culture, of course, cannot and is not the exclusive territory of

Persian language, or vice versa. The historical land we now know as Iran is marked by the literary, historical, and artistic traces of many non-Persian speakers. Before the rise of nation states, I imagined Iran to be its own *donya*, where history, philosophy, literature, and devotional texts were written in an assortment of regional languages, from Arabic to Turkish to Persian. The current tendency to define and equate a nation and its people, cultures, and places with one language, in the name of national pride and identity, runs counter to the historical reality of our region, flattening the differences that constituted premodern cosmopolitan sensibilities. In the case of Iran, some nationalists seem unable or averse to recognize that in its earlier history, affection for a place, be it a village, city, or region, was one element of associating with the world, a process more imaginative than today's fixed identities. Many Iranian poets and thinkers carried their birth cities as names (or *nisbahs*) but they traveled and lived elsewhere too, and often considered these new places their own, just as they did the languages they picked up during their education and travels. That some are today engaged in a nationalistic fight over the identity of Rumi, a thirteenth-century poet and a Sufi mystic who was born in Balkh (in present-day Afghanistan) and died in Konya (present-day Turkey) would appear absurd to Rumi, who wrote principally in Persian, but lyricized with ease in Arabic, Turkish, and even Greek. Just as Rumi captures the plural and fluid personhood typical of an earlier Iran, so too are the proprietorial squabbles over him today indicative of our hardened borders and identities. Moving from Iran's provinces to its metropolitan heartland in Tehran during my adolescence and adulthood, however, taught me that despite our impulse for fixed categories, other, more generous forms of relating to place are possible.

4

Zahra's Paradise, 1977–1978

Homa Nategh Defends our Faith

It was early one October morning when our family phone rang. Mozafar, a friend of mine from Kurdish Sanandaj who lived not far from our Tehran home, was on the other end of the line. A major demonstration, he hastily explained, was underway at Tehran's main cemetery, Behesht-e Zahra (Zahra's Paradise). He was moments from stepping out the door when he decided to call me, so we agreed to meet there. It was a mild sunny day, and by the time I finished the walk from Aryashahr, our neighborhood in Tehran, to Behesht-e Zahra, it was late in the morning. Taking in the sea of people that had already filled the cemetery's vast grounds, I realized it would be no use trying to find Mozafar. After aimlessly wandering the cemetery for some time, a group of people outfitted with microphones and recording equipment caught my eye. I stepped closer to study the scene. Three or four foreign reporters were interviewing two women, one of whom I recognized as Dr Homa Nategh, a professor of history at the University of Tehran and a well-known Marxist critic of the Shah. I had met Dr Nategh a few times as a student. I attended several of her classes and raised the intellectual and political questions they raised for me with her after class. She was always kind and made herself available to students.

I waited for the foreign reporters to pack up and leave before I, along with some other members of the remaining crowd, approached the interviewed women. One bystander praised their intelligence and thanked them for representing the women of the revolution so graciously before the foreign press. More compliments followed. Then Nategh, who spoke confidently and in eloquent Persian, addressed us: "We put the foreign reporters in their place. They were questioning Islam's treatment of women, raising all sorts of concerns about revolutionary religious forces and the status of women. We, of course, defended our faith, telling them that in our revolution no difference exists between men and women. We are not at all worried," she concluded, "about what will become of women after the Shah's fall."

Nategh's certainty surprised me, but I stayed silent, respecting her too much to say otherwise. I kept to the background, waiting for the crowd to thin out. Once it did, I approached her and asked, "Dr Nategh, perhaps we are young and inexperienced, but it is hard not to find fault with certain religious activists and leaders. Just this morning in the cemetery I overheard a group of Khomeinists berating others for not saying 'Allahu Akbar' after a talk. I am afraid they will soon try to dictate how we live, think, and behave. Some of the *hezbollahi*s at the university already harrass our women comrades for dressing as they please, not as the *hezbollahi*s think they should.

Is it not unfair that we should keep quiet for the sake of the revolution? What do you think we should do?"

A scowl had settled on Nategh's face by the time I finished talking. She abrasively replied, "This attitutde is precisely what I fear. Everyone wants to march to the beat of their own drum [*har ki be saz-e khod del mi navaze*]. This is a revolution, not a game. We need to respect the masses of people. We cannot afford to make a mountain out of straw [*kah*]." "But Dr Nategh," I responded, "the pro-Khomeini crowd is powerful and in some cases militantly opposes the freedoms the left upholds. They target and berate women, yet here we have a respected woman of the left worried about alienating them. We expect more from you as our spokesperson, Dr Nategh." At this point, Nategh impatiently snapped back that she did not know what I was talking about before walking away, leaving me vexed and alone in the vastness of Behesht-e Zahra. Had I perhaps been too certain of my own feelings? Surely it could not be that everyone was wrong except for me. Perhaps the intoxicating effects of revolution, of reclaiming our future from the Shah were overpowering us all. Caught in this dizzy time, we could not think clearly.

Years later, in August 1983, I had the chance to renew my acquiantance with Nategh, this time in Paris. Although we had met on one other occasion since our October 1978 encounter in Behesht-e Zahra, we had not revisited our fleeting exchange, and I was keen to know whether she had any memory of it. Sitting across from her in a Parisian café, I politely asked if she remembered me from that day a few months before the regime toppled. She hardly let me finish my sentence before interrupting, "I do not understand why everyone is so interested in my life during the revolution! It was a confusing time and situation. Everyone did stupid things and you can count me among them. Now everyone claims to have known everything about Khomeini before the revolution. They blame me," she vented, "for all that this regime has done." It took me a moment to gather myself, before I replied: "I only wanted to remind you that we briefly spoke that day. I did not mean to upset you." She paused, as if the severity of her reaction was setting in, surprising even herself. She softly added, "I am sure you agree." I joked that, even then, she reacted harshly to criticism. I said this believing the possiblity of any kind of relationship between us had by now been squashed. With the past off limits, the conversation drifted to more trivial topics, like my planned return to the U.S. and a paper she had written to deliver to another person.

Homa Nategh died on January 1, 2016, in Arrou, a French village south of Paris. She is remembered as a distinguished historian of the Qajar empire and Constitutional Iran who at the time of the revolution supported Khomeini's leadership only to later oppose him and leave the country for a life in exile. Supporters of the fallen Pahlavi regime found in her remorse the figure of a salvageable revolutionary. It was in a public letter published in 2003 that a penitent Nategh denounced the revolution and her role in it.[1] The unwritten story of Nategh's political evolution is part of the revolution's unthought afterlives and leaves questions worth pondering. How did a scholar well acquainted with the history of Iran

1 Homa Nategh, "It was my own doing, I should be damned for it," *London Kayhan*, February 26, 2003.

and of Islam, an activist who pushed for women's inclusion in politics, come to feel comfortable supporting the clerical leadership of a revolution?

Nategh's own explanation does not address this essential question, seeking instead to absolve herself of the shame and guilt witnesses to the Islamic Republic's ascendency feel. Her public letter attributes her political missteps to a revolutionary fever, which led her and other oblivious Iranians astray: "I am perhaps more culpable for my role in the revolution than others. I was a teacher and a scholar, but I was so moved by revolutionary excitement that I dispensed with all I had learned and joined the ignorant masses in the streets."[2]

Tehran Revisited

It was the summer of 1974 when I graduated from Tehran University. Fresh out of college, what awaited me was not the beginning of my adult life but compulsory military service. At the time, the state required all male college graduates to serve two years in the military prior to assuming a professional job or to leaving the country. I had already served six months over two summers as a university student, which reduced my post-graduation service to eighteen months, but I still roiled at the thought of giving over more than a year of my life to the "Royal Military." The summers I had served had been futile and even degrading. Imagine a young radical who seized any chance he had to resist authority sequestered in a military camp. The military commanders were single-mindedly

[2] Nategh, "It was my own doing, I should be damned for it," *London Kayhan*, February 26, 2003.

obsessed with enforcing discipline and exacting obedience to senior officers. Away from the watchful gaze of our commanders, others and I did our absolute best to sabotage their plans and cause what trouble we could. We openly questioned our commander about the role of Iran's military and foreign policy in the Middle East, and its military dependence on the U.S. Why was it, we asked, that our army was so quick to further U.S. policy in Yemen but could not be bothered to lift a finger in the interest of Palestinians? Our commander, too resigned to quarrel, rarely offered our provocations real answers. He shrugged us off with the reply that this was the Shah's military, not the people's; we were simply there to follow his orders and commands.

I spent the first three months of my eighteen-month service training in an infantry base in Shiraz, where the militaristic pomp I witnessed reached its height. General Jahanbai, the commander of the Shiraz Infantry Division, would call us to attention. We cadets motionlessly remained in place as he lectured at length about the miseries of life in the Soviet Union or some other calamity caused by "collectivism." After three months of his speechifying, I was sent to Sar-e Pol-e Zahab, a small town near the Iran–Iraq border, where I completed the remainder of my service as a unit commander. As a second lieutenant I had a group of about twenty-four military men under my command. I was given a pre-planned schedule for training my unit, which did not allow for much improvisation, except during regularly blocked discussion times. After a few months I decided I would no longer lecture the soldiers under my charge on military subjects and instead turned my attention to current affairs, literature, and history. I spent these periods discussing politics, principally conflicts in the Middle East, with my unit. As with the two summers I served in Tehran, I scarcely learned new skills or knowledge in Sar-e Pol-e Zahab.

While my service was short on useful training, it did introduce me to several activists, and our shared experience forged friendships that endure, even forty-five years later, to this day. During our time serving together, the three of us, Javad, who now lives in London, Ahmad, who spent several years in prison after the revolution and now lives in the Princeton, New Jersey area, and I decided we would travel abroad together for graduate studies. I completed my service in the fall of 1975, and by November of that same year, Javad and I left Iran to continue our studies in the U.K. We stayed in London for a few days before settling in Bournemouth, a town on the English south coast, where Javad had relatives and where I studied English at a nearby school while rooming with a local family. Ahmad had friends and relatives living in the U.S. and left for Washington, D.C. a few months after Javad and I left Iran.

Figure 4.1 Ali Mirsepassi, Sar-e Pol-e Zahab, 1975.

I had planned to stay in the U.K. for a few months at most, long enough to improve my English and to continue from there to my ultimate destination, the U.S., where I would complete graduate studies. A series of unexpected events, however, extended my time in the U.K. I was attending an evening English class, when the instructor, a bookish middle-aged man, discovered my interest in literature and encouraged me to register for classes at the college where he lectured. I did not hesitate to follow his advice and began a program in English literature at the local college right away. At the same time, a different kind of love fell into my life, and this was the more essential motivation for staying in the U.K. This unexpected relationship, which had compelled me to stay, however, proved rather complicated and was over by the winter of 1977.

In a way, its dissolution could not have been better timed. By early fall of 1977 friends in Iran were writing to me with increasing regularity about the unprecedented situation there. New opportunities for mobilization, they reported, were opening daily, unleashing a torrent of political and cultural activity. With the fall of the Shah looming on the horizon, I

Figure 4.2 Ali Mirsepassi (left) and a friend, Bournemouth, U.K., 1977.

decided to postpone my trip to the U.S. for graduate studies yet again and return to Iran at once. I had been craving a freer and more open Iran since I was thirteen or fourteen years old. Now that hopeful intimations of a democratic Iran were surfacing, however early and unpredictable, I could not bear to remain far away. I desired nothing more than to experience these events first-hand, not as an observer, but as a participant on the ground. Yet leftist arms of the resistance had not outmaneuvered the Shah's suppression as religious dissidents had, so I was not certain we were prepared to play a leading role in the revolution, wherever it might take us. I left for Iran nonetheless hopeful that the secular left would somehow muster at the eleventh hour the resources needed to reorganize and emerge as a major political force on par with our religious counterparts.

Saying goodbye to the U.K. proved easy. It was only toward the end of my two years there that I began to develop an attachment to its places and people, most of them students, teachers, and other intellectually minded folks I met in bookstores, workshops, and art events in London. While I loved these friends, I never developed a synchronicity of feeling with them and sensed I would always be to them a *gharibeh*. I had been routinely reminded in the U.K. that I was an Iranian, an identification that alerted me to a new scale of difference: being an Iranian in the U.K. opened me to more isolation than being an outsider in a neighboring Iranian town ever had. I particularly loathed the term used to remind me of my difference—"alien." The first time I encountered it, I felt sick to my stomach. I was attending an English language institute and was given a form to fill out.

At the top of the page, in large, bold lettering read, "Alien Students Information." It did not suffice here to refer to me as a stranger. I was an alien, an outsider to the designator's known human world, an ontologically lesser being. While a close circle of Iranian friends provided me an island of familiarity, I otherwise kept a deliberate distance from Iranian and English activists, not feeling at home with either group, since they seemed more preoccupied with criticizing each other than cultivating solidarity.

Home is not a place, I learned during my time abroad, but the company you keep. Even as I was returning to Iran, I knew my travels abroad were an incomplete project I would soon revisit. With the words of Dr Enayat still heavy on my mind, I intended to stay in Iran for two or three months and then leave once again to pursue graduate studies in the U.S. Although I hoped to contribute to the struggle for a freer Iran, my ambitions to train abroad as a social scientist were growing and pulling me in a different direction. By the time I left the U.K. I had taken college-level courses in English literature. Although I was beginning to feel comfortable with the language, two years were not enough time to accrue the ability needed to study English-language classics in the social sciences and humanities, a requirement, Dr Enayat reminded me, any intellectual worth their salt should meet. I envisioned myself continuing this endeavor in the U.S., this time studying international relations, a field I thought would provide me with a better understanding of the world. I was told by several friends studying there that it was more welcoming of Third World students. Despite my commitment to this vision, I could not let my studies, something I figured I could always resume, obstruct my chance to participate in a once in a lifetime political transformation.

Poetry Readings, 1977

I returned to Tehran through Mehrabad Airport one early November morning. As the plane rumbled to a landing, a warm mesh of memories welcomed me. The label "Tehrani" still did not fit comfortably, but I felt at ease back in the capital. After exiting the plane and collecting my luggage, I was greeted by a friend from my university days who had agreed to give me a ride. As soon as we climbed into his car, he began rattling off a list of recent anti-regime events, each more important and spectacular than the last, including the now well-known nights of poetry readings at Goethe Institute. The Institute had partnered that year with the oppositional Writers' Association of Iran, almost spontaneously transforming the Institute into a forum for mass political communion. Soon after returning to Tehran, I attended one of these poetry readings. The celebrated poet Mehdi Akhavan Sales, a mentor to my instructor Dr Shafi'i Kadkani and my favorite contemporary Iranian poet, was the main speaker, making the night instantly memorable. Akhavan sat center stage before a brimming room, a cloud of excitement hanging thick over the air. Although a month had passed since the famous "Ten Nights" of poetry readings in October 1977, which attracted crowds of thousands to the Institute and its surrounding streets, that night carried with it too the solemnity of an almost religious experience, as if we men and women, true believers, had pilgrimaged here to meet our saint. This aura of spirituality struck me, not a person prone to contemplating such things, as profoundly real. Our long-held dream of a new Iran was finally coming true.

The crowd assembled at the Goethe Institute resembled a scene from the 1940s, when Tudeh activists and sympathizers gathered in clubs (*kolb-ha*) to discuss new ways of approaching art, culture, and politics during a more humanistic and cosmopolitan period of the party's history. When the First Congress of Iranian Writers, sponsored by the Perso-Soviet Cultural Society, convened in Tehran in the summer of 1946, its participants, who included Karim Keshavarz, a pro-Tudeh writer, Sadegh Hedayat, a pioneer of modern Persian literature, and Ali Akbar Dehkhoda, a lexicographer, famously set off a double debate: first, on the meaning of modern literature and, second, how younger writers and poets might go about challenging the literary status quo.

The environment of the lectures, art exhibits, and theater performances I attended as a university student, however, differed from that of the 1940s. Speakers had by the 1970s internalized the consequences of censorship and carefully refrained from directly criticizing the government, relying instead on innuendo and metaphor to communicate critical ideas. The same was true of the plays and films produced during that period. There were, however, certain domains in which the government permitted a measure of intellectual and artistic freedom. Journalists, playwrights, and filmmakers had leeway to condemn urban decay, Western cultural decadence, and the corruption of Iranian morals and society by materialist consumerism so long as they cast the state as the heroic defender of Iranian tradition. In fact, Channel 2, a state-run television network, encouraged moral and cultural criticisms of secular democratic values that invoked the sanctity of Islam, which it claimed the West imperiled. This argument of course made little sense to Iranians who had taken to the streets to demonstrate against the Shah and recognized his government as the real derider of civil rights.

A few nationally televised debates on the idea of Iranian-Islamic spirituality were even more puzzling. Most of the participants were foreign-educated professors or writers whose comments often veered into critiques of the West. Why, I wondered, did they feel such hostility for the West? The participant I found most strangely captivating was the "oral philosopher" Ahmad Fardid (1910–94), who had coined the term Westoxification (*gharbzadegi*) in the 1950s to describe how Western ideas and institutions, such as progress, the rule of law, parliamentary elections, and so on, had enfeebled Iran. The concept would be made famous by Jalal Al-e Ahamad, whose book of the same name launched a popular paradigm for critiquing Iranian modernity in the 1960s and 1970s. Fardid's views were often scattered and incoherent, yet he seemed more genuinely anti-Western than the others. Most of the participants, I felt, pandered to popular sentiment or whatever message the government expected of them, combining populist anti-urbanism with New Age spiritualism. I had become acquainted with these tendencies through some of my upper-class Western-educated relatives, partisans to this cultural reaction. Yet Fardid was different. He saw himself as a prophet, but perhaps a failed one, and his ideas had become fashionable among people who scarcely understood them. I remember, one day, talking to a university friend about a recently televised debate. He ventured that Fardid's incoherence verged on mental instability.

He asked in genuine bewilderment, "How could the other panelists treat him with such respect?" I responded, "Fardid is the real thing, the only person who sincerely believes in the need to cleanse Iranians' collective mentality of the West. The others are merely performing [*bazi mikonand*]." Yet his sincerity only made him scarier: Fardid meant what he said, and what he said was thoroughly reactionary.

The Joy and Anxiety of Revolution

Back in Tehran, and a year prior to the revolution's climax, amidst a flurry of political excitement and heady optimism, I felt I was once again, as with my adolescence in Golpayegan, living in two different worlds simultaneously. My home life in Golpayegan had been marked by the comfort and privilege afforded the son of a government official. Yet at school most of my friends were locals of farming extraction, making the classroom a profound space for thinking and learning about the world. Now, back in Tehran, the epicenter of a national uprising, I once again felt myself entering one world then lapsing into another. I experienced in the company of friends and on the streets of Tehran the harmony of united opposition to the government. At home, however, my father, now retired to our family residence in Tehran, remained steadfast in his support for the Shah, only incensed by the government's passive response to protesters.

Within my circle of leftist friends, we did not worry about recalcitrant royalists like my father but instead about religious activists who had at their disposal resources we did not dream of. Although we remained open to learning from religious friends and family members and did not oppose religion outright, we were less generous about the idea of handing the reins of government over to Shi'i clerics. Our aspirations and views were a world away from those of Ayatollah Khomeini and his supporters. Based on my experience in Golpayegan and what I had learned about the ulama, I feared that if they were to govern, their hostility to the institutions and achievements of post-Mashruteh Iran would ruin the country. Despite the growing popularity of religious resistance, still the left toiled. My friends in the Ministry of Foreign Affairs, the National Iranian Television Organization, and several private companies helped us distribute political flyers, usually messages by the Fedayeen encouraging protests of the Shah and alerting us to the government's anti-opposition activities. As leftists, we were anxious when, by late spring and early summer 1978, we realized that religious dissidents under Khomeini's leadership were seizing control of the movement.

My overall thinking about Ali Shari'ati one of the chief ideologues of Iran's religious resistance, remained until then ambivalent. His writing and speeches were stirring and an improvement on the rhetorical style of orators like Taghi Falsafi, who communicated only by way of arrogance and anachronism. Shari'ati spoke the language of young Iranians. There was a modern sensibility to his orations that was at once radical and instructive. I was, however, put off by his quasi-Marxism. Either he was dressing Islam in Marxist garb to sell it to the youth, I thought, or he was a Marxist using Islam instrumentally. I found him an unreliable interpreter of either tradition at any rate.

Still, Shari'ati was an unavoidable subject of debate. He was arrested in 1973 and jailed for two years. Following his release from prison, he published a series of essays entitled "Man, Islam, and Marxism" in *Kayhan*, a major daily newspaper. These essays generated heated debate and divided the public. Many felt that the attack on Marxism waged under Shari'ati's name was a SAVAK fabrication meant to discredit the recently freed thinker in the eyes of his radical supporters. Others argued that the essays were in fact consistent with ideas he had articulated elsewhere, but that they had been published to stoke tensions between the secular and religious left. I later learned that Shari'ati had in fact written the essays, although SAVAK publicized them. Hamid Algar, in an introduction to his English translation of the essays published years after the fact, gives a detailed history of SAVAK's intervention in the publication of Shari'ati's writings on Marxism. Still, I read them with interest and was disappointed with the criticisms credited to Shari'ati. While other scholars like Vardasbi and Enayat had their own arguments against Marxism, largely refutations of materialism in defense of Islamic theology, in Shari'ati's essays, something else was afoot. His views resembled those of Ehsan Naraghi, Ahmad Fardid, and other cultural conservatives consumed by the idea of a clash between East and West and a prophecy of Western decline and "Eastern" spiritual resurgence. At the time, I saw Shari'ati's essays on Marxism as fodder for the Shah's assault on leftist activism. Yet his intervention did more than that. It bolstered the Islamic forces challenging the Shah.

Approaching what we would later mark as the downfall of the Pahlavi state, public spaces and institutions opened their doors to a variety of oppositional gatherings, activities, and lectures. My days between the spring of 1978 and January 1979 started with demonstrations in the morning, were punctuated by lectures or student gatherings in the early afternoon, and ended with an evening debriefing at a friend's apartment. We exchanged observations about the political situation of the day, sometimes analyzing them intensely, before planning the next day's activities. We spent a fair share of our time and energy attempting to contact other leftist groups, a task that proved almost impossible, since the state had driven the left underground, isolated its members in prison, and otherwise reduced it to splinter organizations.

During this period, I traveled to three towns in western Iran: Sanandaj, Boroujerd, and Nahavand. In Sanandaj, I spent a few days with Khalu, or Mehdi, a charming and affable friend from my military days. Sanandaj, the capital of Kurdistan province in Iran, was Khalu's hometown, and he was working there for the province's Labor Ministry. When my bus pulled in, one late spring afternoon in 1978, to the station, Khalu was there waiting for me. As we started walking to his house, I was struck by the city's calm. There was no sign of recent protests, rallies or other political activities in sight.

The next day, Khalu took me to the town's main square. Several Kurdish political prisoners had been released from Evin Prison that day, and thousands had gathered to welcome them home. A caravan of cars arrived late in the afternoon, but the crowd, it turned out, would not have the chance to see or hear from any of the recently freed political prisoners. A middle-aged man apologized, "Our brothers are tired, and they need to go home. They thank you for your support and ask that you go home in peace." I heard several younger boys near me sneer "*tarsuh*" (coward). With this news, Khalu, whose face wore a look of sullen disappointment, and I walked back to his home.

That night I asked Khalu why Sanandaj was so quiet. He seemed to detect an insinuation in my question and responded somewhat defensively, "We are all against the Shah. The Fedayeen and Tudeh Party have strong bases among Iranian Kurds. But the situation is confusing for us as Sunnis and Kurds. It's hard not to harbor misgivings about backing a Shi'i-led movement. Khomeini's vision of the future has left many apprehensive." My trip to Sanandaj reminded me of Iran's tremendous internal diversity, which compounded the complexity of the political situation we faced.

Later that year, I decided to visit a few other places outside of Tehran to see what the state of affairs was along Iran's fringes. That I had friends and relatives in Boroujerd and Nahavand made travel to these two towns, each an hour away from the other, easy. In October 1978 I visited Boroujerd, where I stayed with a distant relative for three days. My father had been transferred to Boroujerd from Malayer when I was three years old, and we lived in Boroujerd for four years, including for the birth of my sister, Susan. The town was alive with frenetic political energy. City streets were sprayed in revolutionary graffiti, with "death to the Shah" a crowd favorite. Every day I witnessed huge demonstrations, and I perhaps met more leftist activists during my few days in Boroujerd than I did any other town during the revolution. Several distant relatives and their friends were Marxist activists with some leadership role in the town's political activities. I learned from them that while the Fedayeen in particular had a strong presence, there was a network of intellectuals and political activists organizing and vying for leadership of the local opposition. The atmosphere in Boroujerd was very encouraging. The activists I met were confident in their work and vision and had created a community of like-minded leftists.

On my last day in town, I was walking in a residential neighborhood made up of large, elegant, newly built houses. Despite or perhaps because of its affluence, political graffiti covered its walls. I was absorbed in reading the graffiti when I heard a group of people chanting. A crowd of about fifty people appeared from the opposite side of the street. They all gathered around a house with a dark blue gate and broke into it. I decided to stop and see what would happen. It did not take long for people to emerge running from the house holding chairs, rugs, paintings, bicycles, and shoes. I saw a young boy of maybe ten or twelve years old passing by and asked him whose house it was. He smiled and said it was the house of a rich doctor before running away.

I took a bus from Boroujerd to Nahavand the next day. I had not visited my mother's home town since my return from the U.K., and I was eager to see my grandmother and to learn about the political situation in Nahavand. I arrived around three in the afternoon and it took me no more than fifteen minutes to walk to my *madar*'s house, where I had spent so much of my childhood. I went directly into my grandmother's room and as soon as our eyes met, she leapt up to hug me. After having tea and sweets, Madar, in her own measured and detailed fashion, filled me in on the latest news from our extended family. She did not say much about town politics except to let me know that "*shahr khayli sholugh shodeh*" (there is a lot going on in town). She then mentioned that a distant relative, Ali Shahbazi, had been released early from Evin Prison and was now back in Nahavand, before urging me to go see him. Ali was a few years my senior, and I had looked up to him when we were in high school. He was a successful student, exceedingly polite and mature for his age, and sort of acted as my mentor. He was knowledgeable of Persian literature and each time we met he introduced me to a new book or two.

Ali was born in 1947 and completed high school in Nahavand before moving to Tehran to attend college. After graduating from university in the early 1970s he started working for Encyclopedia Dehkhoda in Tehran. But he was arrested and sentenced to ten years in prison for anti-Shah activities not before too long in 1973.

The next morning, I had breakfast with my grandmother and a few of my cousins. Around ten o'clock, I walked to the other side of town to see Ali at his parents' house. When I arrived, the front door to the house was open and several people were milling around the yard. I figured a party was underway. I entered the main room of the house. The house felt instantly

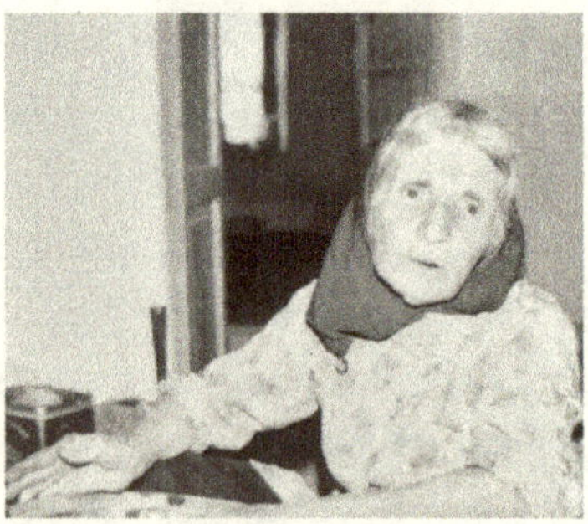

Figure 4.3 My grandmother, Nahavand, early 1970s.

familiar. During Ali's time in prison in Tehran, whenever I was in Nahavand I made sure to visit his mother and express my solidarity and sympathies. A hush fell over the room, full of young men, as I entered. Everyone stopped their conversation to greet me. Ali stood up and walked over to embrace me. He then took my hand and asked me to sit next to him.

Ali and I spent the next half hour speaking about his time in prison. He identified himself and the other men seated in the room as members of the Tudeh Party and spoke of his connections with the party leadership. During his five years at Evin, he had the chance to meet Mohammad Ali Amoui, a long-time political prisoner who had first been imprisoned in 1954 after being uncovered as a member of the Tudeh Military Network. Amoui would spend the next twenty-five years in prison before his release in 1979, only to be imprisoned again in 1983. I asked Ali what he thought the left's policy toward Khomeini and the Shiʿi clerics should be. Ali did not hesitate to say that we need to act rationally, that is to avoid alienating the religious forces. "But the left," he continued, "has a considerable base in Iran and a long history of fighting for social change; we need to make sure that Khomeini and his followers remember this and respect us."

All that Ali said that morning pleased me. His optimism about the left's future, nestled in a confident but sober analysis of the revolutionary situation, revived my flagging hope. Before I left his family home that day, Ali asked me to come back and see him again another day so that he might introduce me to his friends in Tehran. I agreed to this, but decided on my way back to my grandmother's that I would not return. I was a leftist activist, but I also had deep-seated feelings for Iran. I was unhappy with the Soviet Union's policies toward Iran and rather distrustful of their internationalism. For similar reasons, I disagreed with the Tudeh Party's policies and thought the organization as a whole was too close to the Soviet Union and lacked the independence needed to act as a radical organization interested in the well-being of Iran.

Sadly, both Ali and Amoui were arrested again during the 1983 crackdown of the Tudeh Party. At that time, Amoui was a member of the Central Committee of the Party and Ali was a high-ranking member. Amoui and other leaders of the Tudeh were tortured in prison, and they were forced to appear on Iranian national television recanting the party. It was there that Amoui confessed that the Tudeh Party functioned as a front organization for the Soviet Union and that its principal activities in Iran were espionage. It became clear later that Tudeh leaders had made these confessions under brutal physical and psychological torture. Ali, however, would not repent and was sentenced to ten years in prison. He would only live another five years, however, before he was hanged in 1988 during what is now known as a mass execution of political prisoners on the direct orders of Khomeini.

Back in Tehran, I spent most of my days either on city streets, or at the university. Tehran University was a prime place to gather for lectures, art exhibits, theater performances, and teach-ins. I took these experiences as proof that a freer Iran was materializing under our care. Writers, artists, and political activists were remaking the cultural and political life of their own nation in real time. Yet my fears of a religious takeover following the state's collapse persisted and were compounded by the fact that I scarcely heard any practical ideas as to how we might proceed in its aftermath. Most demonstrations and discussions focused on enumerating the wrongdoings of the Pahlavi state, with the future imagined as free and open arena in which anything would be possible. This seemed naïve and conflicted with what I had encountered in Golpayegan and later on the streets of Tehran, where Islamist activists organized themselves against the state on a new scale. Although I cherished a great many things about Golpayegan, I worried its insularity would be universalized across Iran, with the only change being a swap of political figureheads. I feared that a post-Pahlavi Iran, as with the Golpayegan of my adolescence, was on track to becoming a place where religious values and authorities dominated and deviation from these norms was only begrudgingly tolerated. While I did not have a practical idea of what post-revolutionary Iran should look like either, I desired the kind of collective Alavi imagined in *Chashmhayash*, an Iran where enlightened and good people ruled, working to make our nation a place we might be proud of.

Although the fortress of Pahlavi power showed serious cracks, the revolutionary movement continued to grow within the mold of existing political institutions. Nearly eliminated as an organized force, the left was sorely lacking in leadership and resources. Its presence was limited to high schools, universities, and prison cells. The revolutionary movement, then, was for the left not a moment of triumph but of learning and reflection, one that laid bare its failure to communicate its vision to Iranian society. Yet this failure was not entirely of its own making, since the state had eroded the left's wherewithal to organize and narrowed its access to public spaces. Religious forces inserted themselves into this vacuum to lead the movement. The clerical leadership, under Khomeini, was present both in and outside of Iran. In nearly every Tehran neighborhood, people consulted their local cleric, who presided over a bounty of revolutionary symbols, from the martyrdom of Imam Hossein, revolutionized by Ali Shari'ati, to the exile of Khomeini. These local representatives of the religious movement moved resources through the well-worn channels of the mosque, bazaar, and other established institutions, relative to which the presence and wherewithal of left and secular forces were rather thin.

During the fall of 1978 I attended a series of events, each of which offered a different vision of the revolution's outcome. As I write about these encounters today, I ponder how many other forgotten events are absent from our stories of the revolution, buried in the remote, sometimes inaccessible recesses of memory.

Karim Lahiji, an Unlikely Revolutionary

My experience of the revolution does not align with the popular narrative of it, according to which Iranians, including liberals and leftists, under a trance, volunteered their loyalty to Khomeini, enabling the rise of a post-revolutionary Islamic State. Yet I cannot say that we had no idea what Khomeini and his associates desired after the fall of the Pahlavi state either. Nor can I deny that Iranians from all walks of life did in fact support Khomeini's bid for leadership. However, to do justice to those who participated in the revolution, it is only fair to try to recover the revolution's hidden conflicts and forgotten traces.

Several events from the fall of 1978 capture some of these ephemeral traces. These were public events inspired by a revolutionary spirit that dissolved boundaries, challenged conventional modes of thought and social categorization, and burned with the fire of hope. People desired direct action and representation, harboring little regard for institutions and their rules.

What would an activist lawyer do in a situation that vitiated the rules and order he had taken an oath to uphold? One clash I observed between a custodian of the law, the young litigator Karim Lahiji, and the masses, whose demands for justice cared little for legal niceties, brought this question to the fore. The occasion was a sit-in at Aryamehr University (now the Sharif University of Technology) in Tehran. A crowd of young students and other activists had assembled in the university gymnasium. I knew the speaker, Lahiji, as a defender of democratic rights and advocate for political prisoners. Lahiji, a trim and stately looking man, took to the podium and after a few words of introduction, began, in keeping with his profession, methodically exposing the Shah's corruption and despotic disregard for the rule of law. As evidence he offered a careful catalog of the regime's human rights violations, expressing sympathy for the leftist activists who the government had wrongfully detained, imprisoned, and, in some cases, tortured and killed. Yet Lahiji's political leanings were not readily discernible. He struck me as a liberal nationalist, perhaps sympathetic to the Mujahedin, since he referenced several of their early leaders, like the Rezai brothers, Majid Sharif-Vaghefi, and Mohammad Hanifnejad, with respect. What was evident from his talk was that he was no proponent of the Shah.

Although Lahiji's talk did not reveal anything that the state's wanton and sometimes fatal use of force against demonstrators had not already communicated, I was happy to learn that we could count a tempered lawyer among our ranks. Lahiji offered a new way to think about our grievances and demands, one that was measured and legalistic but compelling for that very reason: It turned the language the state had sanctioned against it. His moderation acquired a more interesting meaning against the frenetic energy of social revolt. However, no sooner had Lahiji stopped speaking than several men in the hall rose to confront him. One protested that the Shah's brutal regime was worse than Hitler's Germany; his crimes were so obvious that Lahiji's legal arguments were nothing but a pedantic waste of time. Others stood to ask whether the people's will, including their chants of "Death to the Shah" that everyday filled the streets, was not referendum enough on the regime's criminal culpability.

I sat taking in the scene, watching the young activists' opprobrium grow increasingly disconnected from what Lahiji had said. It was clear Lahiji believed that the Shah's regime was criminal and that people had the power to void his authority. I thought Lahiji's legal argument could only help our cause, since many outside Iran were surely ignorant of the Shah's atrocities. Yet I sympathized with the detractors in the audience and their point. How could anyone ignore the fact that Iranians had for years been massively and publicly condemning their government? Unambiguous and ubiquitous denunciations of the regime had been issued by the will of the people and were mightier than any legal edict.

Despite the audience's onslaught of objections, Lahiji refused to abandon his legal reasoning. Once his detractors quieted down and returned to their seats, he responded with a defense of the rule of law, which, he emphasized, only justified our protests. Our aims were ethical, he announced, and our intentions fair and just. He then enquired of the audience: If we agree on these premises, then why fear the rule of law? The regime had violated the letter and spirit of the law when it chose to plunder the country of its wealth rather than prioritize ordinary Iranians. And when people decided to protest this, the regime used every possible means, up to and including violence, to suppress them. This was possible because no institutional mechanism or legal recourse existed to hold state policies accountable to the people. However, Lahiji argued, we were launching a revolution precisely to end such wanton abuses of power. Therefore, we should offer everyone—even members of SAVAK—the right to trial through an organized legal system.

With this qualification, Lahiji opened himself up to a fresh round of challenges. Members of the audience rose, this time to assert that his argument was inapplicable to the Iranian context, since strict adherence to rule of law could only work in a democratic and law-abiding society. The autocratic Shah, however, did not and would not compromise his singular authority, and so popular will must have the last word on justice. "If we all agree that the people of Iran want justice," Lahiji responded, "then why not serve it in a proper manner? The law," he went on, "is our best guarantee against arbitrary and capricious exercises of power." Precisely because the Shah's government violated the rule of law, revolutionaries needed to teach dictators that with ordinary people in power, society will be fairer and more just.

Lahiji's composure in the face of such intense questioning moved me. I felt, however, that this was a losing battle for him. How could anyone play the role of revolutionary and still call for law and order, which the revolution aimed to overturn? One might argue that Lahiji was involved in a self-defeating project. His situation was not unlike my friend Levi's, who I had met during my undergraduate years at Tehran University and reconnected with in the fall of 1978.

One day, Levi, Masoud, a friend of ours working for national television, and I sat in a tea house near the university pondering how our lives might look after the fall of the regime. Should the day come, I declared, I would stay in Iran. I would enjoy our newfound freedom, practice politics, and perhaps seek a job at the university. Masoud was certain he would lose his job at the television office but added that he was fine with this, since he had resolved to set up a studio and work as an independent artist should the regime fall. When we asked why he thought he would lose his job, he explained that everyone at the office knew he was not religious. It seemed to him a foregone conclusion that the Khomeinists would seize power and, immediately upon doing so, oust him or, at best, ask him to leave. As I tried to process this reality, Levi, who was Jewish, interjected: "You guys are lucky to come from Muslim families. We are selling our house and everything we have. We plan to leave for Israel before Nowruz." My heart sank. I wanted to comfort my friend but, still recovering from this blow to the imagination, was unable to offer much consolation. So the three of us sat quietly, each contemplating to himself how the situation could have gotten so far out of hand.

Nasser Zarafshan: The Left and Religion

Among the events I participated in around the time of the revolution, a few remain vivid in my mind. One was a lecture the well-known Marxist writer, translator, and human rights activist Nasser Zarafshan gave at Tehran University's Faculty of Fine Arts. The second was a talk by Taghi Falsafi, dubbed by Khomeini *zaban-gu-ye Islam* (spokesperson of Islam), who I had first encountered by way of his tape-recorded speeches in my Golpayegan classroom. While I had heard religious dissidents lecture many times before, this event was a reminder of my adolescence and a chilling warning of events to come. Yet another awakening was set off by an interview, mentioned earlier, I overheard between foreign reporters and the Marxist historian and activist Homa Nategh at Behesht-e Zahra cemetery.

When I recall these experiences and encounters, I am reminded of how many participants in the revolution renounced, decades later, what happened between 1978 and 1979 as a "grave mistake" or an "alliance with evil." These former revolutionaries blame the left with which they identified not too long ago for giving way to a tyrannical, theocratic dystopia in their naïve pursuit of "ideological paradise." This dissonance points perhaps to the active construction of another "unthought," a barrier keeping them from reckoning with the pain and contingencies of the revolution's outcome. Recanting the revolution is not just an act of self-erasure, but also captures the immense suffering Iranians continue to experience at the hands of the government it begot. Some now apologize for their role in it, pinning their supposed miscalculations on youthful ignorance. A sociologist might interpret this show of despair as a sign that the renunciants (an educated group of scholars, artists, and activists) lived a rather privileged life under the Pahlavi state. They joined the revolution expecting to attain an even higher material and cultural position. Failing to achieve this, they became embittered with what they had hoped to create and in some cases even nostalgic for the Pahlavi monarchy and the supposed golden age it introduced to Iran.

In the thick of the revolutionary moment, however, even those of us aware of the possibility of clerical cooptation held out the hope that the left might squeeze an autonomous role for itself after the downfall of the state. Nasser Zarafshan's talk at the Faculty of Fine Arts was a remarkable display of such hedged hope. Zarafshan, a lawyer, is best known for being imprisoned in 2002 while representing the family members of several Iranian dissidents assassinated in the post-revolutionary "chain murders" of November 1998. That day in 1978, a crowd had gathered in the reception area of the auditorium. When I spotted Zarafshan, hard to miss with his thick swatch of grey hair and large frame glasses, out of the corner of my eye, I decided to peel away from the crowd and introduce myself. I noticed a book on the Iranian Constitutional movement in his hand and asked, "Mr Zarafshan, what message is there for us in a book about the Mashruteh?" He smiled and said, "My dear [*azizam*], I am afraid we have forgotten the important achievements of our people. We may think we are starting a revolution from scratch, but we owe a lot to the Mashruteh and still have much to learn from its successes and mistakes." I was taken by what he said and wanted him to explain his thoughts. However, he was called at that same moment to the podium to start his talk.

Zarafshan took to the stand and proceeded to give a sweeping history of the Iranian left, reminding and reassuring the audience that the Iranian left had a proud history which we were nurturing today. We should not forget, he maintained, that the left had made major achievements in the fields of politics, culture, and the arts. His talk, thoughtful yet accessible, revived my faltering faith in the left's future, but I sensed his apprehensions about the road ahead. He recounted the sacrifices the Iranian left had historically made in service of the larger goal of national independence and prosperity. Other political forces, he cautioned with a view toward the future, had taken advantage of the left's willingness to broker coalitions only to sideline it. Zarafshan's perspective and suggestion, both rooted in history, that we were still struggling to fulfill the goals the Constitutional movement introduced decades ago left an impression on me because it had strategic weight to it. It provided a left counternarrative to those Islamic forces who defined the revolutionary movement in terms of the realization of a deferred Shi'i vision of Iran.

Yet it was the audience questions which followed that shifted my outlook. A cascade of questions culminated in a spontaneous back-and-forth between Zarafshan and the audience about the historical relationship between Iranian Marxism and religious movements. The discussion spanned the Jangali movement, headed by Mirza Kuchak Khan, the Iranian Communist Party, Marxist guerrilla organizations, like the Fedayeen and the Mujahedin, and ended by broaching the anti-Marxist attitudes of Khomeini and Mehdi Bazargan's

Freedom Movement. I figured some of the audience members were recently released political prisoners, for they specifically questioned and commented on the dynamic between Marxist and religious activists in prison, noting, for instance, that many religious prisoners considered their Marxist cellmates *kafir*, refusing to talk to them as they considered them *najes* or unclean.

The questions, comments, and ensuing discussion together suggested that history was about to repeat itself, this time as tragedy. The relationship between leftist and religious resistance forces, Zarafashan and the audience argued, was largely one of cooptation, not collaboration. Each time the possibility for social change had surfaced in Iran, the secular left, numerically smaller than the more popular and better entrenched religious establishment, entered into coalitions with Muslim reformists. In each case, the left's collaboration ended with their betrayal. Given this record, the activists present expressed fear of playing into Khomeini's hand, as the Tudeh Party and, to a lesser extent, other Marxist organizations had done by supporting the Islamic leadership and hoping, against the historical track record, that they would not turn against them. Other comments referred to present-day issues, mentioning, for example, the rising number of vigilante attacks on women demonstrators by *hezbollahi*s, a pejorative for young, black-clad Khomeinists. These vigilantes disrupted leftist gatherings on campus, chanting "there is only one party, the party of God [*hezbollah*], and one leader, Ruhollah [Khomeini]," and singled out "inappropriately" dressed leftists, and unveiled women in particular, for abuse. I had experienced this myself when *hezbollahi*s insulted our female friends in order to provoke my friends and me into a confrontation. Zarafshan encouraged the concerned activists to find a tactful way of dealing with small bands of harassers, since a premature conflict in the movement would only benefit the government. His analysis that the left was more an inspirational than institutional force articulated a truth I did not want to admit. Yet I knew that scores of dissidents had been imprisoned or killed, leaving organized leftist forces crushed by the government.

Zarafshan also touched on post-Mashruteh movements, from the oil nationalization efforts of the 1920s and 1940s to the 15 Khordad, or June 1963, uprising, a spate of nationwide protests following the arrest of Khomeini for his public denunciation of the Shah, which eventuated in his exile to Iraq, to the Marxist and Islamist guerrilla movements of the 1970s. For four years, I had studied political science at one of Iran's leading universities, yet so much of what Zarafshan shared that night was new to me. None of our professors dared broach the subjects he spoke so commandingly of. My instruction in Iranian political thought and history had come to me by way of non-academic books written by Fereydoun Adamiyat or Bijan Jazani, many of which I acquired in England. This lecture was an organic learning experience, and I hoped to fortify my knowledge of Iranian social movements through talks and debates as the revolutionary movement proceeded. Unfortunately, this would be the first and the last time I participated in such a thoughtful discussion on contemporary Iranian politics and the relationship between Islamists and secular leftists.

In Golpayegan, I had been introduced to secular leftism by my Marxist teachers Mr Amjadi and Mr Eshraghi and to politicized Islam by my pious, Falsafi-promoting teacher, Mr Tavakol, and later the Hojjatiyeh. A decade later, I was participating in a mass movement, yet what was occurring intellectually and politically in Tehran—anti-clerical leftists and pro-Khomeini Islamists uneasily jostling for power and public presence—still resembled my Golpayegan years. Activist Muslims dominated the revolutionary movement, and I saw everywhere signs of cultural conservativism. I could feel the secular left fading from the political scene, too absorbed in its own issues and too disconnected from its history to conceive a way forward.

The Eloquent Spokesman of Islam

Our lives change with time, but the past, as they say, is always present. As I transitioned to adulthood and moved in 1969 from small-town Iran to the major metropolis of Tehran, I was sure I had entered a brand-new world. My old life and all its unpleasantries, I imagined, would wither away. Every now and then, however, an observation would bring the past flickering before my mind's eye, revealing yet another continuity across time and space. One night in Tehran-now (New Tehran), a working-class neighborhood on the outskirts of Tehran, brought the past again to my door, just as the revolution seemed inevitable. It was November 1978, and control of Tehran's streets had been wrested from an almost paralyzed government and taken into the hands of protesters.

Several friends and I had gathered at an apartment that night. I made the acquaintance of a tall young man named Ebrahim, who was introduced to me as the leader of a political group connected to the religious leadership in Qom, a celebrated center of Shi'i learning in Iran. Ebrahim, a soft-spoken man in his late twenties, thanked us for our company and the opportunity to learn from us. He then told us about his activities and how we might help the movement at a time when it was critical that opposition forces work in tandem. I thought back to Zarafshan's lecture as the discussion veered toward an abstract analysis of Iran's future. What would happen now that the success of the revolution seemed irreversible? Would power transition smoothly from the monarchy to the people, or would a major mistake give the regime the opportunity to divide the opposition and stage a comeback?

After that night, Ebrahim regularly met with me and my cadre of friends. Our association grew, yet I continued to think of the young man as a mystery. He was cool and polite but persistent in his support of the ulama and Khomeini, even though we often dismissed his ideas even before he had the chance to express them. Rather than relent, however, Ebrahim always listened when faced with leftist perspectives, asked questions, and offered advice, usually a cautionary note on how to avoid alienating more moderate individuals.

Our religious friend was not without his criticisms of us. For several nights he argued that we lived in an ideological bubble, congregating only with other leftists and secular people. The hopes, ambitions, and worldviews of most Iranians, the base of the revolution, he warned, were alien to us. After a series of arguments failed to convince Ebrahim that we could work across our differences, my friends and I overcame our reluctance and agreed to accompany him to a gathering of "real" Tehranis opposed to the Shah. We met him at Shahnaz Square, a busy center in Tehran-now. As he guided us through a thicket of cheaply constructed houses no bigger than sheds, I wondered where he might be taking us. After walking for several minutes, we approached the garden of a building complex. He showed us inside. To my astonishment, the building's doors opened onto a vast courtyard flanked by open French doors and where a crowd of hundreds of people had already gathered.

At the center of the courtyard stood a balcony, perched on which was a large, empty pulpit (*minbar*). By the time we arrived, it was already eight or nine at night and the courtyard was nearly overflowing with an expectant audience. The five of us, Ebrahim, my friends Hamid, Mozafar, Masoud, and I struggled to find someplace empty where we might squeeze to sit together, so I separated from the group and found a corner for myself at the very end of one room. Still unaware of precisely what, other than Ebrahim's promised glimpse into the authentic dissidents of Tehran, was in store, I asked the middle-aged man seated next to me who would be speaking that night. The corners of his mouth turned up in amusement. He responded, his eyes fixed on mine, that we had the fortune of being addressed by Mr Falsafi that night. As soon as I heard Falsafi's name, my curiosity plummeted. The man asked whether I had heard of him. I decided to answer that I had not, hoping the conversation would end there. Another man nearby, however, jumped in to lecture me about Falsafi. He guessed, based on my looks, that I was a university student and a modernist (*motajadded*). "Let me tell you," he began, "we religious people are not as old fashioned and ignorant of the world as you might think." He proceeded, "Mr Falsafi is not an out of step *akhund* [cleric], but a man of our time with a deep knowledge of psychology, ethics, world cultures, and the issues facing our youth." Falsafi, the man went on, was politically discerning and had opposed the idea of a republic so long as Reza Shah advocated it. In his very early teenage years, Falsafi had joined Hassan Modarres, a constitutionalist cleric vigorously opposed to British interventions in Persia and to the first Pahlavi state, and other religious leaders in an unsuccessful campaign to prevent Reza Khan from abolishing the Qajar dynasty and forming a republic. During the 1940s and early 1950s, Falsafi, the stranger added, also led efforts to curb the growing influence of the Tudeh Party and of Baha'is. Having secured the support of the Shah and the military, Falsafi, with his own hands, participated in destroying a principal Baha'i Center. By June 1951, foreign services recognized Falsafi as an influential cleric whose criticisms of Baha'is and the U.K., U.S., and U.S.S.R. had stoked riots. Falsafi's rabble-rousing and popularity publicly compromised the Shah's situation, so he was ultimately banned from preaching in public, although he continued to rail against Baha'is and other supposed agents of subversion in private sermons.

I was growing tired of listening to the stranger catalog Falsafi's life and activities when a sudden silence fell upon the crowd. Falsafi entered the balcony and took his seat at the pulpit. He began with a routine recitation of Quranic verses in Arabic, an act expected of all preachers. He then proceeded to speak for what felt like hours, although his remarks could not have exceeded sixty minutes. The Muslim nation of Iran and its Shi'i leadership, he declaimed, anticipated a major change. A cultural and moral transformation was coming, one that would touch the innermost depths of our public and private lives.

"There will be nothing," he prophesized, "as it once was." "The Shah and his stooges have transformed," he continued, "our way of living, promising us happiness and satisfaction. In the name of *taraqqi* [progress] and *tajaddod* [modernity], they have taken away our religion, offering us only the illusion of a better material life. But today, as I am speaking to you, millions of Muslims all over the country are chanting 'death to you.' We are neither happy nor content. We call for the return to our faith and of our honorable leader."

Falsafi spoke in code, although the "you" whose downfall he spoke of was clearly the Shah and his "honorable leader" Khomeini. Although Khomeini went unnamed that night, Falsafi praised him for rightly diagnosing that the Shah intended to destroy Islam in the name of women's rights, progress, and development. Khomeini's courageous 1963 *ghiyam* [uprising] had alerted the Iranian people to a conspiracy to corrode Islam orchestrated by Baha'is, Israel, and other British lackies who exercised free rein over Iran's government. Why, he thundered after commenting on the friendly relations between Iran and Israel, was Iran's own government party to everything that Muslims so deeply detested?

He then pivoted from Islam's detractors to the resources, in the form of ethics and institutions like the family, that religion offered as defenses against this onslaught. Islam, he contested, reserves a special place for women and mothers, who safeguard the stability of the home and oversee the religious edification of children, while respecting the central role of men as head (*ra'is*) of the family. His crude gender stereotyping did not push me to the brink of frustration, perhaps since I had already heard such comments in his recorded lectures in Golpayegan. It was the rest of his talk that was more aggravating. He accused the Shah of conspiring to destroy Islamic values by encouraging women to dispense with the commitments necessary to be upstanding Muslims. The delicate nature of women, he claimed, would be sullied should they became involved in matters of public life, such as police work, the legal and criminal justice system, or the economy. He called the Shah's policies of gender equality a manifestation of Westoxification, and a "war" against our faith and ethical beliefs.

Falsafi's rebuke of the cultural changes introduced under Pahlavi Iran was by that point a familiar song to me. I had heard teachers and others in Golpayegan speechify about our "moral" decline more times than I could remember. Even then I sensed a reactionary undercurrent to the nostalgic rhetoric of the older generation, who seemed unable to accept that Iran had simply changed. Normally, I comforted myself with the thought that their ideas would vanish as soon as they themselves did. That night in Tehran, however, sitting in a sea of Falsafi's devotees, many of them as young as my friend Ebrahim, the reality of this discourse's transmission and longevity disturbed me. I realized, all at once, that the hundreds of people listening to this man celebrated his assault on our lifestyle. In my mind, Iranian reforms of the post-Mashruteh period, including the principle of women's rights, were hard-fought gains that generations of Iranians, from early constitutionalists to contemporary feminists, had toiled for. Why should we renounce our own victories?

A day or two later, we were in our usual gathering place, my friend Masoud's apartment. Masoud Dashtban was an artist working at the time for national television. I first met

Masoud in Sar-e Pol-e Zahab, where we were completing our military service together. I raised this question with my friends, mostly secular Tehranis. I asked if they too sensed a different narrative of the revolution forming, one hostile to our way of life and which hid its true intentions behind popular anti-Shah sentiment. Every one of them, it turned out, worried that what had been a struggle against authoritarianism was now morphing into a internecine cultural battle. One friend, a journalist, said that he had learned that Shapour Bakhtiyar, a nationalist statesman and opponent of the Shah who repeatedly warned Iranians of the tyranny of clerical government, had indicated to the press that the clergy was gaining upper-hand dominance in negotiations with the Shah. It was in the same round of negotiations in 1978 that Bakhtiyar, in a last-ditch effort to save the crumbling government, agreed to become prime minister. "What should we do?" asked my journalist friend. We sat in a ruminative silence, when Masoud sprang to his feet and announced: "There is no way we can turn back the clock and have millions of Iranian women enclosed at home. Iranians must continue to fight against the risk of becoming victims of the clerics." While I feared the future would not unfold as I had hoped, I could not have imagined that Iran after the revolution would be even more stifling than my high school or university years, when I feared, not only for my life, but for my family and friends, that the authorities might learn of my political activities.

Homa Nategh in Zahra's Paradise

By the time that I arrived at Behesht-e Zahra (Zahra's Paradise) cemetery on that October 1978 day, the crowd had splintered into smaller groups, each debating and discussing a different issue. The political parties and organizations that had turned out busied themselves with sloganeering. After ambling through this political patchwork, I joined a gathering of about twenty-five young people. I recognized a few of them as leftists from Tehran University, but roughly half of them, bearded men clad in grey and black, had the appearance of pro-Khomeini activists. When I joined the group, a discussion was already underway about the proper manner of showing support for the revolution. One person among the religious faction, growing visibly agitated as he spoke, his brow furrowed and hands flying, maintained that although we were in the midst of a revolution, propriety under these circumstances did matter. This was not an ownerless (*bi-saheb*) revolution; its leader was Khomeini and its ideology Islam. Another younger bearded demonstrator stepped forward and angrily shouted at others to stop sabotaging the revolution. It was then that one of my friends intervened: "Slow down please. You don't own the revolution. We are not sacrificing our lives for Islam or Mr Khomeini. This is a revolution for all Iranians, Muslim or not. It has many leaders, and Khomeini is but one of them. We have many others, including those on the left who have been struggling for decades. Now we are benefiting from the fruits of their struggle to free Iran."

Having entered this conversation midstream, I asked the person to my left what the issue was. A human rights activist had earlier given a talk on the memory of revolutionary martyrs, he explained. At the end of the talk, some in the crowd showed their respect by chanting "Allahu Akbar," while others, the leftists, clapped. This, the difference between chants and applause, had brought us to the present confrontation. I was not surprised. This was but one skirmish in a larger competition between Islamists and leftists. Some resisted the idea that Islam should be the language of the revolution. Rather than generalize religious sentiments to the whole revolutionary movement, we encouraged others to applaud speakers or to celebrate with nationalist or leftist slogans.

At some point, I decided the argument with the Islamist activists was a waste of time and began wandering the cemetery to see what else was going on, at which point I stumbled upon Homa Nategh and the foreign reporters I earlier mentioned. Many years later, in August 1983, Nategh and I had the chance to renew our acquaintance. I was a graduate student living in Washington, D.C., where I had grown involved in the pro-Fedayeen student movement. A violent purge of opposition forces, and of the Mujahedin, Fedayeen, and Paykar in particular, was underway in post-revolutionary Iran. Not a day went by without news of another wave of mass arrests or executions. The left, moreover, had continued to fragment, and factional disputes begot bitter conflicts. As this conflagration reached its climax, my friends and I in the U.S. joined a small group of radicals who had managed to escape from Iran to Paris, where they, under the leadership of Alireza Mahfoozi (alias Rahim) and Homa Nategh, had formed a new group, the Project of Revolutionary Socialists, in coalition with an Iranian Trotskyist organization. Sometime in August 1983 my friends in the U.S. proposed that I travel to Paris to meet with the project's leadership to learn how we might help them. I agreed to act as a liaison with the Paris leadership, which also included Torab Sales (an alias for Hormoz Rahimian), a member of the Trotskyist group.

This was a peculiar and trying interval in my own life. Against the backdrop of ideological battles within the pro-Fedayeen movement, I came under tremendous skepticism and scrutiny from people I had considered to be friends and comrades. Despite suffering their hostility and blame, I had difficulty thinking of them as horrible people. Yet I increasingly realized that I was nearing the end of the long road I had first taken in Golpayagen.

For these reasons, my trip from Washington, D.C. to London and Paris proved to be about more than party politics. While I was in London and before I had made it to Paris, word spread that our two comrades there, Rahim and Nategh, had disapproved of the views I expressed in my exchanges with U.K. student activists. One of the London activists, a friendly, reserved man in his twenties also named Ali, pulled me aside one day to warn, "Rahim and Nategh called from Paris and said, 'Watch Ali from Washington, D.C. He is having second thoughts about Marxism-Leninism and our ideological principles.'" The message from Paris had inflamed tensions within the group. Dismayed, I called a friend in Paris to ask what was going on. Nategh may have been behind this, he said, before adding that she herself was under pressure from the Trotskyists, who saw me as hostile to them.

I called Torab, the leader of the Trotskyist organization, with the intention of asking why he and his Paris associates were maligning me before we had even had the chance to meet. To my surprise, Torab answered my call with an invitation to his apartment. He was disarmingly friendly, and it was only after I got off the phone that I remembered I had called to ask if he was peddling accusations about me. In the end, my near three weeks in Paris were mostly spent in his company. He was an extremely kind and admirable political leader, if too orthodox and hung up on matters of ideological purity for my taste.

Years later, Nategh and a few other activist academics in exile formed *Dabireh*, a journal of pre-Islamic Iranian history and culture. She converted to Zoroastrianism and continued to produce historical works, but our tracks as researchers never crossed. Although I remembered her for her stern temperment, she remained someone I liked and even admired. We had our clashes, but she possessed a sharp mind I could not ignore.

Thirteen years before her death in 2016, Nategh denounced in a public letter the revolution and her role in it. Nategh recast her former revolutionary fervor as a fever dream that led her and the oblivious Iranian masses astray: "I am perhaps more culpable for my role in the revolution than others. I was a teacher and a scholar, but I was so moved by revolutionary excitement that I dispensed with all I had learned and joined the ignorant masses in the streets."[3] Nategh's recantation captures what she believed in 2003, but it is not a compelling explanation of her thinking and actions at the time of the revolution, when she was a leading figure in theorizing and strategizing the movement. Our earlier encounters suggest that her understanding of Islam and Khomeini's role in the revolution were not mere afterthoughts but areas of careful consideration. She made these views known to me that day at Behesht-e Zahra and publicly endorsed Khomeini's leadership and position on gender issues.

[3] Nategh, "Liberation of Women is not apart from Liberation of the Toiling Masses," *Kayhan*, Marhc 12, 1979.

Only a few months after the revolution's eventual triumph against the Shah, Nategh delivered a talk on Women's Day, March 5, 1979, which was reprinted in a national newspaper. Nategh beseeched Iranian women to join ranks with the Mujahedin and Khomeini in support of the revolution:

> Raising the women question, at this phase of our struggle, is a mistaken proposition. We should not be concerned about the women issue in the current situation. A person may have said something about *hijab*, but then rescinded it. Therefore, we should not instigate tensions around this matter [compulsory hijab]. We should join ranks with the Mujahedin, even if it requires us to wear a head cover . . .[4]

These do not strike me as the words of a reluctant follower, or a scholar swept up by revolutionary sentiment. Nategh offered a calculated argument for why Iranian women ought to unite with and follow the leadership of Ayatollah Khomeini:

> We are all part of the same nation [*mellat*] Imam Khomeini speaks about. We likewise desire to partake in the reconstruction of our country. We too are cognizant of the fact that this reconstruction is not achievable unless all militant forces who support democracy and are for an utter eradication of the imperialist and corrupt institutions of the old regime come together. We also believe that the freedom of women is not separate from the liberation of the toiling masses. And Imam Khomeini too advocates on behalf of toiling masses.[5]

[4] Nategh, "Liberation of Women is not apart from Liberation of the Toiling Masses," *Kayhan*, March 12, 1979.

[5] Ibid.

Although Nategh's unthought is perhaps irretrievable to us now, by casting comparative light on her, my own, and other revolutionaries' spontaneous participation in those heady days and our retrospective remembrances and recantations of them, I hope to lay one brick in what must be a collective effort to recuperate these fading traces.

5

Our Dreams On Trial, 1979

Revolution without Revolutionaries

Kazem had been released from prison only a few days when I met him at an apartment in central Tehran, close to the American Embassy, one October 1978 afternoon. He was not a particularly imposing man, but his wrinkled blue button-up shirt and faded pants clung to him, hinting at his muscles beneath. My friends and I had spent months toiling to arrange a meeting with a representative of the Fedayeen-e Khalq (People's Fedayee Guerrillas). I was not sure what I had expected a Fedayee, a member of the elusive Marxist-Leninist guerrilla group which the Pahlavi state's massive security apparatus had forcefully driven underground, to look like, but Kazem, an unassuming man of twenty-some years, scarcely resembled the hardened guerrilla I had imagined to find before me. In that apartment on Bahar Street, however, Kazem let loose a stream of stories of his years incarcerated at the notorious Evin Prison. His tales were laced not with boastful arrogance, however, but with care and caution.

He recounted conflicts he had with pro-Khomeini inmates and imprisoned Shi'i clerics. "They considered us Marxists *najes* [impure]," he explained, "and avoided touching or sharing meals with us." He warned us that though we may struggle for the same cause, certain clerical elements of the resistance abhorred the left more than they did the Pahlavi regime we were supposedly united against. All we could do, he encouraged, was to stay active in circulating Fedayee views, leaflets, and announcements.

I sat politely listening, but by October 1978 I had heard my share of such premonitions and borne the brunt of enough Khomeinists' hostilities to develop worries of my own about the course the revolution was taking. Growing impatient but hopeful that Kazem and the Fedayees had strategized an exit from this impasse, I put a blunt question to the recently freed guerrilla: Had they prepared for the possibility of a counterrevolutionary coup? At first, he was reluctant to respond to my question, simply emphasizing that "we are all Fedayees" and need not worry, since the group had behind them the support of hundreds of thousands of Iranian youths. But the pro-Khomeini forces have a clear, determined leader and sizeable resources to draw on, dwarfing anything the left might muster, I responded. "Do the Fedayees," I asked, thinking a second go at the question might do the trick, "have the leadership needed to respond to and meet the demands of the revolution?" Kazem looked vigilantly to his left and right before whispering, "The *sazeman* [organization] does not exist as an active body much outside of prisons, so it is up to you supporters to conduct yourselves as if you were the organization. You, our comrades, need to buy us some time."

He was right. The Fedayeen enjoyed the support of thousands of young Iranians, particularly high school students, yet by 1978, police surveillance had left them scattered across prisons and ill equipped to channel their supporters' energy into any productive outlets. Despite our efforts as eager young leftists to anticipate and actively shape the revolution, so much of it unfolded unpredictably, thwarting any blueprint we could have designed. Yet years later some observers opined that the revolution had been "planned" and carefully orchestrated by Marxist groups. The effective absence of the Fedayeen, as an organized party, exacerbated my worries about the future and made Khomeinists' claim to revolutionary leadership all the harder to challenge. While my willingness to protest the Shah earned me the respect of several Khomeinists at the university, our shared struggle was not enough. They insisted that all Iranians should abide by Ayatollah Khomeini's direction; anything less than full loyalty led to scornful charges of separatism and reactionary subversion. I argued with them that Khomeini, who had been exiled from the country for fifteen years, first in Turkey and then Iraq, no longer grasped the revolutionary hopes and desires of the people. Without discounting his political prowess and ability to mobilize the masses even from abroad, I maintained that we needed smart people steeped in the local dynamics and concerns of Iranians to lead the revolution. To this, the pro-Khomeini students responded that Khomeini was a wise man and that his aides and advisors, men like Ebrahim Yazdi, Sadegh Qotbzadeh, and Mehdi Bazargan (all of whom would go on to hold key posts in the post-revolutionary government only to denounce it shortly afterwards), would help manage the county and rid it of corruption and injustice. I found my argument that no real revolutionary could, after calling for the rights and self-determination of the people, consent to a group of outsiders leading the revolution compelling at the time. It was only after the downfall of the Shah that the irony that leftist parties, like the Fedayeen and Tudeh Party, largely existed and operated either outside the county or in prison dawned on me.

But that fall I had little wherewithal for reflection. Instead I threw myself into countless hours of organizing and demonstrating through near daily participation in public protests and behind closed doors in furtive agitation. By pooling together and tapping our contacts in government offices and private companies, my friends and I, an informal activist group of diverse political orientations, printed and disseminated flyers, communicated with better established revolutionaries, organized revolutionary art exhibits, and distributed censored books and other materials. Yet, despite our efforts to shore up a leftist bloc, a coherent and organized left never materialized. What does one do when revolution begins to surface, but the "professional revolutionaries" are nowhere to be found? As I said goodbye to Kazem and exited from Bahar Street, this question rang in my head. I was no closer than ever before to understanding how we had come to find revolution at our door and ourselves too late to answer it.

A Post-Pahlavi Iran

In early spring of 1978, I decided to apply to a graduate program in political science at the National University of Iran. I could not predict how things in Iran would go and in the absence of clarity, I wanted to remain in Iran long enough to see what political possibilities, the fruit of years of agitation, would blossom. But I did not want my academic goals to languish either. At last, one day the ranking of students who had taken university entrance exams was published in the paper, and to my pleasant surprise, I was placed second, behind a woman applicant. I took a copy of the newspaper, *Kayhan*, to my father. My father was very pleased with the news. Always thinking of my future, he said that being a top student in the program would go a long way toward helping me become a university professor one day. In short order, I matriculated as a graduate student to the National University. Despite the accomplishment, I felt no special attachment to the institution. My life still orbited around Tehran University, where my friends were either former or current students and where we met almost every day for protests, lectures, and our smaller debriefings. But all the time I had poured into political activism and organizing left my undergraduate GPA rather low, and I was not allowed to sit for its entrance exam.

By late September 1978, with my graduate student ID in hand, I ventured onto the campus of the National University to begin my program in political science. The National University straddled what was then the northernmost edge of Tehran and its outskirts. The campus, like so many other spaces where students concentrated, was a center of protest. Several younger faculty members from the political science department sometimes attended these rallies and dared to discuss politics with us. Despite their support for our endeavors, when later that month, talk of a university-wide strike cropped up, they chaffed at our plan to strike classes. With diplomatic tact, they asked that we let the university function alongside our protests.

We students felt, however, that only a complete shutdown of classes would signal student-faculty solidarity with the revolutionary movement and maybe even force the university administration to take action. Their concerns seemed shockingly out of step with the magnitude of what was transpiring before us. A revolution was playing out before their eyes, yet they expected us to ease up so that they might go on with their normal work of teaching. I confronted one of the professors and asked, how could one call himself a scholar of political science and at the same time willfully ignore politics beyond his classroom, all for the sake of ensuring the university's operations? Did he not, I continued, support the revolutionary movement and if so, why not join us? The young professor asserted that of course he was for the revolution. "In fact," he added, "university faculties are among the Shah's chief victims." But, he argued, it was precisely at this moment that faculty sympathetic to protests should keep their classrooms open so that they might teach what they had always wanted and transform the classroom into a radical learning place. Surprised by the thoughtfulness of his objections, I admitted that we shared the same goal, but that it was only after the fall of the Shah that classrooms might realize their full pedagogical potential. Until then, I reasoned, our energy ought to be focused on the singular task of removing him from power.

By October 1978 the downfall of the regime seemed imminent. Riots were engulfing the nation with increasing frequency and intensity, particularly after Black Friday, when, on September 8, 1978, clashes with military forces resulted in some 100 deaths and hundreds more injuries. Ministerial resignations revealed growing fissures even within official ranks. I was confident Iran was on the precipice of cataclysmic change and wondered whether there would be any need for me to go to the U.S. to continue my studies. By November 1978 the Pahlavi state had entered the irreversible process of collapse. Khomeini had defied attempts to negotiate a unity government with the Shah, who was at this point making desperate appearances on national television "approving" the revolution and promising to make amends. By November, Iranians began to wake to the fact that protesters were ruling city streets, university campuses, mosques, and even some state offices, since government institutions, including the military, had tipped toward the general strikes. The state was suddenly shorn of its ability to maintain even a semblance of control. Even a few members of parliament took to lambasting the state and lauding protestors, and their public denunciations and declarations were circulated on television and in national newspapers. I remember one particular parliamentary deputy, Ahmad Baniahmad, who publicly criticized and even moved to censure the government in March 1978 for its handling of riots in his native Tabriz the month prior, when police forces shot and killed twelve people and injured over a hundred others. As for those government officials who had not flipped, the growing opposition overwhelemed their confused and ad hoc responses. It was at this time that I began to turn my attention to what might replace the Pahlavi state in earnest.

The idea of building a new government was equal parts exhilarating and bewildering. Despite the growing and palpable presence of Khomeinists, the particularities of who might take power and in what capacity were not yet clear. A few leading politicians, such as Karim Sanjabi and Mehdi

Bazargan, seemed like natural candidates to lead an interim government. Sanjabi was the leader of the National Front and a loyal member of Mosaddegh's government in the 1950s. Bazargan was the leader of Nehzat-e Azadi (the Freedom Movement) and a respected Muslim who had cultivated close relationships with the ulama. Despite their anti-Pahlavi credentials, Sanjabi and Bazargan were ultimately liberal nationalists. It was difficult to picture a reformist leading a revolutionary government, let alone one possibly helmed by Ayatollah Khomeini. Yet neither was the left prepared to assume leadership, with its most experienced figures either dead, imprisoned, or exiled. Uncertainty, not hope, ruled my thinking about the future, and almost every day I found myself debating the unknowable with friends and strangers: a post-Pahlavi government.

Who Speaks for Revolution?

It was during these tumultuous days that my own experience of the revolution came to a head. I had helped nurture the revolution and thought it would treat me and others who had sacrificed for it kindly in return. With the state's power daily attenuating, I stole a glimpse into the collective kindness I had hoped for and began living a freer, less fearful life. But we, the leftist activists, had been designated the lesser revolutionaries, granted admission but no right to action. The Khomeinists expected us to follow their lead, mistreated our sister activists and, to the extent possible, marginalized the left's discourse, symbols, and history from the rituals of the revolution. They aspired to absolute control, but their success was partial, and the left's legacy lived on in traces. The students shot and killed for protesting Nixon's visit to Tehran continued to be commemorated, the Fedayeen were almost universally respected, and leftist literature proliferated so widely across Tehran that censorship, either from the state or rival political camps, proved futile. All this even though the revolution for religious activists meant foremost the country's moral and cultural renewal.

While the Khomeinists relented when it came to circulating censored writings and tracts that exceeded their sense of political propriety, Khomeini's leadership of the revolution was a point on which they would not compromise. Khomeini's uncontested right to the mantle of the revolution was a matter not just of revolutionary but religious faith for them. Clerics and other Khomeinists vigilantly asserted their authority over the proceedings and demonstrations I attended, not least by stamping them with massive posters and banners bearing their leader's visage, relegating others present by default to the position of followers. This endlessly frustrated me and my friends. We believed that we, the ordinary people who did the everyday work of showing up on the streets, were the genuine revolutionaries and feared the Khomeinists were short-changing the revolution by foreclosing other, useful ideas, which were not necessarily religious or sanctioned by the ulama.

The event that not only defined the revolution for me but also altered my life was set in motion by a proclamation from Khomeini. This communique in question directed Iranian students to cease at once all strikes and closures of offices, schools, and universities. The rationale for this curious pivot was murky. Some rumors had it that government and military officials were negotiating with Khomeini's representatives in Tehran, and Khomeini's order was meant to signal a good faith effort at cooperating. But many felt that hope for compromise had been shattered and could not comprehend why Khomeini would call for calm as the Shah's regime teetered toward collapse. I was at Tehran University the day Khomeini issued the declaration, which quickly monopolized the conversations underway. Those of us on the left were prepared, in defiance of Khomeini, to keep universities closed, but the pro-Khomeini camp insisted that his call could not be without reason. Khomeini, they argued, must know something we did not; he would not ask us to end the strikes if it simply meant capitulating to the Shah. I and others argued that whether he was privy to special knowledge or not, his judgment was misguided. It was easy to call a strike off but difficult to rebuild the momentum to resume it later. After some discussion, we decided we would not try to force an agreement between us that day. We would reconvene at the National University the next day to reach a resolution.

The following morning, I drove my old red Paykan, a popular Iranian-made car, to northern Tehran and parked it outside the National University in what appeared to be a no man's land. It was only when I reached the center of campus that I realized, for all the quiet on the fringes of campus, that hundreds of students had already congregated there. As the crowd waited for speakers to start the demonstration, students busied themselves with side discussions, and in some cases emotions ran high.

I slipped my way into a small group and listened to them debate how we ought to proceed. Some argued that perhaps going back to classes may not be such a bad idea. Protestors were at the zenith of their power, and if needed we could close classes in the future. But most others in the group felt that going back to classes would harm the revolution by redirecting thousands of students on to university campuses. Their absence from the streets, some feared, would help the government control opposition.

These splintered conversations continued for an hour or so until one student shouted, asking for everyone's attention. The crowd came to a standstill. Once the silence was total, he began to explain that we had gathered that day to determine whether to end the months-long student strikes that had swept across campuses and resume university classes or not. A few others came forward to speak. Some argued that this was not our decision to make, since the leader of the revolution, Khomeini, had already instructed us to allow universities to return to their regular operations. While some regarded his word as final and infallible, others dissented and argued that the strikes ought to continue, since without them, student leadership would splinter and our grip over the universities would loosen.

After an increasingly fractious volley of comments, the crowd started to come quickly undone. A contingent of pro-Khomeini students disrupted the speaker, branding him a traitor and an agent of the Soviet Union. Others were quick to return their insults, calling them stupid and brainless. It was then that one friendly looking student tried to restore order to the gathering. He called for everyone's attention and asked that we all stop talking. "Please let me remind you," he began, "that we are all part of one revolution, and we have already paid a dear price for what we have achieved. Let's be reasonable and find a rational solution to our disagreement." His sincerity calmed the crowd, who stood in a hush, wondering what he would propose. "Opinion is divided among two groups of students. You know where you stand," the mediator continued. "Half of us hold religious views, and the other half are leftists. Yet it is important that we come to a unified position about this. Resolution is possible," he continued, "since our disagreement today is not about faith or ideology, but political strategy." He then proposed that we take a ten-minute break, during which each group would delegate a person their representative. Each representative would then have fifteen minutes to make a case for or against the continuation of strikes.

But no such time was needed to select a spokesperson for the two groups. As soon as the mediator finished speaking, someone among the crowd of religious students shouted out a name as their leader. Their faction, without missing a beat, roared a collective "yes" in agreement. As if not to be outdone, a friend of mind next yelled out my name and a unanimous "aye" followed from our section. After the pro-Khomeini representative took a few minutes to prepare himself, the mediator who had proposed this process invited him to speak. He would have no more than fifteen minutes to explain why we should follow Khomeini's call to end the strikes and return to classes.

Everything was moving so quickly that I had no time to understand what I was being asked to do. It was only when my eyes met the sea of faces staring at me that I appreciated the weight of the burden placed on my shoulders. I must not fail, I thought to myself, to make a convincing case. Just as I felt my grip on the situation slipping again, however, the other speaker's words came into focus. "This revolution is not without a *saheb* [owner]," he began, "Imam Khomeini is the undisputed leader of our movement, and it is our moral and political duty to follow his *farman* [order]. Our decision is as clear as *aftab* [the sun]: Khomeini has asked us to return to class and stop the strikes, and so we must obey his order." He concluded his comments by reiterating the importance of unity and of throwing our energy behind the shared goal of creating a new society. The student's argument (more a reiteration of Khomeini's supremacy than anything else) came as no surprise. It was the same line of reasoning almost all Khomeinists invoked when someone challenged their leader's claim to the revolution. Their emphasis on one man's right to rule and on the clergy's "ownership" of the revolution struck me as a poor, undemocratic way of motivating Iranians to mobilize against the Shah. While it lit a fire in me that day, their unrelenting claim to leadership now seems like a strategic move meant to naturalize Khomeini's post-revolutionary assumption of power, even if it meant alienating some members of the opposition.

When my turn came to speak, I felt positive that I could deliver a restrained but resolute case for continuing the strikes. "Dear friends and all who have gathered," I started, "please ask yourself, why are we here today? What has compelled us, we who come from different parts of Iran and may not know each other, to assemble together? What are we here for as a community? That we are here is no coincidence. We are not sheep who have lost their way. We are here because we are revolutionaries. We have clear goals and are ourselves leaders of this amazing movement. We are here because the Shah and his regime do not believe in us and because they see university students and Iranian youth as either educated servants or a deviant and infantile bunch. I am saddened, as I am sure you are too, that our friend used a similar line of reasoning to convince us to obey a leader who, despite his remove from the country, gets to decide that we should stop protesting." Then, in my own way, I attempted to build a bridge between the two groups, "Yet I am happy to see Ayatollah Khomeini and other Shi'i leaders support the revolution. He has suffered at the hands of the Shah, but his suffering is no greater than those of us who wish to continue the strike. I agree that we need to maintain unity and a common purpose to the struggle. But if it is to remain ours, I humbly ask that you do not do as you are told but as you think is reasonable and correct. Listen to your own hearts and minds and I am sure we will vote for the continuation of the strikes." And on that note, I ended my comments, hoping I had succeeded in convincing everyone that we should stay the revolutionary course.

The crowd did not wait for me to finish my talk before bursting out in shouts of support and applause. Our moderator, based on the crowd's cheers for me alone, concluded that the overwhelming majority of those present agreed with me and, so it followed, were in favor of continuing the university strikes. I was elated, but a nagging apprehension ate at me. Perhaps I had gotten carried away and, in a rush to win, had been excessively harsh when I should have been searching for more common ground. A stream of students approached me afterwards, some congratulating me, others chiding me for dismissing the Imam, who, unlike leftists, they reminded me, was supported by Iranians outside the university. I responded as calmly as I could that the power of student activists should not be minimized; hadn't youth movements and the May 1968 protests sent shockwaves throughout the world, after all?

And universities may be rarefied places, but when the Shah tightened his absolutist grip on the country, resistance still emanated from universities, which, I reminded, had played a decisive role in leading the revolutionary movement. Of course, they disagreed and credited Khomeini for initiating the *nehzat* (movement) in June 1963, or 15 Khordad, when his denunciation of the government's violation of the constitution as corrupt and servile to foreign powers resulted in his arrest, setting off waves of protests across the nation.

By the time I finished addressing the supporters and critics who had approached me, the campus was deserted. Other than a few idling students, I saw no one in sight. I had been in high spirits and gratified with what happened, but once alone, I felt nervous and sapped of energy. I headed for my car, parked on the edge of campus in a vacant lot. After walking for fifteen minutes, I spotted it, a red speck on an empty stretch of land, and quickened my pace toward it. At the exact moment that I reached into my pocket for my car keys, I felt the weight of the world come crashing down on my head. Everything stopped. When I next opened my eyes (many hours later, I would learn), I was prostrate in a ditch in the middle of a landfill. A few children and two or three adults hovered high above me, flanking either side of the ditch. Seeing my eyes flutter open, they shouted out, "He's not dead!" All I could do was open my eyes; I had lost control of my body and could not stand or turn my neck to look around. My memory was a blank from the moment I reached for my car keys on. I had no idea how I had ended up in a dump. But before I could try to piece together a timeline, an ambulance arrived and rushed me to the hospital.

For the next few hours, in the ambulance and at the hospital, I struggled to remember anything as I drifted in and out of consciousness. When I next woke, I was lucid enough to establish some basic facts: it was night-time, and I was in a hospital. The nurses and a doctor joked that God must have favored me, since I was alive thanks to a *mo'jezeh* (miracle) or else stupendous luck. Before I could concentrate enough to ask what had happened, they explained that some kids were playing in a village outside of Tehran when they saw a white Paykan stop at a nearby landfill. A man stepped out from the car, opened the trunk, and extracted from it a body, which he dumped into the ditch in broad daylight before quickly driving off. The children informed their parents, who called for an ambulance. I had been stabbed many times. Some wounds were superficial, others more severe, and I had lost a significant amount of blood. Fortunately, none of the wounds were to sensitive parts of my body, and I was released from the hospital that night. What tore at me most on that long drive home was thinking that I was targeted not by the Shah's police or security forces, as I had long feared I would be, but by other revolutionaries for the crime of not supporting Khomeini. This realization plunged me into an existential crisis just as our long-awaited dream of revolution was on the precipice of success. With it, the revolution cut into my heart.

Washington, D.C., 1986

After this incident, I decided that I should leave Iran and go to the U.S. to continue my studies. I arrived at the decision in a matter of minutes as my friend, Mohammad, drove me home from the hospital. When I shared the news with my parents, my father enthusiastically approved. The situation in Iran, he reassured me, was unpredictable and going to the U.S. for graduate school would be my best option. My mother was supportive too, but she worried I was being impulsive and might want to stay in Iran after all. Many of my relatives and friends who had no knowledge of what happened to me and knew me as a political activist could not understand my rationale for leaving the country at the revolution's climax. One friend went so far as to confront me and asked why I was leaving and withdrawing my support from the revolution. It was hard to hear such as comment, but I did not want to use what had happened to me as an excuse for leaving the country, and at any rate, I hardly felt ready to confide in even my closest friends about it. I just reminded everyone that my plan had always been to visit for a short time before moving on to the U.S. to study. I would leave for Washington, D.C., where I would stay with my uncle, as soon as I was well enough to travel.

On the way to the airport that day, I sat in the back seat listening to my parents plot my future with a hand resting on my bandages, too absorbed in the unreality of all that had happened to say a word. The life I knew in Iran was now nothing but a blur, dissolving with the same ease as the streets we whirred past. And so weeks later, I watched the Shah leave Iran from a television in Washington, D.C, unable to celebrate the revolution's triumph. I would not step foot in Iran again for fifteen years, only to become in a few short years a *persona non grata*, culturally shunned and figuratively non-existent.

It was the summer of 1986 when I first tried to return to Iran. I had just defended my doctoral dissertation and was preparing to start the next stage of my life working and teaching at a uniersity. I felt strongly that I should work at a university in Iran, and perhaps be to a younger generation of Iranians what my mentors had been to me. This had been my plan when I left Iran for the U.K. And even after the attack on me, I felt compelled to work in my country. I was prepared to endure a month or two in jail when I arrived in Tehran, given my ongoing student activism in the U.S., but I did not think the authorities would hold me much longer than that or seriously harm me. So one late August day, around four in the morning (since they could only process a limited number of visa applications per day), I drove from my home in northern Virginia to the Islamic Republic's Interests Section in Washington, D.C. and waited in line to apply for a new passport. After idling for hours in a linoleum-floored and fluorescent-lit waiting room, at around ten in the morning a staff member finally called my name. I jumped from my plastic seat and walked to the window, where he collected my application, passport pictures, and documents and instructed me to return after three that afternoon to pick up my passport.

I returned later that day, expecting to retrieve my passport and be on my way. Instead, the same man showed me to a small private room. Behind its unmarked door was nothing other than two chairs and a gray table, and the only thing gracing its four walls was a framed picture of Khomeini. I was told to wait and sat there for maybe fifteen minutes, wondering why the officers had separated me from the others. Then a young man opened the door, entered, and apologized for the delay. He sat down and quietly passed me a piece of paper. He whispered, leaning in close to me, "There is a telephone number written on the paper I have given you. Please call

Mr Kashani. He will explain everything." He then showed me to the door and calmly said, "*Shoma mas'aleh darid* [you have a problem]." If leaving without a passport wasn't enough, these words confirmed my fear: I had been blacklisted. I did not argue and asked only for the documents I had submitted that morning. The young man again said, "Call the number on Wednesday. Mr Kashani will explain everything to you."

I returned to my apartment in northern Virginia, confused and depressed. Visions of my Iranian homecoming had carried me through the last hard months of graduate school, but now that was gone. I called Mr Kashani on Wednesday knowing full well I had been barred from entering the country. Mr Kashani was expecting my call, and as soon as I introduced myself, he said, "Hello. We were surprised to learn that you had decided to return to Iran. May I ask the reason for your visit?" I could sense the sarcasm in his voice, but I pretended not to notice and blithely replied, "There is no plan. I have completed my studies and am going back home." Annoyed, he thundered, "I mean no disrespect but allow me to be frank and tell you that you will never again set foot on Iranian land. Please make your goodbyes to Iran; you won't be returning for the rest of your life. You are a counterrevolutionary and Iranians will not welcome you. Make a home in the United States for yourself." His words were heartrending, and I could tell how it pleased him to crush another person's hopes and dreams. He was wrong, I told him; one way or another, I would make it back. I was only sorry that a revolution I had participated in now had such a callous man speaking on its behalf. He suddenly changed his tone and politely replied, "I did not mean to upset you. You are a leader of the opposition, and it is in your own best interest that you do not go to Iran."

My Teacher is in Town

Today, I split my time between New York City, where I work at New York University, and the small town of Cranbury, New Jersey, located just outside of Princeton. One afternoon, in late October 2009, I was visiting an Iranian scholar who also lived in Princeton. He had been a professor in Iran when I was an undergraduate student at Tehran University in the 1970s. We usually met or spoke on the phone several times a year, but I had arranged this meeting specifically to interview him about Ahmad Fardid, who I was in the early stages of writing a book about. My friend's first-hand observations of Fardid provided important information I had so far been unable to attain from other sources and helped confirm the impression I had formed of Fardid's politics and fondness for the Shah. But to my dismay, my friend asked that I not use his name or the information he provided in what ultimately became the book. However, my disappointment subsided when he casually mentioned toward the end of our conversation, "You know, Dr Shafi'i Kadkani is in town and will be at Princeton University for almost a year." I excitedly asked him to please let Kadkani know that I would be thrilled to see him. He agreed to bring it up but added warily that Kadkani had been spending most of his days at the library, and that it would be difficult to tear him away from his research when his time here was limited.

That one of my dearest university teachers and I should land in this tiny corner of New Jersey at the same time made a reunion, after almost four decades, seem fated. That night, still animated by the prospect of seeing my old professor after so long, I started looking up Kadkani online. The website of the Institute of Advanced Studies, where Kadkani would be affiliated from September 2009 to July 2010, announced that "Mohammad-Reza Shafi'i-Kadkani will be studying manuscripts related to the Karramiyya sect in the context of wider debates about Sufism and notions of asceticism in ninth-century Khorasan and their social and political background." By the end of the night, I had downloaded a folder full of writings I planned to read before our upcoming meeting.

The Sufi Karramiyya order did not ring a bell, but its connection to Khorasan established a clear through line with Kadkani's other research and writing. That night I continued my research, and more recently, I consulted with my colleague at NYU, Ismail Fajrie Alatas, a scholar of Islam. I learned from him that the Karramiyya are a relatively marginal sect whose writings are not easy to access. He explained, "Sufi production of literature was dominated by Arabic until the eleventh century. Only in the eleventh century do we begin to see Sufi literature written in Persian . . . [and] we can speak more confidently of a Sufi contribution to Persian literature. That development was part of the development of Baghdadi-style Sufism in Khorasan, becoming more prominently part of that region's religious landscape."

Still giddy with excitement, I answered a call from my friend the next day, expecting to hear that he had arranged a meeting between Kadkani and me in the not too distant future. I was in for some disappointing news instead: "I do not think Dr Kadkani wants to see you. He has already explained that he has no desire to see other Iranians. He is analyzing a set of Arabic texts, and all he wants to do is read them." Dr Kadkani was the kindest professor I had. Now that he was on leave, staying in my small town, he had no time to meet me or other Iranians. The revolution speaks to us in strange ways. Because of it, I cannot return to my country of birth, nor can I see my favorite teacher, even when he is only a fifteen-minute drive from me. All of it is too much to bear. Perhaps Michel Foucault was right to describe the Iranian revolution as "the most modern and maddest form of revolt." As a child of *ghorbat*, I sought sanctuary in political activism and the company of others who shared my desire for a new Iran. Now I sadly recognize that the revolution has driven Iranians farther apart than they have ever been. Dr Kadkani's disinterest in seeing me, or any other Iranian living in the U.S. for that matter, is a reminder of how our lives have been torn to pieces one cannot patch back together.

Conclusion
East Coast, U.S., 1980–2021

The Forbidden Box of Unthoughts

Time is not a friend of revolutions. With the passage of time, revolutions grow distant from their ideals, opening their successes and shortcomings up to fresh contestation. This perpetual flux makes thinking about them difficult, not least because "popular" remembrances of revolutions, including of the Iranian revolution, tend to be filtered through the prism of present feeling. The judgment of those writing in proximity to revolutions is often warped by the still receding shadow of upheaval, and so they write of solidarity, hope, and boundless promises. But post-revolutionary power struggles have a way of stifling the spirituality of revolutions (that is, their electric sense of shared purpose and hope). Stories sediment into orthodox narratives of loss and despair. Yet the ossification of and disenchantment with revolutions forms part of their histories too, so we ought to confront these aspects by reverting to a view of the revolution in its early days.

My memories of the revolution's end are clouded by my flight from Iran on the threshold of its success and my entry into a movement opposed to the post-revolutionary government. Yet distance has only deepened my affection for Iran. It was only after I spent several years in the United States that I came to appreciate it as my home, as a unified idea. In Iran, I had been a stranger everywhere I went and so thought of the country as a project still in the making. It was one member of a worldwide community of developing nations striving for self-actualization. But with distance comes perspective, and I now see Iran has much to tell us. Unearthing and sharing its stories with the world has been my life's work. My appreciation for Iran's specificity, however, has been replaced by a new kind of *ghorbat*, since little hope remains of my returning and living there.

The Algerian philosopher Mohammed Arkoun once argued that thinking and remembering always happen within the bounds of the unthinkable and the unthought. The moments we cannot or do not remember may seem incidental to our life narratives but are in fact at the core of them. These unthought moments, a curious feature of our lives and psyches, cannot be readily retrieved by conventional ways of thinking. This is not to suggest that humans are estranged from themselves, or incapable of self-reflection. In fact, the unthought is not about the absence or avoidance of thought but about the extent to which forgetting is central to thinking. Our thoughts, a substantive world of images and convictions, occupy and derive from individual and collective minds. To think about the unthought, or those opaque moments in our life, requires confronting the unfamiliar, the undesirable, and all else that we take for granted and leave unexamined, as sources of knowledge. It is often in moments of crisis and malaise, when hope is in short supply, that we may reach for memories, ideas, and experiences we had stopped thinking about.

I recently came to the alarming realization that Iran is splintering into pieces, a million fragments adrift in the world each with its own story to tell. The Iran I see fragmenting is not the country in its territorial sense, but an idea remembered and reconstituted by Iranians across generational, political, and geographical faultlines. These imaginative nationalisms are untethered to land, borders, and the ideologies that cohere them. Iran is encountered as fragments, but each of its parts is imagined as a totality to be celebrated. But with the revolution, which once united so many Iranians, this totality is coming undone as Iranians grow physically distant and emotionally alienated from the country. These are my private thoughts, or to be more precise, my attempts at remembering my "unthoughts," as Arkoun explained the term.

While I am still far from reflecting fully upon all that I long ago pushed to the corners of my mind, recalling the individuals I mention in these pages came naturally. I often think of the lives of my mentors, Dr Hamid Enayat, Abuzar Vardasbi, and Dr Shafi'i Kadkani, and our predicaments after the revolution. I was denied the opportunity to visit and talk with these three individuals I so admired after becoming one of the revolution's early "casualties." I had spent my days and nights in meetings and demonstrations fighting Pahlavi authorities until my departure from Iran. Yet I was far more enthusiastic about the revolution a year before it succeeded than when it happened. Every day that passed, I became more unsettled with the situation unfolding before my eyes.

Reflections on a Strange Time

Life as an intellectual and activist was complex and often confusing, yet amid the disorder and changes enveloping Iran, there was a certain continuity. From Golpayegan to Tehran, religion and Marxism operated alongside one another, however uneasily, in public spaces of opposition. Both Islam and Marxism colored my high school environment in Golpayegan. Although Islam was undoubtedly dominant, Marxism, as embodied by my two Tehrani teachers, Mr Eshraghi and Mr Amjadi, was fully alive, if marginalized. At Tehran University, by contrast, the boundary separating the two was blurred. Individuals, parties, and movements drew on both freely, never thinking of the two as mutually exclusive, as we might understand the terms to be today. If this presents an ideological conundrum, it can only be explained with reference to a wider national and even geopolitical context.

The Pahlavi state throughout the 1960s and 1970s actively attempted to manage the boundaries of acceptable political and intellectual discourse by suppressing public or even academic discussion of the political history of post-constitutionalist Iran. Reflecting on the two decades prior to the revolution, five decades later, I realize that a striking part of our political and intellectual lives was the collective amnesia administered by the state, which marshalled and manipulated history to serve its repressive ends. Our professors were often handmaidens to rewriting the past. They submerged whole episodes of Iranian history into oblivion in favor of disseminating in lectures and literature a "national" history and memory friendlier to the state. The unthought was constructed for us, constraining the possible limits of our intellectual horizon and political vision.

The state's local counterparts, intellectual elites and educators whose jargon and references situated ordinary people outside the borders of belonging, made public forgetfulness possible. The frequent and pointless debates dominating the university about alienation, existentialism, and Hegel exemplified this. What presented itself as radical debate was often a form of jockeying for status and power. This is perhaps what Dr Enayat implied when he advised me to forsake the shallow intellectualism of Pahlavi Iran to study in Europe. However, the stakes were even greater than he suggested. Enayat had implied that there existed "another world"—the West—where students and scholars engaged with these issues substantively. Iran, like so many other countries politically, economically, and ideologically assailed by European colonialism, was gripped by a crisis of meaninglessness and intellectual impotence.

What does this mean for understanding revolutionary and post-revolutionary Iran? This confusion was what, at least at an intellectual level, fueled the revolution, which also attempted to resolve it. Khomeini's purified religious revival, with its promise of a white-hot path to worldwide salvation, offered an unequivocal answer to this vexation. A convenient way of describing the political and intellectual climate of the 1970s is perhaps to describe Iran as gripped by a split personality. This is ironically how one man at the center of the madness, Daryush Shayegan, attempted to explain it. Shayegan, a disciple of Henri Corbin's doctrine of eastern spirituality and of Ahmad Fardid's anti-Western nativism, which transformed into a call for clerical rule in Iran, diagnosed Iran, along with many other Muslim countries caught between "tradition," on the one hand, and the hegemony of Western modernity, on the other, with a case of "cultural schizophrenia." One wonders if Shayegan's idea of cultural schizophrenia is adequate to the reality of Iran in the 1970s, or whether it projects a state of mind prevalent among the Iran elite until recently.

Another approach to understanding the revolution involves stepping back to reflect on the constellation of ideas motivating intellectuals and activists. Were we so enthralled by what was going on in the world that we failed to grasp the magnitude of what was unfolding in our own streets? Or were we so motivated by radicalism or nationalism that we failed to think practically about politics? Was the idea of the nation the organizing principle to our efforts, and Islam and Marxism merely the resources at our disposal to address a crisis of national identity? The future of the country was undeniably important to those of us protesting. Yet we did not use the language of nationalism to tell our stories. Instead, protestors, whether Marxist, religious, or any of the shades in between, insisted on bringing an international perspective to bear on all matters related to Iran.

Perhaps the idea of transnationalism—and the sense of networked interactions and exchanges between communities, cultures, and political ideologies it invokes—could help clarify the situation. The 1960s and 1970s were global decades, a fact mirrored in the proliferation of ideas such as the Third World, the East, Marxism (whether its Soviet, Chinese, or Latin American schools), political Islam, and Westoxification. The Pahlavi state ironically encouraged transnational thinking. Government censorship limited our discussion of Iranian history and social movements, while permitting the coverage, translation, and dissemination of writing and reporting on the Third World. Given the state's official and public patronage of anti-imperialist, anti-Western, and even some anti-Western Marxist materials, a transnational perspective was partly cultivated from without.

Third World resistance movements and revolutionary ideas helped make sense of ourselves and our national predicament. While newspapers and magazines—like *Keyhan*, *Ferdowsi*, *Negin*, *Tamasha*, *Bonyad*—wrote extensively on Iran's membership in the East or the Muslim world, the left invoked the Third World to emphasize inequality and injustice as a global consequence of First World exploitation and to signal solidarity with Latin America, Palestine, and elsewhere. While most of us cared little about the idea of Westoxification (gharbzadegi), a term preferred by the Third Force (*niru-ye sevvum*), a splinter group of former Tudeh intellectuals with a strong print-media presence in the 1950s and 1960s, state-run television programs and publications latched onto this idea. They, especially in the 1970s, gave air to seemingly radical ideas like eastern spirituality (*ma'anviyat-e sharqi*) and Westoxification with surprising frequency. Ehsan Naraghi's nativist arguments for prioritizing Islamic values over modern democracy and spirituality over scientific thinking, especially in light of the decline of the West, were publicized widely. This development was hard to grasp, since we were used to encountering these ideas through the work of anti-state thinkers like Shari'ati, Al-e Ahmad, and Samad Behrangi. That a pro-western and modernizing state would engage in public criticism of its own value system was indeed confusing.

One day in 1972, after listening to Ehsan Naraghi lecture on *Gav* (The Cow), Dariush Mehrjui's 1969 classic of Iranian New Wave cinema, I began to doubt my own understanding of the film. *Gav*, Naraghi argued disdainfully, exemplified the inability of westernized Iranian writers and artists to understand so-called traditional life in rural Iran. The film, with its depiction of a marauding bandit's assault on a village where the stability of life is held together by silence, distorted the reality of rural Iran. Naraghi instead argued that in rural Iran, the close, paternalistic relationship between landlords and peasants is an ideal model for communal care, not a model superior to the parliamentary monarchy established after 1906. Yet it was Naraghi, who having spent much of his life in Europe and ingratiated himself to the royal court, made a career for himself promoting a fictive image of Iran's rural past. Similar feelings stirred in me watching the philosopher-provocateur Ahmad Fardid's TV appearances, where he defended so-called Eastern and Iranian culture against Western cultural hegemony. How did these people, educated in Europe and close to the government, become radical anti-Western intellectuals?

At Tehran University, I witnessed similar intellectual confusion. Hamid Enayat had once been a Marxist and translated the works of modern European thinkers, but he ultimately joined the company of cultural conservatives like Ahmad Fardid and Morteza Motahhari. How do we reconcile the cosmopolitanism of Enayat's biography, studying and working in London and Oxford, with the purposeful provincialism of his intellectual outlook? What does this compound of provincialism and cosmopolitanism teach us about the unthought in the

Iranian Revolution? These contradictions were not only true of Iran, but societies where the desire for a cohesive identity capable of transcending communal strife becomes mired in a logic that blames the persistence of conflict on the "other" and so sets out to destroy it.

Shadow Revolutionaries

The Islamist movement and Shi'i clergy in post-revolutionary Iran found no space for shadow revolutionaries after their rise to dominance and success. Instead, they compelled Iranians who had been eager to free their country to flee for exile and imagine their nations from afar. This turned out to be true for Hamid Enayat, Abuzar Vardasbi, Homa Nategh, Karim Lahiji, myself, and countless others.

In the months immediately after the revolution, Vardasbi, my university friend and fellow activist, returned to his home in Mazandaran, a lush and beautiful province nestled against the Caspian Sea in northern Iran. He threw himself into aiding the farmers of the region. In those years, land distribution and agricultural reform were subjects of national importance. I was not surprised to learn that Vardasbi chose to dedicate himself to advocating for distributive policies that would ameliorate some of the poverty and insecurity farmers faced. During our days at Tehran University, Vardasbi was fascinated by Iranian agrarian history and its land tenure systems. It was through him that I first learned of the British historian of Iran Ann Lambton. Vardasbi explained that an English diplomat who had conspired to stifle prime minister Mohammad Mosaddegh's nationalization of the oil industries had recently written a comprehensive book on the history of

Iranian land tenure, *Malek va Zarra' dar Iran* (Landlord and Peasant in Persia). In that same conversation, Vardasbi also mentioned that he was researching the history of *malekiyat-e arzi* (land ownership) in Iran, which he saw as a corrective to Soviet arguments about the feudal nature of pre-modern Iran. Sometime in 1978 I visited a bookstore in Tehran and stumbled by chance upon his book *Iran dar Puye-ye Tarikh* (Iran in Historical Perspective). Reading him tackle Soviet and European assessments of Iran's pre-modern economy and extensively discuss revolts against the Arab conquests and rule, I was reminded of the Vardasbi I knew in my student days.

But as it turns out Vardasbi's work in Mazandaran was short lived. Two years after the revolution, as groups like the Mujahedin violently confronted the Islamic Republic, Vardasbi fled for France and later Germany. As the Mujahedin degenerated into a cult, Masoud Rajabi, their leader, appointed Vardasbi the group's philosopher. After a few years in Germany, he moved to Iraq to build a library for the Mujahedin camp there. In 1988, at the end of the Iran–Iraq War, the Mujahedin, mobilized, armed, and supported by Saddam Hussein and the Iraqi army, advanced toward southwestern Iran as part of Operation Forough Javidan (Eternal Light). My old friend and mentor joined the reckless operation along with his wife and, with it, both plunged to their death.

My old professor Hamid Enayat stayed in Iran for some time after the revolution. To my surprise, I learned that the man who earlier assiduously avoided politics, even in private conversation, had developed a public political profile. After the revolution, he joined the *Jebhe-ye Demokratik-e Melli*

(National Democratic Front), a coalition of left and liberal nationalists formed after the revolution. The NDF championed political freedom, the rigorous protection of individual rights, a free press, and economic equality. It boycotted the referendum to make Iran an Islamic Republic and supported a loose system of local councils as an alternative form of decentralized governance. Shokrallah Paknejad, a well-known leader of the Palestine Group, led this coalition, and Enayat accompanied him to Dr Mosaddegh's grave where they announced the NDF's platform shortly after the revolution.

For his refusal to remain quiet as the Khomeinists undemocratically seized power, Enayat was targeted during the purges of the cultural revolution. He lost his university position and left Iran for the U.K. in 1980, where he joined the faculty of Oxford University. Only two years later, during a flight from Paris to London, Enayat died of a heart attack. His death was untimely, but those who knew him admired that he passed with his integrity intact.

Dr Shafi'i Kadkani remained in Iran and is, by all indications, flourishing under the Islamic Republic. As far as I know, Kadkani abandoned politics following the revolution in favor of cultivating his status as a scholar of classical Persian literature. However, recently he engaged in a series of commentaries regarding the right of minorities (Azeris, Arabs, Kurds, and others whose native language is not Persian) to preserve their linguistic and ethnic particularities through separate educational systems. A few months ago he commented that Persian literature is the essence of Iranian culture, demoting Turkish and Kurdish literature to merely local works. This excited debate in Iran, but saddened me, since his stance seems estranged from the broad-minded and cosmopolitan literary critic I once knew.

As for my upstanding and somewhat uptight high school teacher Mr Tavakol, a friend recently shared startling information about his life after the revolution. It was a YouTube clip featuring Bahram Moshiri, an Iranian talk-show host living in the U.S. Moshiri was born and raised in Golpayegan, where he graduated from Ferdowsi High School a few years ahead of me. In this short segment, he describes Mr Tavakol's life before the revolution in terms entirely familiar to me: Moshiri remembers him as a decent and quiet man, respected for his learnedness in Arabic and erudition in etymology, or the origin of words. In the run-up to the revolution, Mr Tavakol played a leading role in mobilizing students and teachers against the Shah and, once again within the realm of what I thought to be true, was recognized by the people of Golpayegan as a revolutionary leader. Because of his known commitment to Islam and reputation as an upstanding man and a respected teacher, after the revolution Mr Tavakol became a leading political authority in the town. Yet I was shocked to learn what he did with this power.

According to Moshiri's report, Mr Tavakol quickly organized several flogging stations at public intersections. He ordered the arrest of anyone even suspected of misconduct. The accused would be brought to one of the public flogging tables, before hundreds of spectators, for a beating. Mr Tavakol himself, according to Moshiri, stood at the head of the flogging podium, reading Qur'anic verses aloud as the accused man was whipped.

Mr Tavakol's excessive cruelty and abuse of public confidence and power, however, did not go unchallenged.

As Moshiri, an eyewitness to his downfall, tells it, his extrajudicial abuses eventually sparked popular backlash and the people of Golpayegan, fed up with his abuses, assembled to find and perhaps kill him. Tavakol, in turn, quickly fled Golpayegan, never to return.

Theater of Madness?

My life is but one story of the triumphs, turmoil, and terror that engulfed Iran as people there struggled to realize freedom in the shadow of an oppressive police state. To the same extent, my life between *ghorbat* and religious and secular activism capture the conflicting worlds that combusted in 1978 to unleash a social and political fire that, in many ways, continues to burn from Europe to Africa, to the Middle East and South Asia, and to the United States. Iranians are stranded today between the good society they desired to create, and the unbearable situation they find themselves in today. If my generation risked material comfort for a "higher good," was our failure a political defeat or a delusional mistake, as Homa Nategh bitterly suggested? The idea that material comfort (which was, in any case, still only enjoyed by a narrow portion of Iranians) should be prioritized above human dignity, social justice, and democracy produces an existential challenge for us. If the revolution in Iran was a transitory setback, then it is the task of today's generation to change the course and right what went wrong. However, if the revolution was a theater of madness, smart people performing a reckless game, the task is greater and more unavoidable. Either way, one may say that today we are all the children of the 1978 revolution in some measure. The rise of Bin Laden, ISIS, and extreme populisms in the twenty-first century are perhaps a reminder of the global reach of what started in the late twentieth century.

Reflecting on my memories of the decades preceding the revolution has helped me better understand the nature of revolutions and ideological power (or lack there of) in autocratic states, including in the post-revolutionary Islamic Republic. It is a mistake to conceive of public discourse as an extension of state ideology and its socio-economic support system. The Pahlavi state lacked the omniscience to control public thought, as if by a massively labored conspiracy. Nor was there an alien episteme burying an indigenous imagination. Rather, the state, in its often half-blind efforts to secure political longevity against the rising wrath of the masses, deliberately suppressed or discredited intellectual lines that threatened its legitimacy. In this context, the state succeeded in marginalizing certain secular ideas, but at the expense of letting religious political discourse capture the public imagination.

The state encourages the public to latch their rage onto imaginary enemies—malevolent foreign powers, ethnic minorities, regional conflicts—to spare itself the scrutiny that would threaten its legitimacy and stability. Yet precisely because it is the same state that leads its citizens into disaster, it cannot muster the ideological self-defense needed to secure its survival. This was the unhappy fate of the Pahlavi regime. It believed that by fermenting an anti-Western, spiritualist nationalism, it could crush the memory of the Constitutional Revolution and of Mohammad Mosaddegh's Nationalist movement. By labeling these movements contaminations wrought by "Western disorder," the regime believed it could secure approval for its project of autocratic modernization without democratic participation. The propaganda strategy failed and brought to power a tortured ideological hybrid of colonial humiliation and autocratic control of all public institutions.

Small Towns, Big Stories

I can find no better tableau for understanding the revolution's course than the almost forgotten world of Iran's small towns which stood in curious relation to Tehran. My family followed the pattern typical for civil servants of moving from one town to another every few years, stretching my adolescence across the small towns of Dorud, Nahavand, and Golpayegan. We spent our time in the company of other government officials stationed along western and central Iran. Although my father's vocation set us apart from others, places like Nahavand and Golpayegan, neither fully rural nor urban, were home to the vast bulk of Iran's national population at the time.

Yet such towns have received little attention in discussions about the revolution. This is perhaps because they militate against our models of modern social change. A small town such as Golpayegan is not a likely candidate for incubating radical politics. However, it was the sixties. Even in Golpayegan, we were aware of the youth movement in Paris, the anti-war movement in New York, and of our own radical groups in Tehran, Tabriz, Mashhad, and Shiraz. So did even our humble town join the radical 1960s? I am inclined to think it did, which should provoke new thought about the circulation of ideas and what the local and global may mean.

When it comes to the Iranian revolution, the experience of Tehran is typically centered. However, there is much to learn about Iran's political and intellectual life in the 1960s and 1970s from the perspective of its overlooked towns. Golpayegan can help us get at smaller stories buried beneath official ones. The distance between how small-town Iranians thought and lived and what the government claimed on their behalf, the internal diversity among them owing to class, religious, and other differences, and their willingness to resist local and national elites is greater than we might have realized. Although the experience of living and growing up as an activist outside of Tehran differs from and occasionally conflicts with the Tehran experience, it is similar in one fundamental way. Small towns too drew inspiration from political struggles occurring internationally. Every corner of Iran, even conservative and religious towns, was touched by the radical ideas and movements of the 1960s. In general, Iran was more dynamic—in the circulatory movement of people and ideas—than conventional narratives from Tehran or the West might have us think.

This is the wider vista for the story told here, which is a collection of ephemera from my life and a snapshot of the world as I experienced it. Little can happen outside of the political-institutional complexes stretching the globe, providing a system of pathways, pressures, and triggers. My life story may provide the basis for reconstructing the "unthought" of the Iranian revolution, which we have still barely learned how to reckon with. The unthought cannot be erased from our minds, as it is waiting for us to think and speak about it. These buried memories may supply us with the courage to think beyond the conventional narrative of our time and to offer comfort to our anxious minds.

I have opened the forbidden box of my unthought life in the hope that my story will shed some light on the dynamics and varieties of human conditions I witnessed prior to and during the revolution. For what is the purpose of one person telling their story, except to help confirm that we are not alone, that we live and dream together, and that we may ultimately build a new world of mutual respect?

Bibliography

Abrahamian, Ervand. *Iran Between Two Revolutions*. Princeton. NJ: Princeton University Press, 1982.

———. *Khomeinism: Essays on the Islamic Republic*. Berkeley, CA: University of California Press, 1993.

———. *Radical Islam: The Iranian Mojahedin*. London: I. B. Tauris, 1989.

Adamiyat, Fereydoun. *Andisheh-ha-ye Mirza Fath-Ali Akhundzadeh* [The Thoughts of Mirza Fath-Ali Akhundzadeh]. Tehran: Entesharat-e Kharazmi, 1349 [1970].

———. *Fekr-e Azadi Va Moqaddameh-ye Nehzat-e Mashrutiyat-e Iran* [The Concept of Liberty and the Beginnings of the Constitutional Movement in Iran]. Tehran: Gustarih, 1961.

———. *Ide'uluzhi-ye Nehzat-e Mashrutiyat-e Iran* [The Ideology of the Iranian Constitutional Movement]. Tehran: Payam Publishers, 1355 [1976].

Afary, Janet. *The Iranian Constitutional Revolution: Grassroots Democracy, Social Democracy, and the Origins of Feminism*. New York: Columbia University Press, 1996.

Afary, Janet and Kevin Anderson. *Foucault and the Iranian Revolution: Gender and the Seductions of Islamism*. Chicago: University of Chicago Press, 2005.

Ahangar, Reza-Akbari. *Darsnameh-ye Anjoman-e Hojjatiyeh: Sayri dar Andisheh-ha va 'Amlkardeh-ha*. Tehran: Haqq-pezhuhi, 1394 [2016].

Akhavan Sales, Mehdi. *Zendagi mi'guyad amma baz bayad zist. bayad zist, bayad zist* [Life Says: Still We Must Live]. Tehran: Entesharat-e Tuka, 1357 [1978].

Akhavi, Shahrough. *Religion and Politics in Contemporary Iran: Clergy-State Relations in the Pahlavi Period*. Albany, NY: State University of New York Press, 1980.

———. *Gharbzadegi* [Westoxification]. Tehran: Entesharat-e Ferdowsi, 1341 [1962].

Al-e Ahmad, Jalal. *Modir-e Madrasa* [The School Principal]. Tehran: Amir Kabir, 1337 [1958].

Alavi, Bozorg. *Chamedan* [The Suitcase]. Tehran: Negah, 1313 [1934].

———. *Chashmhayash* [Her Eyes]. Tehran: Negah, 1331 [1952].

———. *Her Eyes*. Translated by John O'Kane. Bibliotheca Persica, Modern Persian Literature Series. No. 9. Lanham, MD: University Press of America, 1989.

———. *Namah-ha va Dastan-ha-ye Digar* [Letters and Other Stories]. Tehran: Bongah-e Matbu'ati-e Setarah, 1331 [1952].

———. *Panjah-o Seh Nafar* [Fifty-Three Persons]. Tehran: Negah, 1330 [1942].

———. *Varaq Pareh-ha-ye Zendan* [Scrap Papers from Prison]. Tehran: Negah, 1320 [1941].

Algar, Hamid. *Roots of the Islamic Revolution*. London: Open Press, 1983.

Alvandi, Roham ed. *The Age of Aryamehr: Late Pahlavi Iran and its Global Entanglements*. London: Gingko Library, 2018.

Ansari, Ali. *The Politics of Nationalism in Modern Iran*. New York: Cambridge University Press, 2012.

Arjomand, Said Amir. *The Turban for the Crown: The Islamic Revolution in Iran.* New York: Oxford University Press, 1988.

Azimi, Fakhreddin. *Iran: The Crisis of Democracy, 1941–1953.* London: I. B.Tauris, 1989.

Bakhash, Saul. *The Reign of the Ayatollahs: Iran and the Islamic Revolution.* New York: Basic Books, 1984.

Bayat, Asef. *Street Politics: Poor People's Movements in Iran.* New York: Columbia University Press, 1997.

Behrangi, Samad. *Mahi Siyah-ye Kuchak* [The Little Black Fish]. Tehran: Entesharat-e Kanun Parvaresh Fekri Kudakan va Nowjavanan, 1347 [1967].

Behrooz, Maziar. *Rebels with a Cause: The Failure of the Left in Iran.* London: I. B. Tauris, 1999.

Boroujerdi, Mehrzad. *Iranian Intellectuals and the West: The Tormented Triumph of Nativism.* Syracuse, NY: Syracuse University Press, 1996.

Chubak, Sadegh. *Kheyma-shab-bazi* [The Puppet Show]. Tehran: Javidan Publisher, 1324 [1945].

Cronin, Stephanie. *The Army and the Creation of the Pahlavi State in Iran, 1910–1926.* London: Routledge, 1997.

———. "The Left in Iran: Illusion and Disillusion," *Middle Eastern Studies* 36, no. 3. (July 2000): 231–43.

Cronin, Stephanie ed. *The Making of Modern Iran: State and Society Under Riza Shah, 1921–1941.* New York: Routledge, 2007.

Dabashi, Hamid. *Close Up: Iranian Cinema, Past, Present, and Future.* New York: Verso Press, 2001.

———. *Iran: A People Interrupted.* New York: The New Press, 2008.

———. *Theology of Discontent: The Ideological Foundation of the Islamic Revolution in Iran.* Edison, NJ: Transaction Publishers, 2005.

Davari, Arash. "A Return to Which Self? 'Ali Shari'ati and Frantz Fanon on the Political Ethics of Insurrectionary Violence." *Comparative Studies of South Asia, Africa and the Middle East* 34, no. 1 (2014): 86–105.

Enayat, Hamid. "Ensan az Khod Biganeh" [The Alienated Man]. *Negin*, Esfand 1346 [February/March 1968].

———. *Modern Islamic Political Thought*. Austin, TX: University of Texas Press, 1982.

Falsafi, Muhammad-Taqi. *Khaterat va Mubarezat* [Memories and Struggles]. Tehran: Entesharat-e Markaz-e Asnad-e Enqelab-e Eslami, 1373 [1994/95].

Farahmand Rad, Shiva. *Dar Gam-ha-ye Faje'yeh* [In the Steps of the Debacle]. Berlin: Democratic Party of Iranian People Press, 1989.

———. *Ghatran dar Asal* [Tar in Honey]. Brentford, UK: H&S Media, 2014.

Fazel, Javad. *'Eshq va Ashk* [Love and Tears]. Tehran: Ma'refat Publisher, 1948.

———. *Salma, Dokhtar-e 'Arab* [Salma, the Arab Girl]. Tehran: Khazar Publisher, 1968.

Fischer, Michael M. J. *Iran: From Religious Dispute to Revolution.* Cambridge, MA: Harvard University Press, 1980.

Floor, W. M. "The Revolutionary Character of the Ulama: Wishful Thinking or Reality?" *International Journal of Middle East Studies* 12, no. 4. (December 1980): 501–24.

Gasiorowski, Mark. *U.S. Foreign Policy and the Shah: Building a Client State in Iran*. New York: NCROL, 1991.

Ghani, Cyrus. *Iran and the Rise of Reza Shah: From Qajar Collapse to Pahlavi Power*. London: I. B. Tauris, 1998.

Golestan, Ebrahim. *Asrar-e Ganj Dareh-ye Jenni* [The Ghost Valley's Treasure Mysteries]. Tehran: Baztab Negar Publication, 1353 [1974].

Gorky, Maxim. *Velgardan va Dastan-ha-ye Digar* [The Outcasts and Other Stories], translated by Ali Kasmai'i et al. Tehran: Negah, 1398 [2013].

Hedayat, Sadeq. *Zendeh Be-gur* [Buried Alive]. Tehran: Chapkhaneh-ye Ferdowsi, 1309 [1930].

———. *Buf-e Kur* [The Blind Owl]. Bombay: Self-published, 1315 [1937].

———. *Seh Qatreh-ye Khun* [Three Drops of Blood]. Tehran: Amir Kabir, 1341 [1932].

Hegland, Mary Elaine. *Days of Revolution: Political Unrest in an Iranian Village*. Stanford, CA: Stanford University Press, 2014.

Hooglund, Eric. *Land and Revolution in Iran, 1960–1980*. Austin, TX: University of Texas Press, 1982.

Keddie, Nikki R. *Roots of Revolution: An Interpretive History of Modern Iran*. New Haven, CT: Yale University Press, 1981.

Keddie, Nikki R. and Rudolph Matthee, eds. *Iran and the Surrounding World: Interactions in Culture and Cultural Politics.* Seattle, WA: University of Washington Press, 2002.

Keshavarzian, Arang and Ali Mirsepassi, eds. *Global 1979: Geographies and Histories of the Iranian Revolution.* Cambridge: Cambridge University Press, 2021.

Kurzman, Charles. *The Unthinkable Revolution in Iran*. Cambridge, MA: Harvard University Press, 2004.

Martin, Vanessa. *Iran between Islamic Nationalism and Secularism: The Constitutional Revolution of 1906*. London: I. B. Tauris, 2013.

Matin-Asgari, Afshin. *Iranian Student Opposition to the Shah.* Costa Mesa, CA: Mazda Publishers, 2002.

———. *Both Eastern and Western: An Intellectual History of Iranian Modernity.* Cambridge: Cambridge University Press, 2018.

———. "Twentieth-Century Iran's Political Prisoners." *Middle Eastern Studies* 42, no. 5 (September 2006): 689–707.

Meskub, Shahroukh. *Ruz ha dar Rah* [Days on the Path]. Paris: Khavaran, 1979.

Mirsepassi, Ali. *Intellectual Discourse and the Politics of Modernization: Negotiating Modernity in Iran.* Cambridge: Cambridge University Press, 2000.

———. *Iran's Quiet Revolution: The Downfall of the Pahlavi State.* Cambridge: Cambridge University Press, 2019.

———. *Iran's Troubled Modernity: Debating Ahmad Fardid's Legacy.* Cambridge: Cambridge University Press, 2018.

———. *Transnationalism in Iranian Political Thought: The Life and Times of Ahmad Fardid.* Cambridge: Cambridge University Press, 2017.

Mosta'an, Hosseingholi. *Rabe'a* [Rab'e], vols. 1–3. Tehran: Negarestan Ketab, 1340 [1961].

Mottahedeh, Roy. *The Mantle of the Prophet: Religion and Politics in Iran.* New York: Simon and Schuster, 1985.

Nafisi, Azar. *Reading Lolita in Tehran: A Memoir in Books.* New York: Random House, 2004.

Naraghi, Ehsan. *An Hekayat-ha: Goftogu-ye Hormoz Ki ba Ehsan Naraghi.* Those Stories: Hormoz Ki's Talk with Ehsan Naraghi. Tehran: Jame'eh-ye Iraniyan, 2002.

———. *Ancheh Khod Dasht* [What Oneself Had]. Tehran: Amir Kabir, 1355 [1974].

———. *Azadi, Haq va 'Edalat: Munazireh-ye Esma'il Khu'i bah Ehsan Naraghi* [Freedom, Right, and Justice: A Talk Between Esma'il Khu'i and Ehsan Naraghi]. Tehran: Javidan, 1356 [1976].

———. *Azadi: Majmu'ah-ye maqalat va musahebeh-ha* [Freedom: A Collection of Essays and Interviews]. Tehran: Afkar, 2004.

———. *Eqbal-e Namomken* [Impossible Fate]. Tehran: 'Elm, 1372 [2003].

———. *From Palace to Prison: Inside the Iranian Revolution*, translated by Nilu Mobasser. Chicago: Ivan R. Dee, 1994.

———. *Ghorbat-e Gharb* [The Alienation of the West]. Tehran, Amir Kabir: 1353 [1974/75].

———. *'Ulum-e Ejtema'i va Sayr-e Takvini-ye An* [The Social Sciences and the Course of their Formation]. Tehran: Tehran University Press, 1344 [1965].

Nategh, Homa. "Khodam kardam keh la'nat bar khodam bad!" [It was my own doing, I should be damned for it!]. *Kayhan*, February 26, 2003.

Nehru, Jawaharlal. *The Discovery of India.* New York: John Day Company, 1946.

Parizi, Bastan. *Az Pariz ta Paris* [From Pariz to Paris]. Tehran: 'Elm, 1371 [2002].

Parsa, Misagh. *Social Origins of the Iranian Revolution.* New Brunswick, NJ: Rutgers University Press, 1989.

Petrushevsky, Ilya Pavlovich. *Islam dar Iran: Az Hejrat ta Payan-e Qarn-e Nohom-e Hejri* [Islam in Iran: From the Hijra to the End of the Ninth Hijri Century], translated by Karim Keshavarz. Tehran: Payam, 1350 [1971/72].

Rahnema, Ali. *An Islamic Utopian: A Political Biography of Ali Shariati*. London: I. B. Tauris, 1998.

———. *Call to Arms: Iran's Marxist Revolutionaries.* London: Oneworld, 2021.

Roozbeh, Khosro. *Eta'at-e Kurkuraneh* [Blind Obedience]. Tehran: Mardom-e 'Asgari, 1356 [1977/78].

Sa'edi, Gholamhossein. *Ahl-e Hava* [The People of Air]. Tehran: Mo'asseseh-e Motale'at va Tahqiqat-e Ejtema'i, 1345 [1966].

———. *Ilkhchi* [Ilkchi]. Tehran: Mo'asseseh-e Motale'at va Tahqiqat-e Ejtema'i, 1358 [1979/80].

Sadr, Hamid Reza. *Iranian Cinema: A Political Story*. London: I. B. Tauris, 2006.

Schayegh, Cyrus. *Who Is Knowledgeable Is Strong: Science, Class, and the Formation of Modern Iranian Society, 1900–1950.* Berkeley & Los Angeles, CA: University of California Press, 2009.

Shafi'i Kadkani, Mohammad Reza. *Dar Kucheh Bagh-ha-ye Neyshabur* [In the Garden Alleys of Nishapur]. Tehran: Tus, 1389 [2010/11].

Shamlu, Ahmad. *Ketab-e Kucheh* [The Book of the Alley], vols. 1–15. Tehran: Entesharat-e Mazyar, 1357–1387 [1978–2008].

Shari'ati, Ali. *Marxism and Other Western Fallacies*, translated by R. Campbell. Berkeley, CA: Mizan Press, 1980.

Shayegan, Daryush. *Cultural Schizophrenia: Islamic Societies Confronting the West.* Syracuse, NY: Syracuse University Press, 1997.

Sohrabi, Naghmeh. "The 'Problem Space' of the Historiography of the 1979 Iranian Revolution." *History Compass* 16 (2018): 1–10.

———. "Remembering the Palestine Group: Global Activism, Friendship, and the Iranian Revolution." *International Journal for Middle East Studies* 51, no. 2 (2019): 281–300.

Tabarra'ian, Safa al-Din. *Chon Esfanj, Narm: Bazshenasi-ye Naqsh-e Doktor Ehsan Naraghi dar Hakemiyat-e Pahlavi-ye Dovum* [Soft Like a Sponge: Evaluating Ehsan Naraghi's Role in the Second Pahlavi Reign], vol. 1. Tehran: Mo'assaseh-ye Motale'at-e Tarikh-e Mo'aser-e Iran, 2013.

Tahbaz, Sirus. *Yush*. Tehran: Nashr-e Mo'aser, 1362 [1983/84].

Talebi, Shahla. *Ghosts of Revolution: Rekindled Memories of Imprisonment in Iran.* Stanford, CA: Stanford University Press, 2011.

Vardasbi, Abuzar. *Jazmyat-e Falsafe-ye Hezbi: Naqdi bar Ketab 'Islam dar Iran'* [Dogmatic Partisans Philosophy: A Critique of "Islam in Iran"]. Tehran: Qalam Publisher, 1357 [1978/79].

Vejdani, Farzin. *Making History in Iran: Education, Nationalism, and Print Culture*. Stanford, CA: Stanford University Press, 2015.

Weber, Max. "Science as Vocation." In *From Max Weber: Essays in Sociology*, translated and edited by H.H. Gerth and C. Wright, 129–156. New York: Oxford University Press, 1946.

Zamanian, Abdullah. "*Nahavand dar Kudeta-ye 28 Mordad 1332*" [Nahavand during the August 28, 1953 *coup d'état*]. *Farhangan*, no. 42 (Fall 2002): 109–120.

Index

adabiyat (literature), 78–9
Adamiyat, Fereydoun, 146, 166, 211
Afghani, Ali Mohammad, 45
Al-e Ahmad, Jalal, 45, 58, 105–6, 149, 170–1, 191
Ahmadi, Amir, 35–6
Akhavan-Sales, Mehdi, 147, 174, 176, 189
Akhundzadeh, Mirza Fath Ali, 146
Alavi, Bozorg, 6, 25; *see also* *Chashmhayash* (Alavi)
  Chamedan by, 45, 98
  on class, 96, 99–100, 102
  Hedayat and, 99
  Kamalolmolk and, 101–2
  social critique by, 95–6
  in Tudeh Party, 98
Algar, Hamid, 194
alienation (*az khod biganegi*), 148–9
alienation (*ghorbat*) *see ghorbat*
Amanat, Abbas, 150–1
Aminian's Bookstore, 44
Amjadi, Mr, 74–7, 92–3, 96–7, 101–6, 124, 145–6, 211–12, 250
Amoui, Mohamad Ali, 199–200
ancient Iran, 85, 126, 146, 222
Andisheh-ye Siyasi dar Gharb (Enayat), 162
Anjoman-e Hojjatiyeh, 130–6, 170
Antari ke Lutish Morde bood (Chubak), 45
anti-authoritarian politics, in Golpayegan, 88–9, 121–2
anti-Bahaism, 113, 131, 133–5, 215
anti-colonialism, 150
anti-intellectualism (*bifarhangi*), 128
anti-Marxists, 135, 153, 209–10
anti-Shah sentiment and activism, 143–4, 198, 218
anti-war movements, 1960s, 13, 120, 126, 238, 261
anti-Western and anti-modern discourses, 19, 159–60, 164, 170, 251–3, 260
Arabic language, 109–10, 127, 177, 245–6
Arab-Israeli conflict, 90
Arani, Taghi, 65, 124

Arianpour, Amir Hossein, 172
aristocratic (*ashrafi*) genre, of literature, 104
Arkoun, Mohammed, 248–9
Aryamehr University, 19, 203
ashrafi (aristocratic) genre, of literature, 104
Ashura festivals, 38, 70, 87
authentic culture (*salat-e farhangi*), 51
authenticity, place and, 12, 48, 50, 53, 160
authoritarianism, 21–2, 88, 171, 218
autocracy, 2, 9, 205, 251
Azerbaijan, 11, 58, 61
az khod biganegi (alienation), 148–9
Az Pariz ta Paris (Bastani-Parizi), 57

bafarhang (cultured) *versus bifarhang* (uncultured), 129
Baghdad, 37–8
Baha'i faith, 130–1, 133–4, 215–16
Bahman, 141–2
Bakhtiyar, Shapour, 218
Balandier, Georges, 155
Baniahmad, Ahmad, 231
Bastani-Parizi, Mohammad Ebrahim, 57–8
Batul Khanum, 31–8
Bayzavi, Said, 68
Bazargan, Mehdi, 209–10, 227–8, 231–2
The Beatles, 120
BEDAMN operation, of CIA, 110
Behesht-e Zahra (Zahra's Paradise) cemetery, 22, 179, 181, 207, 218–24
Behrangi, Samad
  Amjadi and Eshraghi on, 92
  from Azerbaijan, 11, 58, 61
  on hospitality, 58
  "Kandokav dar Masa'el-e Tarbiyati-ye Iran" by, 59
  The Little Black Fish by, 11, 60–1
  on school textbooks, 59
  Ulduz va Kalag-ha by, 60
Behzadi, Hamid, 151–2
Belgian Marxism, 153
bifarhangi (anti-intellectualism), 128
Bijan (cousin), 32, 55, 72
Black Friday, 230
Boof-e Koor (Hedayat), 45
Book of Kings (*Shahnameh*), 10, 43
bookstores, 44–6, 82, 90, 93, 256
Boroujerd, 196–7
bourgeois literature, 104
Bournemouth, U.K., 186
Bozorgnia, Mostafa, 137
Brecht, Bertolt, 140, 144
Buf-e Kur (Hedayat), 99
bullying, 66–8
bumi (local resident), 48, 154
bumi gera'i (nativism), 48–50, 64, 154–60, 251–2

capitalism, 11
Castle of Nahavand (Ghale-ye Nahavand), 89–90
Castro, Fidel, 14, 122–3
censorship, 5, 46–8, 120, 144, 190, 232–3, 252–3

Chamedan (Alavi), 45, 98
Channel 2, 190–1
Chashmhayash (Alavi), 45, 75
  on class, 96, 99–100, 102
  on collectivism, 201
  Eshraghi and Amjadi on, 93, 96–8, 101–4
  Farangis in, 77, 96, 99–100, 102
  Kamalolmolk and, 101–2
  Marxism and, 99–100, 104
  Ostad Makan in, 94–5, 99–103
  on Pahlavi society, 95, 102–3
  on Reza Shah period, 100–3
Chekhov, Anton, 6, 25, 45
Chubak, Sadegh, 45
CIA, BEDAMN operation, 110
citizenship, 125
civil society, 6, 9, 18–19, 21–2, 170–1
class, 41–2, 92, 105, 145–7
  Alavi on, 96, 99–100, 102
  Eshraghi and Amjadi on, 145–6
classical Persian poetry, 63–4, 175, 257
collective action, 6, 19, 133, 136
collectivism, 98, 184, 201
college education, 79–80
colonialism, 164–5, 251, 261
Confederation of Iranian Students, 15, 133
Confederation of Iranian Students Abroad, 163
consequentialism, 108
Constitutional Revolution of 1905–11, 6, 14–15, 101, 146, 208–9, 260
Corbin, Henri, 251–2
cosmopolitanism, provincialism and, 254–5
The Country and the City (Williams), 54
coup d'état, 1953, 122, 137
crime fiction, 46–7
Cuba, 122–3
Cultural Association of Iran and France, 155
cultural conservativism, 212
cultural Marxism, 168
cultural schizophrenia, 251–2
cultured (*bafarhang*) *versus* uncultured (*bifarhang*), 129

Dabireh, 222
dahatis, 84
Dar al-Fonun High School, 138
Dar Kucheh-ye Baghi-ye Neyshabur (Kadkani), 175–6
Dashtban, Masoud, 217–18
Dehkhoda, Ali Akbar, 190
democracy and democratic values, 83–4, 203, 253
despotism, 5
detective novels, 44, 46–8, 146–7
Discovery of India (Nehru), 14, 121
disinformation, 5
Donya (journal), 124
donya (world), 123–9, 177
Dorud, 31–2, 34, 43, 81
Dostoyevsky, Fyodor, 6, 25, 45

Eastern freedom, 157–8
eastern spirituality (*ma'anviyat-e sharqi*), 253
Ebn-e Sina High School, 78, 91, 130
Ebrahim, 212–14, 217

education reforms, 1920s, 138
egalitarianism, 11
ego, freedom from, 157–8
Egypt, under Nasser, 98
'elm-e dini (religious knowledge), 117
'elm-e in-jahani (life sciences), 117
'elm parasti (worship of science), 157
Éluard, Paul, 63–4
Enayat, Hamid, 16–18, 148–9, 160–7, 188, 249
  in post-revolutionary Iran, 256–7
  at Tehran University, 160–3, 167, 254
  in Tudeh Party, 163–4
  on the West, 251
Encyclopedia Dehkhoda, 198
encyclopedias, 46, 124–5
English language, 127–8, 188
"Ensan az Khod Bigane" (Enayat), 148
Esfandiari, Ahmad, 41
Eshraghi, Mr, 74–7, 92–3, 96–8, 101–6, 124, 145–6, 211–12, 250
Esmaili, Mr, 112–13
eternal homeland (*sarzamin javidan*), 9–10
Ettela'at, 42–3
Ettela'at-e Haftegi, 43
Evin Prison, 195, 198–9, 225
exiles, from post-revolutionary Iran, 255–7

factionalism, 167
Fadai'ian-e Khalq, 17, 22, 60
Falsafi, Mohammad Taghi, 7, 134–5, 193
  Khomeini and, 21, 113, 207, 216
  Modarres and, 215
  on Pahlavi state, 111–12, 216–17
  on Reza Shah, 215–17
  Shahnaz Square address by, 214–17
  Tavakol and, 110–16, 118, 129–30, 211–12
Farah (queen), 53
Farangis (fictional character), 77, 96, 99–100, 102
Fardid, Ahmad, 156, 159–60, 163–4, 166, 191, 194, 244
  anti-Western nativism of, 251–2
  on the West, 192
  against Western cultural hegemony, 254
Fardidiyeh, 164
Farhang (cousin), 72
father, of Mirsepassi, Ali, 38–43, 46, 50–1, 78–80, 114
  in Ministry of Finance, 131
  on Reza Shah, 51, 79, 83–5, 192
Fazel, Javad, 104–5
Fedayeen, 144, 173, 193, 196–7, 209–10, 220–1
  leftists in, 226–8, 232–3
  in Nixon protests, 232–3
Fedayeen-e Khalq, 225–6
Fekr-e Azadi va Moqaddameh-ye Nehzat-e Mashrutiyat-e Iran (Adamiyat), 146
feminists, 217

Ferdowsi, 120
Ferdowsi High School, 68, 258
First Congress of Iranian Writers, 190
Foucault, Michel, 246
fragmentation, of Iran, 249
freedom, 2, 157–8
Freedom Movement (Nehzat-e Azadi), 209–10, 232
French Revolution, 157

Gav, 254
gender equality, 216–17
Ghale-ye Nahavand (Castle of Nahavand), 89–90
Ghandchi, Ahmad, 137
gharbzadeghi (Westoxification), 12, 107, 112, 156, 164, 171, 191, 217, 253
Gharbzadegi (Al-e Ahmad), 149
gharibeh (stranger), 28–9, 48–9, 61, 248
  in Golpayegan, 114
  in Nahavand, 65–6, 69–70, 73
  in Tehran, 139
  in U.K., 187–8
ghorbat (alienation), 88, 246, 248, 259
  az khod biganegi and, 148
  gharibeh and, 29
  Iranian writers and thinkers on, 11–12
  making home in, 78–81
  mother of Mirsepassi, Ali, on, 27–8, 30, 55–6, 81, 148
  in Nahavand, 66, 70, 73
  nativism and, 48–50
  overcoming, 12–14
  pain of, 27–31
  Shamlu on, 11
  as strangeness, 8–9, 12, 27–8
  tajaddod and, 9, 25–6
  torment of living in, 8–13
  trouble with home in, 54–6
global consciousness, 119–20
global politics, Iranian political culture and, 151–2
global radicalism, 137–44
Goethe Institute, 19, 189–92
Golpayegan, 8, 13–18, 44–7, 58, 193
  Al-e Ahmad and, 170–1
  anti-authoritarian politics in, 88–9, 121–2
  Baha'is in, 133
  as center of activism, 78
  civic life in, 91
  community of, 86, 145
  consciousness of youth in, 123
  donya and, 124–8
  Falsafi's Shahnaz Square address and, 216–17
  Finance Office in, 80, 114
  gharibeh in, 114
  high school in, 78, 82, 91, 130–2
  high school teachers in, 74–5, 77, 79, 83, 93–4, 110, 119, 129–31, 133–4, 165, 250
  Iranian nationhood discourse in, 111
  Islam and Marxism in, 87–93, 129
  as "land of tulips," 81–6
  leftists in, 121, 165, 211–12
  locals *versus* guests in, 48–9
  Mirsepassi, Ali, in, photos of, 115, 135, 136, 145

Golpayegan (*cont.*)
Mirsepassi family moving to, 78, 80–2
Nahavand and, 89–91, 149, 154, 165, 261
parochialism and, 164
reading and study groups in, 124–5
religiosity in, 87, 89–91, 107, 145
resistance in, 143, 170
Tavakol fleeing, 259
Tehran and, 14, 89–90, 138–9, 149, 167, 169–70, 192, 201, 212, 250, 261–2
Golpayegani (Grand Ayatollah), 87
Gorky, Maxim, 6, 25, 45, 92
Goruh-ye Felestin (Palestine Group), 142, 166
Greater Khorasan region, 17
guest (*mehman*), 48–9, 72–3
Gurvitch, Georges, 155

Hafez, 64, 79, 122
hamin mardom-e Iran (ordinary Iranians), 65
hamleh-ye Moghol, 35
Hanifnejad, Mohammad, 203
Hasanvand tribe, 34–7
Hedayat, Sadegh, 6, 25, 45, 99, 105–6, 146, 190
Hedayat Bookshop, 44
Hegel, G. W. F., 148–9, 164–5
Heideggerian philosophy, 156, 164
Hejazi, Mohammad, 104–5
hezbollahis, 180, 210–11
history writing, memoir and, 7–8
Hojjatiyeh, 211–12
holy places, of Iran, 37–8
Homa (Hejazi), 104
hospitality, 56–60, 70, 72
Hossein (Imam), 38, 108, 202
Hosseiniyeh Ershad, 16
Hoveyda, Amir-Abbas, 156
Hughes, Langston, 63–4
Hugo, Victor, 104–5
humanism, 65, 118
humanist hospitality, 12–13
Hussein, Saddam, 256

Indian independence, 82, 121–3
individualism, 156–7
insider (*khodi*), 29
Institute for Educational and Scientific Research and Planning, 156
Institute for Social Studies and Research at Tehran University, 155–6, 158–9
Institute of Advanced Studies, 245
internationalism, 200
"In This Blind Alley" (Shamlu), 63
Iqbal, Muhammad, 161–2, 164
Iran dar Puye-ye Tarikh (Vardasbi), 256
Iran-e novin (modern Iran), 41–2, 151
Iranian Communist Party, 209–10
Iranian constitutionalists, 11, 122, 217
Iranian folklore, 64–5
Iranian-Islamic spirituality, 191
Iranian Kurdistan and Kurds, 90–1, 149, 175, 196

Iranian "new poetry" movement, 63–4
Iranian oil, British control of, 98
Iranian Revolution, 1–2, 4, 165
  Black Friday, 230
  collective action and secret operations in, 133
  first-hand account of, 7–8
  Foucault on, 246
  Islam and, 219–20, 222
  Islamists and, 25–6, 220
  Khomeini and, 22, 182, 202, 219, 222, 227, 233–9
  Khomeinists on, 219, 227, 231–7
  Lahiji on legal reasoning for, 19–20, 203–6
  leftists and religious radicals in, 219–20, 234–6
  memories and memoirs of, 23–6
  Naraghi after, 159
  Nategh and, 180–2, 222–4
  nationalism and, 252
  opposition to post-revolutionary government, 248
  against Pahlavi state, 20, 23, 208, 231
  popular remembrances of, 247
  renunciations of, 207–8, 222, 224, 259
  revolutionaries for, 228
  Reza Shah on, 231
  spirituality of, 18–23, 25–6
  students on, 5, 234–8
  in Tehran, 212–14
  the unthought of, 262–3
  women and, 223
  Zarafshan in, 207–12
Iran–Iraq War, 119, 256
Iran Novin Party (New Iran Party), 84, 120
Iran Royal Military, 183–5
Iraq, 37, 108, 113
Isfahan, 81
Islam
  Baha'i faith, 130, 133
  Channel 2 on, 190–1
  on *donya*, 124
  Falsafi on, 216
  in Golpayegan, 145
  humanistic sciences and, 118
  Iranian Revolution and, 219–20, 222
  liberation theology, 168
  Marxism and, 87–93, 129, 163, 165–73, 193, 250, 252
  Nategh on, 22–3
  New Tehran schoolteachers on, 169
  political, 13–14, 89, 129, 164, 211–12
  radical criticisms of, 146
  radicalism and, 169
  as source of ethical instruction, 115
  Soviet Marxists on, 163, 172
  theology, 194
  women and, 22–3, 180, 182–3, 216–17
Islamic Republic, 135, 153–4, 164, 183, 202, 242, 257, 260
Islamic revival movement, of Falsafi, 110–11
Islam in Iran (Petrushevsky), 163
Islamism and Islamists, 17, 20–1
  Al-e Ahmad and, 107
  Falsafi on, 21

Islamism and Islamists (*cont.*)
  Iranian Revolution and, 25–6
  leftists and, 21–2, 220
  Marxism and, 15, 142–3, 167, 211
  Nategh on, 23
  against Pahlavi state, 23, 112
  in post-revolutionary Iran, 255
  in Tehran, 201
Israel, 90, 172–3, 206, 216

jahan (new world), 77, 124–5
Jahanbai (general), 184
Jahan-e Islam, 124
Jaleh Square massacre, 18
Jangali movement, 209–10
Javad, 185
Jazani, Bijan, 15, 211
Jebhe-ye Demokratik-e Melli (National Democratic Front), 256–7
Jünger, Ernst, 149

Kabir, Taghi Khan Amir, 138
Kadkani, Shafi'i, 16, 189, 246, 249
  Dar Kucheh-ye Baghi-ye Neyshabur, 175–6
  on Marxism, 17, 173–4
  on Persian poetry and literature, 173–6, 257–8
  in post-revolutionary Iran, 257–8
  at Tehran University, 167, 173–4, 244–5
Kamalolmolk, 101–2
"Kandokav dar Masa'el-e Tarbiyati-ye Iran" (Behrangi), 59
Karamiyya sect, 245
Karbala, 37–8
Kashan, 155
Kashani (Ayatollah), 110
Kashani, Mr, 242–3
Kayhan, 193–4, 229
Kazem, 225–6, 228
Kermani, Mirza Aqa Khan, 146
Kermanshah, 72
Keshavarz, Karim, 190
Keshavarzian, 44
Ketab-e Hafteh, 64
Ketab-e Kucheh, 64–5
Khalu, 195–6
Khan, Mehr Ali, 34–6
Khan, Mirza Kuchak, 209–10
khan khani (landlordism), 36
Khansar, 87, 90
Khanum, Aghdas, 41
khodi (insider), 29
Khomein, 87, 90
Khomeini (Ayatollah), 192–3, 251
  clerical leadership under, 202
  contempt for the West, among followers of, 19
  Falsafi and, 21, 113, 207, 216
  Freedom Movement of Bazargan and, 209–10
  Iranian Kurds on, 196
  Iranian Revolution and, 22, 182, 202, 219, 222, 227, 233–9
  June 1963 uprising after arrest of, 211, 216
  mass execution of political prisoners by, 200
  Nategh on, 182
  Reza Shah and, 231, 234, 238
  on student strikes, 2–3

Tudeh Party and, 210
ulama and, 213
on women, 222–3
Khomeinists, 180, 206, 226
Iranian Revolution and, 219, 227, 231–7
leftists and, 20, 181, 193, 199, 219, 226, 232, 234–7, 240
Khorasan, 57–8, 174–6, 245

Lahiji, Karim, 19–21, 202–7
Lambton, Ann, 255
landlordism (*khan khani*), 36
land ownership (*malekiyat-e arzi*), 256
Latin American revolutionaries and movements, 92, 167
leftists, 60–1, 75, 88, 168; *see also* Marxism
Alavi, 98–9
in Boroujerd, 197
consequentialism lacking in thought of, 108
in Fedayeen, 226–8, 232–3
in Golpayegan, 121, 165, 211–12
in Iranian Revolution, 219–20, 232
Islamists and, 21–2, 220
Khomeinists and, 20, 181, 193, 199, 219, 226, 232, 234–7, 240
religious radicals and, 142, 211, 219–20, 234–8
resistance to the Shah, 187
secular and religious, 194, 210
Shahbazi on, 199–200
underground, 195
Zarafshan on, 209–11
Lenin, Vladimir, 14, 75–7, 92, 96–7, 122–3
Levi, 206–7
life sciences (*'elm-e in-jahani*), 117
literature (*adabiyat*), 78–9
literature studies (*reshteh-ye adabi*), 78–9, 101, 160
The Little Black Fish (Behrangi), 11, 60–1
localism, *versus* provincialism and traditionalism, 129
local resident (*bumi*), 48, 154
Lorca, Federico Garcia, 63–4
Lorestan, 34–6, 89–91

ma'anviyat-e sharqi (eastern spirituality), 253
mahaligera'i (provincialism), 128–9, 254–5
Mahfoozi, Alireza, 220–1
Malayer, 39–40
malekiyat-e arzi (land ownership), 256
"Man, Islam, and Marxism" (Shari'ati), 193–4
Mansour (brother), 72
Maoists, 144
Marcuse, Herbert, 144, 148–9
marksism-e ghalat (mistaken Marxism), 171
Marx, Karl, 149
Marxism
of Al-e Ahmad, 106
anti-Western, 253
Belgian, 153
Chashmhayash and, 99–100, 104
cultural, 168
donya and, 124

Marxism (*cont.*)
  Enayat on, 17–18
  of Eshraghi and Amjadi, 74–5, 77, 92–3, 97, 102, 104
  factionalism and, 167
  Islam and, 87–93, 129, 163, 165–73, 193, 250, 252
  Islamism and, 15, 142–3, 167, 211
  Kadkani on, 17, 173–4
  Lenin on, 76
  Marxism-Leninism, 221, 225
  mistaken, 171
  Nabavi on, 152–3
  of Nategh, 179–80
  of Palestine Group, 142
  political Islam and, 13–14, 129
  in pre-revolutionary Iranian politics, 16
  religious movements and, 209–10
  of Shari'ati, 171–2, 193–4
  Soviet, 163, 172
  Vardasbi on, 17, 168, 172
  Zarafshan on, 209–10
Marxist activists, at Tehran University, 15–17, 142–3, 145–7
Marxist materialism, 163
Mashruteh movement, 19, 65, 151, 171, 193, 208
Masoud (brother), 55, 72, 109
Masoud (friend), 206–7
Massignon, Louis, 155
mass mobilization, 6–7
mass political action, 111, 212
mass protests, 6, 144
materialism, 194
  Marxist, 163
materialist consumerism, 107, 190
Mecca, 108–9
mehman (guest), 48–9, 72–3
Mehrjui, Dariush, 254
memoirs, remembrance and, 7–8, 24–5
messianic Shi'ism, 171
Ministry of Education, Iran, 59
Ministry of Finance, Iran, 38–40, 80, 131
Ministry of Foreign Affairs, Iran, 193
Ministry of Information and Tourism, Iran, 153
Mirsepassi, Abdolhossein, 39
Mirsepassi, Ali, photos of
  at age fourteen, 47
  at age thirteen, 45
  at age three, 30
  in Bournemouth, U.K., 1977, 186
  with brother and cousin, mid-1960s, 55
  in Golpayegan, 115, 135, 136, 145
  with mother and her friends, early 1960s, 34
  mother and sister of, early 1960s, 31
  in Nahavand, 45, 47, 55, 65–6, 72
  in Sar-e Pol-e Zahab, 1975, 185
  in Tagh-e Bostan, mid-1960s, 72
  in Tehran, 1971, 177
Les Misérables (Hugo), 104–5
mistaken Marxism (*marksism-e ghalat*), 171
Modarres, Hassan, 215

modern Iran (*Iran-e novin*), 41–2, 151
modernity (*tajaddod*), 15
  confusion of, 16–18, 20–1
  ghorbat and, 9, 25–6
  in Pahlavi state, 87
  The Swallows Return to Their Nests on, 51, 53
modernization, 8, 22, 56, 59
  authoritarian nature of, 88
  Golpayegani religiosity and, 89
  of Pahlavi state, 9, 14, 82–4, 88
  Tudeh Party on, 84
  under Reza Shah, 102–3
modernizers (*tajaddodgera*), 128
modern man (*tajaddod-zadeh*), 79
Modir-e Madrasa (Al-e Ahmad), 45, 171
Mohseni, Majid, 53–4, 154–5
Momeni, Baqer, 172
Morgenthau, Hans Joachim, 152
Mosaddegh, Mohammad, 22, 83–4, 98, 152, 232, 255–7, 260
Moshiri, Bahram, 258–9
Mosta'an, Hosseingholi, 104–5
Motahhari (Ayatollah), 163–4, 254
mother, of Mirsepassi, Ali, 31, 34, 41–2, 65, 69–71
  on *ghorbat*, 27–8, 30, 55–6, 81, 148
Mozafar, 4, 179
Mujahedin, 17, 144, 173, 203, 209–10, 220, 223
  Vardasbi in, 256
Mujahedin-e Khalq, 168, 171
Musa, 141–2

nabard Nahavand, 89–90
Nabavi, Jamshid, 152–4
Nafisi, Azar, 25
Nahavand, 6, 8, 25, 28, 30
  Batul Khanum in, 31–3, 35, 37
  Bayzavi in, 68
  Boroujerd and, 196–7
  Ebn-e Sina High School, 78
  father of Mirsepassi, Ali, in, 39, 41, 46
  Ghale-ye Nahavand in, 89–90
  gharibeh in, 65–6, 69–70, 73
  ghorbat in, 66, 70, 73
  Golpayegan and, 89–91, 149, 154, 165, 261
  grandmother of Mirsepassi, Ali, in, 198
  locals *versus* guests in, 48–9
  mehman in, 72–3
  Mirsepassi, Ali, in, photos of, 45, 47, 55, 65–6, 72
  Mirsepassi family's move to Golpayegan from, 80–2
  mother of Mirsepassi, Ali, from, 69–71, 81
  movie theater in, 50
  Pahlavi High School, 78, 91
  sabeqeh and *farhang* in, 70
  school in, 66–9
  Shahbazi in, 198–9
  study group in, 56–7
Naraghi, Ehsan, 155–9, 166, 194, 253–4
Nasser, Gamal Abdel, 90, 98
Nategh, Homa, 22–3, 179–83, 207, 220–4, 259
National Democratic Front (NDF) (*Jebhe-ye Demokratik-e Melli*), 256–7
National Front, 142, 232
national imaginary, 23–4, 126
national independence, 121–2

National Iranian Television Organization, 193
nationalism, 9, 14–15, 65, 84, 128
  identity and, 177–8
  imaginative, 249
  Iranian Revolution and, 252
  liberal, 232
  nativism and, 160
  tripartite temporality of, 123
nationalism class, at Tehran University, 151–2
National University of Iran, 2–3, 228–30, 234
nativism (*bumi gera'i*)
  of Fardid, 251–2
  ghorbat and, 48–50
  of Naraghi, 253
  Shamlu on, 64
  of Tehran, 154–60
NDF *see* National Democratic Front
Nefrin bar Zamin (Al-e Ahmad), 45
Nehru, Jawaharlal, 14, 82, 121–3
Nehzat-e Azadi (Freedom Movement), 209–10, 232
Nesin, Aziz, 45
New Iran Party (Iran Novin Party), 84, 120
Newsweek, 126–7
new world (*jahan*), 77, 124–5
New York University, 244–5
Nietzsche, Friedrich, 144, 148–9
niru-ye sevvum (Third Force), 253
Nishapur, 57–8, 101, 174
Nixon, Richard, 137, 232–3
nomadic tribes, of Iran, forcibly settled, 30–1, 36
Nowruz celebrations, 70, 73, 81
Nun va Ghalam (Al-e Ahmad), 45
Nurbakhsh, Mr, 126–7

"Ofogh-e roshan" (Shamlu), 10–11
oil nationalization movement, 44, 83, 152, 211, 255–6
Operation Forough Javidan, 256
opposition radio, 111, 143–4
oppression, resistance and, 6
ordinary Iranians (*hamin mardom-e Iran*), 65
Ostad Makan (fictional character), 94–5, 99–103

Pahlavi, Farah, 156
Pahlavi High School, 78, 91
Pahlavi state, 2, 5–6, 18, 194
  challenging, 77–8
  Chashmhayash on society of, 95, 102–3
  civil society systematically suppressed by, 21–2
  collapse of, 231
  donya and *jahan*, 125
  elitism of officials in, 42
  Falsafi on, 111–12, 216–17
  geopolitics and, 122
  Iranian political history absent under, 15
  Iranian Revolution against, 20, 23, 208, 231
  Islamists against, 23, 112
  Khomeini after fall of, 202
  on Mashruteh movement, 151
  Modarres on, 215
  modernity in, 87
  modernization of, 9, 14, 82–4, 88

Naraghi and, 156
official discourse, 77
on Radio Iran, 120
religious takeover following collapse of, 200–1
revolutionary movement against, 201
Shari'ati and, 171–2
suppression of political discourse by, 154, 250, 260
transnationalism and, 252–3
Westoxification and, 171
Pakravan, Hassan, 156
Palestine Group (*Goruh-ye Felestin*), 142, 166
Palestinian struggle, 82, 108–9, 120, 126, 141, 172–3
pan-Arabism, 90
parochialism, 164
the pastoral mode, 54
paternalism, 88
Paykar, 220
Peace Corps, 127–8
People's Party, 84
Persian cultural heritage, 122–3
Persian language, 176–8
Persian poetry and literature, 108, 110, 122, 124, 149
classical, 63–4, 175, 257
Kadkani on, 173–6, 257–8
of Rumi, 177–8
Sufism and, 245
Perso-Soviet Cultural Society, 190
Petrushevsky, Ilya Pavlovich, 163, 172
Piaget, Jean, 155
place
authenticity and, 12, 48, 50, 53, 160
late 1960s and 1970s as, 120
relating to, 178
place-based belonging and identity, 49–50
poetry readings, at Goethe Institute, 189–92
political Islam, 13–14, 89, 129, 164, 211–12
positivism, 158–9
post-Pahlavi Iran, 228–32
Project of Revolutionary Socialists, 220
provincial (*shahrestani*), 139, 149
provincialism (*mahaligera'i*), 128–9, 254–5

Qajar rule and rulers, 85, 98, 101, 151, 215
Qom, 212–13
Qotbzadeh, Sadegh, 227–8
Qur'an, 114–15

radicalism, 11, 13, 16, 64–5, 88–9
of Al-e Ahmad, 171
global, 137–44
Islamic, 169
religious, 142, 211, 219–20, 234–8
secular, 165, 170
of Vardasbi, 168
Radio Baghdad, 113
Radio Berlin, 75–6, 166–7
Radio Iran, 120
Radio Moscow, 16, 166–7
Radio Peking, 166–7
Rajabi, Masoud, 256
religious knowledge (*'elm-e dini*), 117

remembrance, memoirs and, 7–8, 24–5
reshteh-ye adabi (literature studies), 78–9, 101, 160
revolutionary movement, 20, 201–2, 212, 220
Rezai brothers, 203
Reza Shah, 14–15, 18–20, 30–1, 170–1
  Ahmadi and, 35–6
  Batul Khanum on, 35–6
  birthday celebrations, 120–1
  Chashmhayash on period of, 100–3
  class relations under, 96
  "collectivist ideology" prohibited by, 98
  demonstrations against, 191
  on economic industrialization and political rationalization, 79
  Falsafi on, 215–17
  father of Mirsepassi, Ali, on, 51, 79, 83–5, 192
  Golpayegani to, 87
  government bureaucracy, during rule of, 38–9
  human rights violations of, 203
  on Iranian Revolution, 231
  Kamalolmolk and, 101–2
  Khomeini and, 231, 234, 238
  Lahiji on, 203–5
  leaving Iran, 241
  on leftist activism, 194
  leftist resistance to, 187
  modernization under, 102–3
  Naraghi and, 156
  Nategh as critic of, 179–80
  national imaginary and, 126
  Persian kingship mythology and, 121
  propaganda of, 121
  protests against, 192–3
  Royal Military of, 184
  on *The Swallows Return to Their Nests*, 53
  Tavakol against, 258
  on universities, 230, 239
  the West and, 107
  on wider world, 125
Rouzbeh, Khosrow, 147
royalist parties, 84
Rudaki, 108
rule of law, 19–20, 191, 203, 205–6
Rumi, 108, 122, 177–8
rural Iran, 54, 158–60, 254
rural life, the pastoral mode on, 54
ruz-e daneshju (Student Day), 137

Sa'adi', 79, 112
sabeqeh (history, background) and *farhang* (culture), 70
Sa'edi, Gholamhossein, 96
Saeed, Parviz Ghazi, 46–8
Safi, Mr, 130, 132
salat-e farhangi (authentic culture), 51
Sales, Torab, 220–2
Sanandaj, 195–6
Sang-e Sabur (Chubak), 45
Sanjabi, Karim, 231–2
Sar-e Pol-e Zahab, 184–5, 217–18
Sarkisian, Aida, 64–5
Sartre, Jean-Paul, 144, 148–9
sarzamin javidan (eternal homeland), 9–10

Sasanian Empire, 89
SAVAK, 134, 156, 159, 162, 194, 205
school textbooks, 59, 109–10
"Science as Vocation" (Weber), 173
scientism, 157
Se Qatreh Khun (Hedayat), 45, 99
shadow revolutionaries, 255–9
Shahbazi, Ali, 198–200
Shahnameh (Book of Kings), 10, 43
shahrestani (provincial), 139, 149
Shamlu, Ahmad
  Arani and, 65
  as *gharibeh*, 61
  Hafez collection edited and recited by, 64
  humanism of, 65
  "In This Blind Alley" by, 63
  Ketab-e Kucheh encyclopedia by Sarkisian and, 64–5
  "Ofogh-e roshan" by, 10–11
  "Sha'ri keh Zendegist" by, 62–3
  Yushij and, 63–4
Shari'ati, Ali, 16, 89, 164, 166, 168, 170, 202
  Marxism of, 171–2, 193–4
Shariatrazavi, Mehdi, 137
Sharif-Vaghef, Majid, 203
"Sha'ri keh Zendegist" (Shamlu), 62–3
Shayegan, Daryush, 159–60, 251–2
Shi'i ceremonies and rituals, 87
Shi'i clerics, 25–6, 192–3, 199, 226, 238, 255
Shi'i Islam, 170
Shi'i Muslims, 37, 110, 196
Shi'i policies, official, 111
Shi'ism, 84, 171–2, 209
Shiva, Azar, 51
Shuhar-e Ahu Khanum (Afghani), 45
sit-ins, 19, 203
small towns and provinces, 261–3
  Behrangi on, 58–9
  cities *versus*, 50–4, 56–7, 138–9, 178, 261
  donya and, 123–9
  education in, 4–7, 13–14
  elitist attitude, of Pahlavi state toward, 84
  rural Iran, 54, 158–60, 254
social change, 2, 59
social classes (*tabaqat-e ejtema'i*), 92
solidarity, 142, 144, 188
sonnat-gera'i (traditionalism), 112
Soviet Marxism, 163, 172
Soviet Union, 122–3, 184, 200
Spillane, Mickey, 48
spirituality, of Iranian Revolution, 18–23, 25–6
standardization, of education, 59
State and Revolution (Lenin), 75–7, 92, 96–7
state media, 100, 120
state-sponsored schools, 5
strangeness, *ghorbat* as, 8–9, 12, 27–8
stranger *see gharibeh*
strikes, by university students, 2–3, 233, 235–6, 238
Student Day (*ruz-e daneshju*), 137–8
Sufism, 177–8, 245
Sunni-Shi'i split, 163
Susan (sister), 72, 109

The Swallows Return to Their Nests, 50–4, 79–80, 154–5

tabaqat-e ejtema'i (social classes), 92
Tabari, Ehsan, 15
Tafresh, 38–43
Tagh-e Bostan, 72
tajaddod (modernity), 9, 15–18, 20–1, 25–6, 51, 53, 87
tajaddodgera (modernizers), 128
tajaddod-zadeh (modern man), 79
Taraqqi, 43
Tarikh-e Jazmiyat-e Hezbi (Vardasbi), 172
Tavakol, Jafar, 91–2, 97, 106–7, 134
  Esmaili on, 112–13
  Falsafi and, 110–16, 118, 129–30, 211–12
  Moshiri on, 258–9
  on Palestine and Palestinian struggle, 108–9
  parochialism of, 164
  on Qur'an, 114–15
  religious teachings, in classroom of, 109–19, 124
Teacher College, Tehran, 92
teach-ins, 19, 200
technologization, 157
technology, 79, 148, 156–7
Tehran
  Aryamehr University, 203
  Baghdad *versus*, 38
  Behesht-e Zahra cemetery, 22, 179, 181, 207, 218–24
  clerical leadership in, 202
  Dar al-Fonun in, 138
  elementary schools, 168–9
  gharibeh in, 139
  Golpayegan and, 14, 89–90, 138–9, 149, 167, 169–70, 192, 201, 212, 250, 261–2
  Iranian Revolution in, 212–14
  Islamists in, 201
  mahaligera'i and, 128
  materialist consumerism, of elites in, 107
  Mirsepassi, Ali, in, photo of, 177
  Mirsepassi, Ali, surviving attack in, 1–4, 239–40
  Mohseni in, 53
  Nahavand and, 69–70
  Naraghi in, 155
  National University in, 2–3, 228–30, 234
  nativism of, 154–60
  Nixon visiting, 137, 232–3
  poetry readings in, 189–92
  Shahbazi in, 198–9
  shahrestani in, 139, 149
  Shamlu from, 63
  small towns and provinces *versus*, 50, 77–8, 178, 261
  Teacher College, 92
  Tehran-now neighborhood, 169–70, 212–14
Tehran University, 19, 22–3, 25, 134, 183, 229
  Amanat at, 150–1
  anti-Shah activism at, 143–4
  Art Faculty, 101
  Bahman at, 141
  Bastani-Parizi at, 57
  Behzadi at, 151–2
  cultural and political life of, 200
  during cultural revolution, 153–4

Enayat at, 160–3, 167, 254
Faculty of Law and Political Science, 137, 139–40, 150–5, 160, 162
French, American, and British faculty of, 150–4
Hamid at, 140
Institute for Social Studies and Research at Tehran University, 155–6, 158–9
Islam and Marxism at, 250
Kadkani at, 167, 173–4, 244–5
Khomeinists at, 227
Marxist activists at, 15–17, 142–3, 145–7
Musa at, 141–2
Nabavi at, 152–4
Naraghi at, 155–6
Nategh at, 179–80
politics as lifestyle at, 145–9
Vardasbi at, 167, 255
Zarafshan talk at, 207–11, 213

Tehran University students
on Behrangi, 58
demonstrations by, 147–8
Mirsepassi, Ali, photo of, 57
as part-time elementary school teachers, 168–9
protests and police attacks at, 1970, 137–42
on Western philosophers, 148–9

Ten Nights of Poetry Readings, at Goethe Institute, 19, 189
Third Force (*niru-ye sevvum*), 253
Third-Worldist ideas, 150, 252–3
Third World movements, 168, 253
Time magazine, 126–7
Tobacco Revolt, 15
torture, 200
traditional culture, Naraghi on, 157
traditionalism (*sonnat-gera'i*), 112
transnationalism, 109, 126, 129, 252–3
transnational media, 5–6, 120, 126–7, 253
Trotskyists, 220–1
Tudeh Military Network, 199
Tudeh Party, 11, 17, 65, 93, 144, 167, 253
activists, at Goethe Institute, 190
Alavi in, 98
Al-e Ahmad on, 106
Enayat in, 163–4
Falsafi against, 215
Fedayeen and, 228
Iranian Kurds in, 196
Khomeini and, 210
on modernization, 84
Naraghi in, 155
Rouzbeh and Akhavan-Sales in, 147
Shahbazi in, 199–200
Soviet Union and, 200
Turkish language, 177

U.K., 185–8
ulama, 116, 193, 213, 232–3
Ulduz va Kalag-ha (Behrangi), 60
UNESCO, 155–6, 158–9
the unthought, 1–2, 135, 167, 207, 224, 247–51, 262–3
U.S.
English language and, 127–8
graduate studies in, 186–8, 240–1
influence, in Iran, 121–2

U.S. (*cont.*)
 interventions in Third World, 141
 Peace Corps volunteers from, 127–8
 Yemen policy, 184

Vardasbi, Abuzar, 16–17, 163, 167–70, 194, 249
 Iran dar Puye-ye Tarikh by, 256
 radicalism of, 168
 Tarikh-e Jazmiyat-e Hezbi by, 172
 at Tehran University, 167, 255
Vietnam War, 90, 106, 120, 122

Washington, D.C., 241–3
Weber, Max, 173
the West, 106–7, 149
 Al-e Ahmad on, 170
 Channel 2 on, 190–1
 Enayat on, 251
 Fardid on, 192
 on freedom, 157–8
 on Islam and political Islam, 164
 Naraghi on, 156–8, 253–4
 Pahlavi elite on, 171
Western philosophers, 148–9
Western science, 157–9
Westoxification (Al-e Ahmad), 171
Westoxification (*gharbzadeghi*), 12, 107, 112, 156, 164, 191, 217
 former Tudeh intellectuals on, 253
 Pahlavi state and, 171
Williams, Raymond, 54
women
 hezbollahis attacking, 210–11
 Islam and, 22–3, 180, 182–3, 216–17
 Khomeini on, 222–3
 Khomeinists on, 181
Women's Day, 1979, 223
women's rights, 23, 216
Wong Kar-wai, 107
world (*donya*), 123–9, 177
worship of science (*'elm parasti*), 157
Writers' Association of Iran, 189

Yazdi, Ebrahim, 227–8
"Yours Truly: Johnny Dollar," 48
Youth Division, UNESCO, 155
Yushij, Nima, 63–4

Zahra's Paradise (Behesht-e Zahra) cemetery, 22, 179
Zarafshan, Nasser, 207–13
Zende be Gur (Hedayat), 45, 99

CPSIA information can be obtained
at www.ICGtesting.com
Printed in the USA
JSHW031719080323
38611JS00003B/4

9 781399 511421